POPULATION: THE VITAL REVOLUTION

POPULATION:
The Vital Revolution

EDITED BY

RONALD FREEDMAN

ALDINE Publishing Company / *Chicago*

CONTENTS

POPULATION: THE VITAL REVOLUTION

INTRODUCTION

Ronald Freedman

The "vital revolution" of modern times is described in this book by nineteen experts, analyzing important world population trends in non-technical language. These essays were originally prepared as lectures for a Voice of America Forum Series, broadcast in 1963 to eighty-five different countries. Their purpose was to acquaint an intelligent world audience of non-specialists with some of the best current scientific knowledge and opinion about population trends. Because of the nature of the audience, statistical tables, footnotes, and other scholarly abracadabra were inappropriate. The resulting product was a series of readable essays by experts on a subject in which there is increasing public interest.

Modern population trends are unique in historical perspective; describing them as part of a "vital revolution" is not an exaggeration. The more popular term "population explosion" is less accurate, because it refers to only one aspect of the current situation—the unprecedented growth rates. In the last two centuries other important trends have developed, also without precedent in all of the previous millennia of human history. While the size of population growth is very important in itself, the essays in this volume demonstrate that there are many other aspects of structure and change in populations which are equally important.

What are the most important population trends of the modern period? Any summary statement is necessarily arbitrary in selection and emphasis, but the following list and brief discussion is one basis for organizing much of the material in the essays which follow:

1. *The rate at which populations are growing is without historical precedent, whether we consider the world as a whole or major continents and regions.*

Hauser's opening essay demonstrates how unique the growth rates are for the world and for major regions. Also, each of the essays about a particular region or country demonstrates that everywhere spectacular rates of growth have occurred or are in immediate prospect. How such rapid growth rates have developed in the past is the central topic treated in the Stolnitz essay on "The Demographic Transition: From High to Low Birth Rates and Death Rates."

Very rapid growth rates today are best illustrated in Latin America, as the essay by Smith indicates. Lorimer's discussion of Africa indicates that growth rates there are still relatively moderate, although faster increase is in the offing. The moderate growth rates for the United States, whose history is described by Vance, are still sufficient for very considerable population growth.

2. *There has been an unprecedented decline in mortality in the developed countries. Similar declines have already occurred or are likely to occur soon in the newly developing countries.*

Of course it is this rapid decline in mortality, while fertility remains high or declines slowly, that produces the large rates of population growth. No significant part of the world population growth is attributable to increasing birth rates, although such increases did occur in some countries in the early part of the demographic transition from high birth and death rates to low birth and death rates.

The essay by Spiegelman indicates how this mortality decline occurred in the United States and where some of the important remaining differences are to be found among various parts of our population. Keyfitz shows how the mortality decline in the developing countries is a central issue in their struggle for higher standards of life. Each essay about a country or region deals with a similar issue in a specific situation, for the decline in mortality, universally desired, is occurring throughout the world and is affecting the basic vital balance of population in relation to the social structure and resources of each country.

3. *Fertility—the birth rate—is becoming the dynamic and problematic factor in population change for the first time in human history.*

It is likely that fertility has been less than the physiological maximum possible in most societies over most of history, and it is also likely that birth rates tended to remain relatively stable in most societies for rather long periods. Short-run changes in birth rates and in average family size were probably rare. Over most of man's history, changes—especially short-run changes—in population growth rates have developed mainly from variations in the death rate. In general, a population was likely to adjust to an unfavorable circumstance, such as a flood or famine or pestilence, by an increase in the death rate rather than a decrease in the birth rate. In especially good times the population grew more rapidly. This essentially Malthusian description of population change probably applies to much of the history of the world before the modern period.

Now, however, in much of the West, the picture has changed. Mortality rates are rather stable at such a low level that further declines cannot be very great.

In addition, for the first time in human history, birth rates and family size are being adjusted both up and down on a massive scale as the cumulative effect of millions of couples' making short-run decisions about the number and spacing of their children. These decisions are implemented by a variety of means for family limitation, ranging from contraception (including the rhythm method) to induced abortion and sterilization. These variations in fertility are now much more important than variations in mortality for the growth rate of Western populations. In such a highly developed country as the United States, death rates are now so low in the crucial reproductive ages (under forty-five for women) that Ansley Coale was able to demonstrate a few years ago that even the achievement of complete immortality (with a death rate of zero!) would have less effect than a 15 per cent increase in fertility rates on the long-run growth rate of the United States population.

Westoff's essay describes how the birth rate fell in the United States, and speculates on the reasons for its recent rise. Since the practice of family limitation and the number of children desired is by no means uniform among major strata of our population, he deals also with the important differences among subgroups.

In the newly developing countries, population growth rates will still be much affected in the coming years by further large decreases in death rates. These declines seem to be fairly certain and predictable. More problematic is what will happen to their birth rates, and, in particular, how long the transitional lag will be between the decline of mortality and the decline of fertility.

4. *The age structure—the proportion of a population that is old or young—depends mainly on the birth rate and not on the death rate. It is only in modern times that populations have become older on a massive scale, because it is only recently that we have had the massive declines of fertility rates that produce an older population.*

Coale, in his essay, "How a Population Ages or Grows Younger," presents a lucid explanation of this very important idea, which has been understood by demographers only in the past ten years. It is still unknown to most intelligent laymen today. The consequences of this idea are very important. It means, for example, that the newly developing countries will not lessen their burden of childhood dependency if their death rates fall. The anomaly Coale explains is that as people live longer, the population structure as a whole becomes somewhat younger rather than older, unless fertility rates fall too. It also means that when a population has an increasing proportion of older people

—as has been the case in most Western countries—it is because the birth rates have fallen and not because death rates have fallen.

Understanding how the age structure of a population changes is important, because so many aspects of the society obviously depend on such changes. The proportions of the population who will be marrying and starting new families, buying new homes, entering the labor market, or retiring—these are only a few of the important social facts which depend on age structure.

The developing countries are all uniquely different from the developed countries in their age structures because all of them have relatively high birth rates compared with the developed countries. Without knowing anything else about the countries, it would be possible to classify them quite accurately in the "developed" or "still developing" categories by an examination of their age structures alone.

5. *The populations of the modern world have been involved in massive movements unprecedented in human history in both scale and numbers of areas involved.*

Since the beginning of modern times, massive population movements have taken place not only within countries but between countries and continents, as part of new settlement patterns appropriate to the new urban and industrial societies. Within the developed countries there has been a massive movement out of rural areas to urban centers. These large concentrations of people are located in centers from which complex relationships over a wide area can be organized, mediated, and controlled. This produces a variation in the density of settlement which is probably greater in the developed societies today than at any time in history.

The developing societies are only beginning to experience this phenomenon of population mobility and redistribution. In most preindustrial societies the population is distributed in close relation to basic resources. It is likely that all of them will experience this trend toward large urban concentrations. Many are already suffering the problems of crowded and rapidly growing cities which seem out of proportion to the less developed hinterlands they presumably serve. In his essay on world urbanization Hawley traces in broad terms the long-run growth of urban centers and its remarkable acceleration in modern times.

But mobility in modern times is not limited to the nonrecurrent transfer of populations from rural to urban centers or from settled to frontier areas. Equally important in this new setting is a new kind of geographic mobility, tied to the economic and social conditions of an industrial world. This type of movement involves the transfer of labor from place to place as occupational opportunities shift with technology and the market. It also involves moves as people shift from one place to another in getting an education, in starting out in the labor market, in taking a better job, in finding a congenial place for retirement. Lee, in describing the very large population movements in the United States, demonstrates that these movements are no longer primarily rural to urban shifts.

This kind of massive recurrent internal migration is especially unique to the modern period. Previously, great hordes of people sometimes moved from one place to another in response to severe and prolonged drought, or to the attractions of a lush and weak society. But these movements were unique and occasional, and touched very few of the people in the world. In traditional preindustrial societies most people spent their lives in the communities in which they were born. Recurrent mobility on a mass basis is something new in the world.

6. *Modern population trends are greatly affected by an expansion of the range of social and economic interchange.*

As Hawley points out in his essay on world urbanization, the growth of cities which characterizes the modern world is an indication that larger populations and areas are being drawn into a single system of exchange, influence, and division of labor. Organizing and coordinating such larger systems is the central function of a city. The trends that we have described are dependent on such larger units of

political, social and economic interaction, crossing political boundaries in many cases. The scientific, agricultural,
medical and public health developments which made
possible the low death rates of the developed countries
could never have taken place while the lives of most people were circumscribed within the narrow confines of local
communities. Such developments depended on a greatly
expanded division of labor and a wider interchange of
ideas and mutual influence. This is clearly illustrated in the
rapid decline of the death rate in newly developed areas
today. Without access to ideas, products, and personnel
from the developed societies, their mortality never would
have fallen so rapidly.

The past decline of fertility in the West and the im-
pending decline in the rest of the world are also related
to the enlargement of social units of all kinds. In the
smaller units of preindustrial societies, almost all of the
major institutions were based on kinship ties, and most of
the goals valued in the society were achieved only with
the help of kinfolk, and particularly of children. In the
expanded modern society, a whole new range of institutions provides many of these satisfactions without reference to children or kinship. At the same time, declining
mortality has made it possible to rear any desired number
of children with a smaller number of births, since almost
all children now live to be adults in the developed countries.

Finally, the exceptional mobility of modern populations
is obviously possible only in the larger social units char-
acterizing the developed societies.

The expansion of the units of social and economic interchange was one of the fundamental prerequisites for the
population trends that distinguish the modern period.

7. *More governments are trying, in more ways, to influence
population trends by explicit population policies now than
at any other time in history.*

All societies have had population policies as an implicit
part of their social arrangements from time immemorial.

For example, every society has as part of its culture social norms controlling the reproduction of the population
by regulating such matters as marriage, sexual intercourse, periods of ritual abstinence, induced abortions, and
so forth. In the preindustrial societies where mortality was
high, only those societies in which these arrangements produced a rather high birth rate could survive at all. But
in large part these social pressures for reproduction were
not conceived as deliberate population policies, and they
were not adaptable to short-run changes in economic or
political conditions. There is evidence that Rome and other
preindustrial societies encouraged the reproduction of
elite groups. It is also true, of course, that there were many
actions by governments or other agencies designed to increase the chances of good health and long life.

But it is only in the modern period that mortality, and
now fertility, have become subjects of government policy,
not only to further the health and welfare of the individual
citizens, but also to influence the rate of growth, size, and
age structure of populations. Various essays in this volume
delineate the role of government policy in public health
programs and other activities designed to reduce illness
and mortality. Good health and long life are so highly
valued everywhere that action to achieve these results is
almost universally accepted as a primary responsibility of
government.

Explicit population policies to affect the birth rate first
became important before World War I, when many European countries appointed population commissions to in-
vestigate their declining birth rates and to develop policies
to reverse the trend.

Apart from concern with population size as compared
with rivals, some countries, for example France, were concerned with the fact that their populations were becoming
older as the birth rate fell. Almost all the countries of the
West, except the United States, have adopted family allow-
ance systems in which there is a more or less explicit
policy objective of preventing a decline in the birth rate.

As Irene Taeuber points out in her essay on Japan, that

country's prewar rulers moved in a variety of ways to keep
the birth rate from falling. Banning contraception and
abortion was only the negative side of a positive program
for emphasizing traditional familial values and maintain-
ing the birth rate. This program was successful enough
only to retard the decline of the birth rate. The spectacular decline of the Japanese birth rate after the war probably was in part a "making up" of the social change that
would have occurred without the unusual restraints previously imposed by the government.

Country-wide policies to reduce the birth rate are really
a phenomenon of the last decade. As Stycos points out in
his essay, many countries have now declared it a matter of
high policy to spread the means of family planning and
to reduce the birth rate. This is done not only for the welfare of the individual families involved at the time, but
also because the governments believe that the success of
general development programs depends on a fertility decline.

There now appears to be a move toward support from
international agencies for countries wishing to pursue such
policies. This is a slow and difficult process, because there
is no complete consensus that small families are a good
thing to match the universal consensus that low mortality
is desirable.

In the United States there is general agreement on an
explicit population policy for promoting low mortality both
at home and abroad, although there are disagreements on
implementation. Fertility policy has been largely implicit
in the past, but there is increasing discussion and controversy about what our policy should be. In our foreign
aid program we seem to be gradually moving to the position that we will give assistance on request to countries
developing family-planning programs, although the first
explicit grant for this purpose is yet to be made. At home
there is an increasing discussion about the role of government in preventing or encouraging family planning for
those who are interested in it.

As Westoff points out, no Western country has ever had

a government program for reducing the birth rate. The low fertility rates described by Petersen for Western Europe developed without government support and often in the face of government and other organized opposition. Therefore the assistance that Western countries might give to developing countries seeking to reduce their birth rates quickly by governmental measures may be limited by lack of relevant experience.

Such countries as India, in the large government programs described by Mauldin and Stycos, will set new precedents, if they are successful. Government policy in the U.S.S.R. and China, as described by Eason and Orleans, is less often openly directed to limiting population growth for ideological reasons. Yet in the Soviet Union birth rates have fallen with industrialization and are similar to those in the United States. China's policy, although erratic and justified as protecting the health and welfare of the mothers and children, has implicit in it the basis for population limitation.

In a number of countries birth rates have fallen sharply since the war as a result of government legalization of induced abortion, apparently with the objective of eliminating the appalling health risks of illegal abortions. This was true first and most dramatically in Japan, but as Petersen indicates, the same pattern is being repeated in Eastern Europe. Apparently it is true that abortion has been the principal means used in all the countries with major fertility declines since World War II.

Explicit population policies are often related to policies for economic development. But population trends and economic development are interdependent, even if there is no official policy recognizing their relationships. The character of the relation between economic and demographic trends is discussed by Spengler in his essay.

8. *Data about population trends are being improved in quantity and quality as interest in population problems increases, but this development is recent and many countries still have little information.*

Almost all of the developing countries are seeking to develop statistical information about their populations as a basis for intelligent planning. The United Nations Population Division and other United Nations agencies render valuable services in this area. But, as Hauser and others indicate, our knowledge of most populations is still rather incomplete and of recent origin. This is not surprising, since interest in a census or accurate vital statistics is of little value to the peasant who lives out his life in a routine relationship to a small group of people whose history he knows well enough without statistics and charts. Most of the world's population has lived in such a setting until recently; a substantial part of it still does.

It is the development of the complex modern society which has led to the demand for detailed and accurate social accounting schemes, including the census and vital statistics. Perhaps the best indication that we still have a long way to go is the statement by Orleans that we do not really know what the population of mainland China is, although we guess that about one fourth of all the people in the world live there.

The essay by Conrad Taeuber on the 1960 U. S. census is intended to describe what is involved in taking an inventory of 180,000,000 people. Our census is perhaps the most complex and comprehensive in the world (although it is not necessarily the most accurate). It is likely that most countries will move toward such more complex and automated statistical systems in order to have accurate information about their populations and to keep abreast of current changes. These facts provide the basis on which the activities of governments, business, and private associations are based.

These statements in outline form are the editor's view of some of the more important trends in world population. While he believes that they are consistent with the detailed treatments in the nineteen essays, he recognizes that the organization and emphasis in this summary might not be congenial to all the authors.

Each author has compressed a vast amount of material into a short essay in which important variations, exceptions and explanations are necessarily omitted. The authors have shown exemplary restraint in omitting the detailed documentation that might bring the reader closer to the truth for specific situations, but might obscure the general overview which was our objective. To help the reader who wants to go beyond the summary statements of the essays, each author presents at the close of his work a short annotated list of suggestions for further reading. The editor is providing, in addition, the following list of more general references in which the topics of many of the specific essays are given more detailed treatment:

United Nations. Population Division. *The Determinants and Consequences of Population Trends: a summary of findings of studies on the relationships between population changes and economic and social conditions.* New York: United Nations, ST/SOA/Series A/17, 1953.

This is the most comprehensive and authoritative single volume available about world population trends, their causes and consequences.

Philip M. Hauser and Otis Dudley Duncan, editors. *The Study of Population: an inventory and appraisal.* Chicago: University of Chicago Press, 1959.

This is an encyclopedic review of the status of knowledge and research about population, with chapters by an international group of experts on the nature of population study, methodology, and the development of the field in important countries.

Joseph J. Spengler and Otis Dudley Duncan, editors. *Demographic Analysis: selected readings.* Glencoe: The Free Press, 1957.

Joseph J. Spengler and Otis Dudley Duncan, editors. *Population Theory and Policy: selected readings.* Glencoe: The Free Press, 1956.

These two volumes contain a wide range of important articles and book excerpts on many aspects of population theory and research.

W. S. Woytinsky and E. S. Woytinsky. *World Population and Production: trends and outlook.* New York: The Twentieth Century Fund, 1953.

A comprehensive treatment of world population trends, country by country.

George W. Barclay. *Techniques of Population Analysis.* New York: John Wiley and Sons, 1958.

This is a good introduction to the methods of analysis used by demographers for persons without much training in statistics or mathematics.

Donald J. Bogue. *The Population of the United States.* Glencoe: The Free Press, 1959.

This is a massive work on all major aspects of population and population change in the United States.

Philip Hauser, editor. *The Population Dilemma.* Englewood Cliffs: Prentice-Hall, 1963.

The papers of an American Assembly Conference on the population problem. An excellent series of essays dealing with some topics (e.g., the world food supply) not covered in the present volume.

Harrison Brown. *The Challenge of Man's Future.* New York: The Viking Press, 1954.

This is an especially stimulating volume for the layman. In addition to a rather brief overview of population trends, there is an excellent treatment of present and potential resources for a growing world population.

Alfred Sauvy. *Fertility and Survival. Population Problems from Malthus to Mao Tse-tung.* New York: Criterion Books, 1961.

This is a popular treatment of many important aspects of the "population problem" by the leading French demographer, whose views on many issues differ from those of his American colleagues.

Warren S. Thompson. *Population Problems.* New York: McGraw-Hill, 4th ed., 1953.

This has been the most widely used textbook in this field. While it is not up to date on some matters, it is still comprehensive and stimulating.

Thomas Lynn Smith. *Fundamentals of Population Study.*
Chicago: J. B. Lippincott, 1960.

A general textbook which emphasizes American data,
but includes some comparative materials.

William Petersen. *Population.* New York: Macmillan,
1961.

This is the newest textbook on population, with more
current statistics than the others.

The Population Index. Quarterly publication of the Population Association of America, Inc.

This journal consists mainly of a superb classified and
annotated bibliography of all current publications related to population. In addition it publishes in each
issue one or two brief articles and some collections of
population statistics.

Population Studies. Publication of the Population Investigation Committee, London School of Economics.

This is a British journal of demography. It publishes
important technical articles on all aspects of population
study.

Population. Publication of the National Institute of Demographic Studies of France.

This French journal is published under the auspices of
the *Institut National D'études Démographiques.* It is
written in French and carries many important technical
studies of population trends all over the world.

Chapter 1

THE POPULATION OF THE WORLD: RECENT TRENDS AND PROSPECTS

Philip M. Hauser

Knowledge about population in the past, the present, and the future enables a person to see himself as an element in world population. It provides perspective of one's self in relation to fellow men in the same manner that astronomy provides one with perspective about this earth as an element in the solar system, the galaxy and the universe. Four numbers summarizing the population history of the world help to provide such a perspective.

Although the first complete census of mankind has yet to be taken, it is possible to reconstruct, within reasonable error limits, the estimated population of the world from the end of the Neolithic period (the new Stone Age) in Europe (8000–7000 B.C.). World population at that time is estimated to have been some ten million, and perhaps was as low as five million. At the beginning of the Christian Era the population of the world probably numbered between 200 and 300 million. At the beginning of the Modern Era (1650) world population had reached about 500 million. In 1962 world population totaled three billion. A relatively simple analysis of these numbers discloses that an enormous increase in the rate of world population growth has occurred, especially during the past three centuries.

Man or very close kin to man has been on the face of the earth for perhaps two million years. Although it is not known exactly when Homo sapiens, the present version of man, first appeared, he was much in evidence in Europe something like 25,000 to 30,000 years ago. It is estimated that for the some six hundred thousand years of the Paleolithic Age (the old Stone Age) population growth perhaps approximated .02 per thousand per year. During the three centuries of the Modern Era, population growth increased from about 4 per thousand to 10 per thousand per year during the interwar years. The rate of world population growth continued to accelerate after World War II, so that in 1963 it approximated 20 per 1000 per year.

In the course of man's inhabitation of this globe, then, his rate of population growth has increased from about 2 per cent per millennium to 2 per cent per year, a thousand-fold increase in growth rate.

If man's precursors prior to the old Stone Age are ignored, it has been estimated that since the beginning of that era there have been perhaps 77 billion births. Of this number only 12 billion, or less than 16 per cent of the total, occurred during the approximately 8000 years encompassing the Neolithic period and history up to the middle of the seventeenth century. Some 23 billion births, or 30 per cent of the total, occurred during the three centuries of the Modern Era. Of the total number of persons that have ever been born, according to these estimates, about 4 per cent, therefore, are now living.

Population data prior to the Modern Era are admittedly speculative as are, also, the inferences and conclusions which are drawn. But they provide a reasonably sound perspective and permit a very firm conclusion—namely, that whatever the precise numbers may be, there can be no doubt that in his habitation of this planet, man has experienced tremendous acceleration in his rate of growth.

This conclusion is supported by placing in perspective the present rate of world population increase, estimated by the United Nations as approximating 2 per cent per year. Although 2 per cent per year may seem like a small return on investment to persons fortunate enough to have funds out at interest, it turns out to be a truly astonishing rate of world population growth. For example, to produce the present population of the world, about three billion, one dozen persons increasing at the rate of 2 per cent per year would have required only 976 years. Yet Homo sapiens alone has been on this earth at least twenty-five to thirty thousand years and some form of man perhaps as long as two million years. Similarly, the same one dozen persons reproducing at the rate of 2 per cent per year since the beginning of the Christian Era could by 1962 have had 300 million descendants for each one actually present on the face of the earth.

Further appreciation of the meaning of a 2 per cent rate of increase per year is gained by observing the population that this growth rate would produce in the future. With an initial population of three billion, the present rate of world population growth would give a population of fifty billion in 142 years. This is the highest estimate of the population-carrying capacity of the globe ever calculated by a responsible scholar. This estimate, by geochemist Harrison Brown, is based on two extreme assumptions: first, that solar or nuclear energy will be developed to a point where the cost of power is so low that it approximates zero. Under this condition it would be possible to obtain the "things" we need from rock, sea, and air to support a population of this size indefinitely. The second assumption is that mankind would be content to forego not only meat, as the Hindu has already done, but also vegetables, and be content to subsist on food products from "algae farms and yeast factories."

A continuation of the 2 per cent rate of world population growth from the present population of about three billion would provide enough people, in lock step, to reach from the earth to the sun in 237 years. It would give one person for every square foot of land surface on the globe, including mountains, deserts and the arctic wastes, in about six and one-half centuries. It would generate a population which would weigh as much as the earth itself in 1,566 years. These periods of time may seem long when measured by the length of the individual lifetime, but they are but small intervals of time measured in the time perspective of the evolutionary development of man.

Projections of this type, of course, are not to be interpreted as predictions. They merely help to indicate the meaning of the present rate of growth. They also permit another firm conclusion—namely, that the present rate of

world population growth cannot possibly persist for very
long into the future. As a matter of fact, in the long run,
given a finite globe and excluding the possibilities of ex-
porting human population to outer space, any rate of population growth would in time saturate the globe and
exhaust space itself. In the long run, man will necessarily
be faced with the problem of restricting his rate of increase
to maintain some balance between his numbers and the
finite dimensions of this planet.

It is possible quickly to summarize the remarkable acceleration of his growth rate which man has experienced.
It took most of the millennia of man's habitation of this
planet to produce a population as great as one billion
persons simultaneously alive. This population was not
achieved until approximately 1850. To produce a population of two billion persons simultaneously alive required
only an additional seventy-five years, for this number was
achieved by 1925. To reach a population of three billion
persons required only an additional thirty-seven years, for
this was the total in 1962. Continuation of the trend would
produce a fourth billion in about fifteen years and a fifth
billion in less than an additional ten years.

Analyses of this type have led the student of population,
the demographer, to use emotional and unscientific language on occasion to describe population developments.
Such a phrase as "the population explosion" is admittedly
non-scientific language, but it serves to emphasize the dramatic increase in man's rate of growth and to call attention
to its many implications.

Why has the rate of world population growth increased
so greatly? The answer may be found by analyzing the
great differences in rates of population growth among the
continental regions of the world and examining the reasons
for these differences. Although the data are subject to
error, it is possible to reproduce with reasonable accuracy
the populations of the continents over the three centuries
of the Modern Era.

Examination of these data discloses that for the three
centuries between 1650 and 1950 the population of the

world as a whole increased fivefold, from about 500 million
to about 2.5 billion. The population of Europe (including
Asiatic U.S.S.R.), however, increased almost sixfold. The
population of Northern America (north of the Rio Grande)
increased 168-fold, from about 1 to 168 million. The
population of Latin America (south of the Rio Grande)
increased about 23-fold, from about 7 to 163 million.
Oceania increased more than sixfold, from about 2 to
13 million; Asia, showing a fivefold increase, grew at a
rate close to the average for the world, of which it constitutes the greatest portion. In contrast, Africa, the slowest-
growing region of the world, merely doubled its population during these three centuries, increasing from about
100 to about 200 million. The regions which experienced
the most rapid growth during the three centuries of the
Modern Era were Europe and the areas of European settlement. The population of Europe and the areas of European
settlement combined increased about sevenfold; the areas
of European settlement alone, the Americas and Oceania,
increased eight- to nine-fold between 1650 and 1950.

Why did the rate of population growth increase so
spectacularly in Europe and areas of European settlement?
The answer is to be found of course in the technological,
economic, and social developments within these regions
during the Modern Era. Acceleration in growth rate may
be traced to the impact of the many technological, economic, and social changes which are summarized by the
expressions the "agricultural revolution," the "technological
revolution," the "commercial revolution," and the "industrial revolution," climaxed by the "scientific revolution."
The profound changes in man's way of life and in the social
order generated by these developments produced the "demographic revolution." More specifically, the combination
of developments accelerated the rate of population growth
because it brought about a sharp and unprecedented decline in death rates, with a corresponding great increase in
average length of life.

Precise information is not available, but in all probability
the expectation of life at birth in Egypt, Greece, and Rome

around the beginning of the Christian Era was probably not above thirty years. During the first half century of the Modern Era, 1650 to 1700, life expectation at birth in Western Europe and North America was at a level of about thirty-three years, and probably had not changed much during the preceding three or four centuries. By 1900 death rates had declined to a point where expectation of life at birth in Western Europe and North America had increased by fifteen or twenty years, reaching a level of forty-five to fifty years. By 1960 another twenty years of life had been gained. Life expectation in Western Europe and North America reached a level of about seventy years.

Although some changes in birth rates were also involved, it is clear that the major factor in the great acceleration of population growth, first evident in Europe and areas of European settlement, was the decline in the death rate. Three factors contributed to this decline. The first was the general increase in level of living resulting from technological advances and increased productivity and the achievement of relatively long periods of peace and tranquillity by reason of the emergence of relatively powerful and stable central government. The second major factor accounting for the decrease in mortality was the achievement of environmental sanitation and improved personal hygiene. During the nineteenth century great strides were made in purifying food and water and improving personal cleanliness, which contributed materially to the elimination of parasitic and infectious diseases. The third major factor is of course to be found in the great and growing contribution of modern medicine, enhanced by the recent progress in chemotherapy and the insecticides.

These developments during the Modern Era upset the equilibrium between the birth rate and the death rate that had characterized most of the millennia of human existence. In eighteenth-century France, for example, of 1000 infants born, 233 had died before they reached age one, 498 had died before they reached age twenty, and 786 had died before they reached age sixty. In contrast, in present-day France, of 1000 infants born only 40 had died before age one, only 60 had died before age twenty, and only 246 had died before age sixty. In eighteenth-century France, of the original 1000 infants only 214 survived to age sixty. In contemporary France, 754 of the original 1000 infants were still alive at age sixty. As a result of such a decrease in death rates, the 100 million Europeans in 1650 three centuries later had about 940 million descendants.

The acceleration in rate of total population growth was the result of sharp declines in mortality while fertility remained at relatively high levels. This pattern, an example of which is given for England and Wales, characterized the demographic transition in Europe and in areas colonized by European stock. At mid-eighteenth century the birth rate in England was at a level of about 37—that is, 37 births per 1000 persons per year. The death rate stood at a level of about 33—33 deaths per 1000 persons per year. Natural increase, the excess of births over deaths, approximated 4 persons per 1000 per year, or a .4 of 1 per cent per year rate of population growth. A century later, by 1850, the death rate had declined to a level of 21, while the birth rate remained at the relatively high level of approximately 34. Natural increase with this fertility and mortality was therefore 13, producing a population growth of 1.3 per cent per year, more than three times the rate of increase a century earlier. As in the case of England and Wales, mortality in Western Europe began its relatively rapid descent toward the end of the eighteenth and early part of the nineteenth century, while fertility still remained at relatively high levels. It is only with considerable lag that the birth rate began to decline and, therefore, to dampen rates of population increase. This is the manner in which the "demographic transition" occurred.

Prior to World War II, the spectacular decrease in the death rate of the economically advanced nations had not been shared by most of the population of the world. Of the peoples of non-European stock, only Japan had managed appreciably to increase longevity. The two thirds of the world's people who live in the economically under-developed regions—Asia, Latin America, and Africa—before World War II had achieved some decrease in mortality, largely through contact with advanced nations. But most of the world's people prior to World War II were character-ized by an expectation of life at birth no greater than that which Western Europeans had during the Middle Ages.

This situation has dramatically changed since the end of World War II. A combination of factors, including the advent of the United Nations and the specialized agencies with programs emphasizing economic development and im-proved health conditions, "the revolution of rising expecta-tions," the development and dissemination of chemother-apy and insecticides, have opened up to the mass of the world's people the achievement of the twentieth-century death rates. Since the end of World War II, declines in mortality among the economically underdeveloped areas of the world have been more dramatic than those in the in-dustrialized areas.

Longevity is increasing much more rapidly in the less developed areas than it did among Europeans and Euro-pean stock, because of the much more efficient means now available for eliminating causes of mortality. For example, the death rate of the Moslem population in Algeria in 1946–47 was higher than that of Sweden in 1771–80, more than a century and a half earlier. By 1955, however, in eight years the decrease in the death rate in Algeria was greater than that Sweden experienced during the century from 1775 to 1875. Between 1940 and 1960 Mexico, Costa Rica, Venezuela, Ceylon, Malaya, and Singapore were among the nations which decreased their death rates by more than 50 per cent. Ceylon's death rate was decreased by more than 50 per cent in less than a decade.

Without question the most important population devel-opment in the twentieth century is the spectacular decline which is taking place in the death rates of the people in the less developed areas. As a result of the decline in mortality rates, population growth among the two thirds of the world's people in the less developed areas is now greater than that previously experienced by European stock. Whereas annual rates of population growth among the industrialized nations rarely exceeded 1 per cent per year through natural increase during most of the Modern Era, populations in the present less developed areas of Asia, Latin America, and Africa are increasing at rates from 2 to 3 per cent per year. The reason for the more rapid rate of population growth in the less developed areas today than was experienced by the economically advanced nations during their period of rapid population growth is to be found of course in relation between the death rate and the birth rate. In the experience of economically advanced countries a decline in mortality was spread out over the entire three centuries of the Modern Era, during the latter part of which, over periods ranging from half a century to perhaps a century and a half, the birth rate also began to decline.

Precise statistics are not available for birth and death rates of the less developed regions of the world. Reasonably good estimates are available through the United Nations which, from the time it was first organized, has devoted considerable attention to population trends. Birth rates in the less developed regions of the world tend to average 40 or more (births per 1000 persons per year), a level little lower, if any, than it was centuries ago. In contrast the birth rates in the economically advanced regions in Europe, North America and Oceania range from below 15 to 25 (births per 1000 persons per year).

The great acceleration in the rate of population growth in the less developed regions is brought about by the retention of their high birth rates while they are experiencing precipitous decline in death rates. The death rates in the less developed continents, although higher than those which obtain in the more developed regions, have now fallen to levels (deaths per 1000 persons per year) from below 10 to about 20 (per 1000 persons per year). This difference between the death rate and the birth rate gives a natural increase of about 20 to 30—a population growth rate of 2 to 3 per cent per year.

At the present time a number of the industrialized countries of the world, largely European nations and Japan, are growing relatively slowly at rates which would double their populations in from fifty to 100 years. Some of the industrialized countries, including the United States, the Soviet Union, Australia, New Zealand, Canada and Argentina are growing somewhat more rapidly, at rates which would double their populations in about thirty to forty years, about the average for the world.

The less developed areas of the world, containing two thirds of the total population, are now the most rapidly growing regions of the world. They are increasing at rates which would double their population in from twenty to forty years.

The less developed areas are now experiencing the demographic transition already experienced by the industrialized nations, but at a much more rapid pace. The implications of the present patterns of fertility and mortality for future population have great significance, particularly in view of the national aspirations of the less developed areas for improving levels of living. To achieve higher levels of living, income per capita must, of course, be increased. Planners must, therefore, be aware of what the prospects are for future population so as to be in a position to set desired economic goals and lay plans for their achievement. The United Nations has made population projections for the world and for individual nations as well as for its various regions. The projections made before the new censuses were taken, in or around 1960, are already too conservative. That is, the acceleration in growth rates of the less developed areas has been so rapid as to have outmoded the population projections since they were constructed in the late 1950s. The United Nations "high" projections serve, however, to illustrate what the present trend would produce by the end of the century.

Should the trends continue, the population of the world as a whole would increase from about 3 billion in 1960 to approximately 7 billion by the year 2000. World population would more than double during the remainder of this

century. The effect of declining mortality in the less developed areas may be readily seen by comparing anticipated growth in the second half of this century with actual
growth during the first half. Between 1900 and 1950 world
population increased by less than 1 billion persons. Between
1950 and 2000 present trends indicate an increase of 4.4
billion persons. That is, the absolute increase in the population of the world during the second half of this century will
be almost four and a half times as great as that during the
first half of the century. During the second half of this
century, there will be a greater increase in world population than was achieved in all the millennia of human
existence up to the present time.

Between 1960 and the end of the century, Latin America
will have the most rapidly growing population—more than
tripling, to reach a total of 650 millions from a level of
about 200 million. Asia and Africa will each increase by
two and a half-fold. Africa's population will rise from 250
million in 1960 to 660 million by 2000. Asia's population
will increase to 4.3 billion in 2000 from a level of 1.7 billion
in 1960. The slowest-growing regions of the world between now and the end of this century will be the industrialized areas. North America and Europe will each
increase by about 50 per cent while Oceania will less than
double during the remainder of this century. The population of Europe will total about 1 billion in 2000, compared
with 640 million in 1960; that of North America will number 330 million in 2000, as compared with 200 million in
1960. Oceania will have about 30 million persons in 2000
as compared with 17 million in 1960. These projections,
it must be emphasized, are estimates of what would happen if the trends observed were to continue for the remainder of the century.

An interesting shift has occurred, and is again in prospect, in the population relationships of North and Latin
America. Latin America contained more people than did
North America before European colonization. The more
rapid economic development of North America gave that
continent a larger population than Latin America during

the course of the nineteenth century. In 1960 the number of persons in Latin America exceeded the number in North America for the first time in more than a century. Despite the postwar boom in marriages and babies in North America, the population in Latin America is now growing so much more rapidly that by the end of this century Latin America will contain about twice as large a population as North America.

It is difficult to comprehend the significance of the population increase during the remainder of this century which present trends indicate. Some understanding of what lies ahead may be gained by historical comparisons. The absolute increase in the population of Latin America during the last half of this century may equal the total increase in the population of the world in all the millennia which man has inhabited this globe up until 1650 when the first colonists in the United States were settling New England. The projected increase in the population of Asia during the second half of this century is as great as the total population of the world in 1958.

The world's population is unevenly distributed over the surface of the globe. About two thirds of the people on the earth live on about 7 per cent of the land area. There are four areas of great population concentration—Eastern Asia, South Central Asia, Europe and Northeastern United States. This distribution of the world's peoples is, of course, the result of the adjustment of population to world resources that has taken place over the millennia.

Differences in rates of population growth, historically and in prospect, alter the distribution of the world's population by regions. In 1650 Asia contained 61 per cent of the world's people. Africa and Europe each had 18 per cent, and the remaining continents—North America, Latin America, and Oceania combined—had less than 3 per cent of the world's total population. By 1950 the effects of the demographic transition in Europe and the areas colonized by Europe were clearly visible. Asia's share of the world's total population had shrunk to 54 per cent and Africa's to only 8 per cent of the total. Europe's share had in-

creased to 23 per cent, and the areas of European colonization, North America, South America and Oceania had
increased their share of the world's total to over 14 per
cent.

Differential growth rates during the remainder of this
century, reflecting the demographic transition in the less
developed areas, will reverse the previous pattern of change
in population distribution by world regions. The economically less developed continents—Asia, Africa and Latin
America—will increase their share of the world's total population at the expense of North America and Europe. Asia's
share of the world's total will increase to about 62 per cent,
Latin America to over 9 per cent, Africa's to close to 10
per cent. In contrast, Europe's share of total population
will decrease to less than 15 per cent, while North Amer
ica's will shrink to less than 5 per cent.

At mid-twentieth century, the industrialized continents
—North America, Europe and Oceania—contained over 30
per cent of the world's total population. The less developed
continents—Asia, Africa and Latin America—contained the
remainder. In the course of the twentieth century, the
proportion of the world's population in the less developed
continents will have increased from less than two thirds in
1900 to about four fifths by 2000. Conversely, the share
of the world's total population contained in the more economically developed continents will have declined from 36
per cent of the world's total in 1900 to 21 per cent in 2000.

Acceleration in the rate of the world's population growth
is still under way. But it is clear that even present rates of
world population growth cannot continue for very long into
the future. Man is the only culture-building animal on the
face of the earth. He not only adapts to environment but
creates environment to which to adapt. In developing his
culture and precipitating the technological, the industrial
and the scientific revolutions, man has profoundly altered
the rhythm of his own reproduction. He has destroyed the
equilibrium between the birth rate and the death rate which
existed for most of the millennia he has been on this globe.

Man has the capacity, however, not only to build culture

but also to perceive the consequences of his handiwork. It is because he is becoming increasingly aware of the implications of accelerating population growth that so much attention is now being paid to population problems. It is because of the increasing awareness of population trends and their implications that the United Nations and its specialized agencies and an increasing number of individual nations are facing up to the population problem. A number of nations, including India, Pakistan, Egypt, Tunisia, Korea and Japan, have formulated population policies and are developing programs to make sure that the Malthusian checks to population growth—vice, misery, famine and war—do not provide the solution to their increasing numbers.

SUGGESTIONS FOR FURTHER READING

United Nations. Population Division. *The Determinants and Consequences of Population Trends*. New York: United Nations, 1953.

A comprehensive treatment of world population trends and problems with a full bibliography.

Political and Economic Planning. *World Population and Resources*. Fairlawn, N. J.: Essential Books, 1955.

Contains excellent regional data on population and resources and full discussion of policy implications.

Harrison Brown. *The Challenge of Man's Future*. New York: The Viking Press, 1954.

Especially good for world-resources picture and implications for population.

Philip M. Hauser. *Population Perspectives*. New Brunswick, N. J.: Rutgers University Press, 1961.

A short book on world, United States and metropolitan population trends and their social, economic and political implications.

Philip M. Hauser, editor. *The Population Dilemma*. Englewood Cliffs: Prentice-Hall, 1963.

An up-to-date presentation by ten experts of population trends for the world, the underdeveloped areas, and the U. S., including attention to problems of population control and policy, and a policy statement by the American Assembly.

Chapter 2

THE DEMOGRAPHIC TRANSITION: FROM HIGH TO LOW BIRTH RATES AND DEATH RATES

George J. Stolnitz

Demographic transitions rank among the most sweeping and best-documented historical trends of modern times. The following discussion of transition patterns summarizes past declines of vital rates and the prospects for future ones in comparatively global fashion. Its focus is on modern population movements in broad terms, on major regions of the world rather than individual countries, and on some major implications only. Details will be kept in the background. It is important to keep in mind, therefore, that the general picture to be described is based upon hundreds of investigations, covering a host of specific places, periods and events. Indeed, it is the very multiplicity of these building blocks which accounts for the impressiveness of the over-all structure.

The main outlines of the structure can be summarized briefly. All nations in the Modern Era which have moved from a traditional, agrarian-based economic system to a largely industrial, urbanized base have also moved from a condition of high mortality and fertility to low mortality and fertility. In so doing they have almost all experienced enormous increases in population along with massive shifts in their relative numbers of children, adults and aged. Partly as cause and partly as result have been associated sweeping changes in the relation between population and natural resources, in the relation between numbers of consumers and size of labor force, in investment patterns and in the distribution of people between rural and urban areas.

To give these generalizations even skeletal form requires

some perspectives. A first perspective is that the periods needed for maturation of the vital trends just outlined have not been short. Although they vary greatly from country to country and case to case, they have always been long-run, more like quarters of a century or generations than decades, and surely more like decades than single years. We need to remember this when considering the relevance of the experience in the industrialized nations for the under-developed economies of today.

A second perspective is that the pace of the trends to modern, lower vital rates marked a vast break with the past, without precedent in human history. The mortality declines which have occurred in many areas over the past century almost certainly exceed by far the cumulative movement in any part of the globe over the preceding twenty centuries. In their own proportions, the declines in fertility have been similarly precipitous by previous stand-ards.

A third perspective is that the trends appear without exception to have become irreversible wherever they have occurred. This too marks a significant break with the past. Premodern decreases in mortality must have been suc-ceeded by more or less equal increases, subject to the vagaries of the harvest and the whims of a threatening natural environment. It is true that one can only surmise this interpretation, but indirect evidence makes it seem most probable. Even apart from wars, the time path of human survival before about 1800 was one of fluctuations rather than sustained movement. In contrast, the modern path has been to ever higher, more secure ground. Given peace, the current levels of medical technology and eco-nomic well-being in the industrialized nations are more than ample to initiate rising longevity. They seem super-abundantly capable of preventing declines.

Similarly, the prospect for significant reversal of past fertility declines in industrialized societies seems remote. The closest to an exception has been the rise in the birth rate of many of these areas after the war. Some partial reversal of the long-term trend in fertility may well have occurred in at least some areas. But at most, the return was to the years before the unusually depressed conditions of the 1930s, not to traditional high fertility. Although childless and small-size families in a number of countries have recently become less frequent than a generation ago, large-size families have also continued to become less frequent. The postwar experience is better described as a "trendlet" rather than a trend, compared to long-run fertility movements, even where the recent increases have been greatest. Moreover the crest of the rise has already been reached and become dated in numerous cases and gives evidence of being left behind in others. But perhaps above all, the context of the postwar fertility increases in industrialized areas has been one of ever spreading family planning and control over its size. It may well be that the nations in the vanguard of fertility transitions have reached something like a bottom plateau, involving the two-child family. Future fertility in these areas may fluctuate sometimes above this level, sometimes below, depending upon economic conditions and social fashion. Or it may resume a further downtrend. In any event a sustained long-run uptrend seems inconceivable. By all available indications, the break with the historical past appears to be complete.

A fourth general perspective to keep in mind is a close variant of an ancient bit of folk wisdom: it's not what you do but the way you do it that makes the final difference. The low birth and death rates encountered today in the modernized economies could have been reached by many paths through time. In fact, however, the death rate has either come down first or has moved more rapidly than has the birth rate. The result almost everywhere among such economies was a rapid acceleration in their population growth rates and numbers, which lasted for decades. Eventually the gap between their birth and death rates closed and decelerated growth ensued, but only after lengthy periods of transition. Experience of a full transition process was needed before the low growth rates of their pre-transition history reappeared.

A fuller account of these effects would have to take

heed of the great transatlantic migrations before World War I, which lessened the acceleration in Europe and enhanced it in the newer nations of North America and Oceania. Also France, Ireland and perhaps the United States provide exceptions to the general prototype, each for its individual reasons.

Nevertheless the proposition stands, with very high probability, that demographic transition implies a substantial speeding up in the growth of population both as compared to the pre-transition period and to its later phases. The probability approaches certainty in the case of the newly developing, low-income countries of today. The initial widening observed between birth and death rates in past transitions has not been accidental, and an analogous widening seems even more likely in future transitions. Among the reasons for this anticipation are several that merit special attention.

Thus, on the one hand, lower mortality is a universally desired and accepted social goal, at least in peace and off the highway. Nineteenth-century declines in death rates among the then developing economies were an outcome of effective new methods of disease control and rising levels of living; they did not result in a significant way from changes in the social order or from altered social values. Today methods exist for reducing high mortality that are more effective in a technical sense than ever before, that require relatively low expenditures and small numbers of skilled personnel, and that can be divorced sharply from the general socioeconomic environment. Applied in the form of public health, sanitation and mass medical programs, such methods can be superimposed by governments upon populations that are technologically backward in most or all other respects.

On the other hand, lower fertility and the means for achieving it have long been subjects of religious controversy and deep-rooted ethical, social and individual debate, both within the household and in the community at large. Previous transition experience suggests that sustained downtrends in fertility often begin as a result of forces whose momentum develops slowly. Such downtrends require a shift in attitudes from the traditional fatalism typical of peasant societies to a belief that one's destiny can be affected by one's deeds, in childbearing as in other spheres of behavior. Another major factor in the past has been the growing importance of secular education, which refashioned old attitudes and proposed new values, along with fresh opportunities for putting these to work. Increasing urbanization was typically a third major factor, with its emphasis on a skilled and better-educated labor force and with its tendency to reduce the importance of the family as a center of employment opportunities, economic security, education and recreation. Children on the farm could be, and usually were, put to work early. In the city equal numbers of children became a much greater drain on family resources, a lesser source of income, a more potent competitor with basic family needs such as housing, and a threat to earning capacity on the part of women. As a rule, therefore, the spread of small-family ideals has tended to be more rapid in an urban context than in rural cultures. The specific knowledge and motivations needed to convert such ideals into effective behavior, in particular knowledge of contraceptive methods and willingness to apply them, also tend to be more rapidly acquired in urban environments. In contrast to medical innovations, whose effectiveness is largely a technological matter, adoption of contraceptive methods may require a wholesale reorientation of social values and attitudes.

All of these classes of causal factors—changing value structures, shifting occupational and residential composition of population, and rising educational levels—are relatively long-run in nature. It is true that the weight and timing of these factors are not easily traced; their causal influence in quantitative terms remains obscure even in the cases where their importance stands out most clearly. It is also true that other factors have sometimes appeared capable of initiating marked fertility downtrends, as in France, Ireland and the United States. As of now, however, the weight of evidence from past transition patterns leans heavily toward the expectation that future departures from traditional fertility patterns will come slowly. And even if this is not the case, mortality in many areas with high birth rates has already come down, or promises to do so, more rapidly than has ever been the case before.

There is another dimension to the point that the process of transition is important, in addition to its end result. The nations with low vital rates today could have had the same increases in numbers if their fertility and mortality trends had been smaller than the ones they actually experienced. In other words, ignoring migration, the rate of population growth depends upon the difference between birth and death rates, not upon their level. A birth rate of 25 per 1000 and a death rate of 15 per 1000 yields the same growth as does a birth rate of 20 per 1000 and a death rate of 10 per 1000. In both cases the growth is 10 per 1000.

Yet there is an important difference between the two, involving the age composition of the population. Declines in mortality tend to have only limited effect on the fractions of a population belonging to the young ages, or roughly under fifteen, the main adult ages, or fifteen to sixty-five, and the old ages, sixty-five and over. If only mortality had declined in the industrially advanced nations while fertility had remained unchanged, their age composition today would be much as it was in 1850. A demonstration of this rather startling conclusion is given in the essay following, by Ansley Coale. For present purposes we can simply accept it as true, though it seems to fly in the face of common sense and in fact eluded the attention of professional demographers until quite recently. Age composition, in short, tends to remain quite unaffected by movements from high to low mortality. In contrast, declines in fertility have a sharp effect on age structure, leading directly to a decline in the fraction under fifteen. The larger the decline in the one, the sharper is the decline in the other. The second side of the coin, of course, is that the fraction of adults increases.

We have here in a nutshell an explanation of one of the great historical shifts of the Modern Era. As fertility in the industrially advanced nations came down rapidly during the late nineteenth and early twentieth centuries, their age profiles shifted commensurately. Young populations became young adult populations and consumers became, increasingly, producers as well. Moreover this was at a time when productive capacity, rather than aggregate demand, was the key to economic progress. Output which would otherwise have gone to support the young could be applied to private and collective investment, without sacrifice of consumption levels. Not only was labor efficiency rising, because of new technology and new forms of economic organization, but the average laborer had fewer persons to support.

A substantial component of the rise in the per capita income of the industrializing nations between about 1870 and 1920 can be traced to these facts. And conversely a substantial segment of the economic difficulties confronting the newly developing countries of today stems from a continuing unfavorable balance among their age groups.

A fifth and final perspective is that only a minority of the world's population has already made a substantial demographic transition or is clearly in process of doing so. As already indicated, all industrially advanced nations have reached a stage of both low fertility and low mortality. A number of other nations, at an intermediate stage economically because development came later or was retarded, are also as a rule in an intermediate stage demographically. But even if both of these groups of areas are combined, they are far outnumbered by the rest of the world, where economic development has not begun or is barely incipient.

The demographic situation in the underdeveloped areas is mixed only with respect to mortality. Substantial numbers of such areas have already experienced large declines in the death rate, especially during the last two decades. The basic reason has been that modern public health methods and medical technology are both cheap and effective enough to keep people living much longer—even in the face of chronic hunger, general economic misery and ever present risks of mass disease. The instances where this pattern has recently occurred in low-income areas are so numerous and so widely distributed that it seems safe to predict its recurrence in many other such areas, where mortality has yet to make a major move pending the introduction of modern disease-control systems.

A central question, especially in the densely settled low-income nations, is how long these achieved or prospective mortality declines can be preserved under unfavorable conditions of life in general. For fertility—the other side of the transition process and the component much more resistant to change—has yet to give any significant signs of decline in the underdeveloped world.

In short, current mortality trends in the world's low-income areas are in good part independent of the pace of development, while fertility remains unresponsive to its first stirrings. The result has been a growing number of burgeoning populations, whose rates of growth are without parallel anywhere in the past. For the present at least, the difficulties of accommodating the growth in numbers are far more clearly in sight than the signs of relief. It is true that past economic development in the industrially advanced nations has always brought with it lower fertility, as an apparently inevitable by-product. But so far as our current information goes, the inevitable in today's newly developing economies may well come slowly.

These summary comments should make it clear that past and current world population movements need to be sharply classified by regions or economic status. In order to take a closer look at international transition processes and their implications, it is useful and convenient to make a threefold classification of populations by area. One group includes the nations of Northern, Western and Central Europe and their offshoot populations overseas in the new lands of the nineteenth century, mainly the United States, Canada, Australia and New Zealand. For simplicity and with no political undertones intended, this group may be termed "the West." A second group is Eastern and Southern Europe, the intermediate-stage region referred to earlier. It is true that the overlap of demographic characteristics in this region and the West has increased rapidly since the war. However, the typical differences between member nations in the two groups have been very substantial in earlier periods, both in terms of the levels of their vital rates and the timing of their transitions. Significant differences exist on the average even today, though with numerous individual exceptions. Thus a good deal more is gained for our purposes by distinguishing the two groups than by lumping them together.

The third group comprises the countries of Latin America, Asia and Africa (really the non-white populations of the last). No doubt a lumping of densely settled India with the sparsely settled Middle East, or the newly created nations of Middle Africa with Latin America, does violence to many facts. Nevertheless the procedure is justified for brevity and as a working approximation. Economic modernization is just beginning or has barely begun in all but a small part of any of these continents, while fertility is at traditional, premodern levels almost everywhere. The exceptions, Japan and a very few other nations such as Argentina, are better treated individually than as a basis for further subclassifications. Moreover, in all three continents the statistical record is scattered and fragmentary up to the end of the interwar period. Enormous data gaps remain the rule today and the generalizations we can safely make must therefore be rather unrefined. All in all, we can make the main points to be indicated for the underdeveloped world by treating it as a whole.

Turning to a closer look at the three groups, the heartland of the transition process has clearly been the West. The nations of the West began their economic modernization first, have progressed the furthest in productive capacity and income levels per capita, and have been exposed the longest to interactions between demographic evolution and rapid long-run economic change. Since economic and statistical development tend to go together, the West also provides the most extensive statistical record of such interactions.

Unfortunately the record is too short even here. We can

surmise only indirectly and in retrospect that mortality in a number of Western areas eased downward during the century or two before the industrial revolution. As suggested earlier, the downdrift was marked by extensive fluctuations about an unemphatic trend. The course of fertility is still more speculative. The first available figures on national birth rates in the West are typically well below the ones encountered today in Latin America and Asia among populations not practicing birth control. Little is known about why this should be the case. Sweden, the only Western nation with records going back to 1750, showed little change in the birth rate for a century thereafter but had already reached the low initial level of 30 to 35 per 1000. France had also attained this level by roughly 1800 and moved slowly to lower levels after the Napoleonic period. The United States apparently started with a much higher birth rate in 1800 and witnessed a much sharper drop in the next half century, although it should be cautioned that the available estimates are extremely tentative. In any event by about 1850, when extensive data first became available, most Western nations may have experienced a kind of preliminary transition, though one whose time path is uncertain and whose causal mechanisms are most obscure.

The middle decades of the nineteenth century constituted a long lull in the demographic history of the West. The forces working for transition gathered strength, as it were, for a more decisive onslaught. The storm broke in the last quarter of the century. In country after country fertility and mortality began to decline at a pace without any previous precedent. Not the least remarkable aspect of the event was its almost simultaneous occurrence in so many areas, despite substantial differences in their political and social structures, in economic conditions and trends, and in historical contexts. A giant diffusion process, so to speak, until then undetected by contemporary observers, was suddenly released and has been alive in the West ever since.

Mortality has continued downward since the 1870s, almost undeterred in trend by the two world wars. It would be difficult, for example, to distinguish neutrals from belligerents by mortality as of 1925 after the First World War or as of 1955 after the Second. For many decades Western nations have experienced ever more similar as well as declining mortality. Expectation of life at birth a century ago in the West averaged about forty years. Today it is close to or above seventy years, the biblical threescore and ten long cited in history as a limit to man's stay on earth. The trend to still higher levels of longevity seems certain to continue, though it may well slow down substantially. In the past the main contribution to increasing length of life came from mortality declines in the young ages. Today mortality before age fifty is already so small that even its total elimination would lead to only moderate gains in average longevity. Of course should major breakthroughs be achieved against the diseases of old age, notably heart and cancer, the horizons would open again much as they did in the past following breakthroughs against the infectious diseases.

On the side of fertility, the trends launched about 1875 gathered momentum for many decades. By the end of the interwar period, birth rates ranged from 15 to 20 per 1000, roughly half the size of the rates about 1850. The fertility increases in many parts of the West since the war therefore represent the first break in trend in close to a century. They also mark an interruption of the convergence of reproductive patterns throughout the region. At the moment, fertility in the European parts of the West is well below the levels found in its non-European parts, i.e. North America and Oceania.

It may be, as previously suggested, that the West has embarked upon a new phase in its fertility history. Only time will permit secure judgment. But it does seem certain that Western fertility in the future will not undo the long-term changes of the past.

The specific time sequences of the vital trends just summarized were such as to produce enormous increases in numbers, together with large-scale shifts in age composition. Among the long-settled nations of the West, population between 1850 and 1950 rose by two to three times in Norway, Denmark, England and Wales, Sweden, and the Netherlands. We need to recall that these increases developed despite very large out-migration. The newer parts of the West increased much more rapidly, of course, partly because of immigration but also largely because of their own excess of births over deaths. The two exceptions to the typical Western experience of rapid growth are France, where population increased only slightly as a result of her long-declining birth rate, and Ireland, where population decreased sharply because of emigration and uniquely low rates of marriage after the potato famine of the 1840s. As to age, in 1850 the percentage of population under fifteen tended to be about 35 in Western nations. By 1950 the typical value was 25 per cent. Although there was also a rise in the per cent over sixty-five, most of the shift went to the intermediate ages, fifteen to sixty-five, the main years of labor-force activity.

Eastern and Southern Europe—the second group of populations singled out—has had a much briefer recorded history of modern demographic movements. These can therefore be summarized more rapidly.

Details apart, perhaps the main point to be noted is that a decided transition process took place outside the West, under vastly different cultural, social, and economic circumstances. Moreover the process was no pale imitation of Western experience but occurred in its own time and manner. In retrospect, to be sure, the movement to lower mortality was quite unsurprising, given the effectiveness of twentieth-century medical technology and the universal appeal of longer life. Much more surprising—even startling—is that the appeal of lower, controlled fertility has also not been space-bound or time-bound. Eastern and Southern Europe shows clearly that this appeal has extended well beyond the centers of Western culture in the past.

As of about 1900, when a sizable collection of data first became available for Eastern and Southern Europe, both

mortality and fertility were typically above the Western
average in 1850. Unlike the West, therefore, the break
with tradition in most parts of the region has been an
event of the present century. And once it began, the transition was far more rapid. In little more than a decade during the interwar period—between the early 1920s and the
late 1930s—birth rates in many parts of Eastern and
Southern Europe dropped by amounts it took the West
more than a generation—about thirty to sixty years—to
achieve during its own early transition. Again unlike the
West, the birth rate has often continued to fall in the postwar period, especially in countries with relatively high fertility, as the transition has continued its course. Today
mortality and fertility in the region are still above the
West on the average, but the gaps of a half century ago
are a relic of the past. Birth rates in many countries are
below 20 per 1000 or not much above this level. Thus
fertility is often well below that in large parts of the West;
Hungary today has the lowest birth rate of any nation in
either region. Expectation of life at birth is typically well
over sixty to sixty-five years, which most Western countries
reached only one or two decades ago.

With respect to the underdeveloped areas, or nearly all
of Latin America, Asia, and Africa, some of the most
salient points have already been reviewed. Fertility remains
at traditional levels almost everywhere in all of these continents. Indeed it may even be rising in some areas as
a result of lower mortality, though the data are often not
reliable enough to judge. Of course it may also be that
some declines have taken place but been similarly obscured. In any event, there is certainly no evidence of any
sharp or even early transition in fertility. Meanwhile mortality in a large and growing number of countries has
been falling at a headlong pace since the war, without
precedent in previous trends. It is a remarkable fact that,
in every underdeveloped country of these continents for
which fairly reliable information exists, the mortality declines in the last decade or two have matched or exceeded
the maximum rates of decline in any part of the West

during its known history. Recent declines in a number of underdeveloped areas with less reliable data have been less dramatic, though they have certainly been rapid. In still other areas, such as Middle Africa and the Middle East, sustained mortality declines can be expected with confidence in the near future, as governments mobilize the tools of known medical technology.

The result, increasingly encountered since 1950, has been population growth at an enormous pace. National rates exceeding 2.5 per cent annually are now common, and rates exceeding 3 per cent not infrequent. The near prospect is for many other areas to reach these levels. We need to remember that such rates imply a doubling of population in only about twenty-five years. It is also worth noting that the same rates are about double the maximum rates of population growth in the European parts of the West during their century-long transition. Since Latin America, Asia, and Africa comprise the bulk of the world's population, an acceleration of their numbers implies also an acceleration in the world total. More important than global aggregates, the greatest increases in the foreseeable future will occur in the very regions with least developed economic resources. Growth in the West or Eastern and Southern Europe will be much slower.

This is not the occasion to examine closely the economic implications of such a rising tide of numbers. The densely settled agrarian areas such as India and China will clearly suffer greatly in terms of human costs, as economic needs for investment come into conflict with human needs for consumption. The less densely settled areas such as Brazil can accommodate added numbers more readily in their agrarian sectors, but even here the density picture will change radically if the expected trends come to pass. And in all underdeveloped areas, continued high fertility will imply an unfavorable age structure, with something like 40 per cent under age fifteen compared to the 25 or 30 per cent found elsewhere. The typical worker in the underdeveloped economies of Latin America, Asia and Africa will have fewer productive resources to work

with and also more mouths to support. Similarly, at the
government level, undeveloped fiscal systems will be con-
fronted with especially severe demands for collective consumption by the young, as in education.

This does not mean, despite the many voices of alarm
one hears, that the population problem in the underdeveloped areas threatens catastrophe. The newly developing economies have so far been successful enough in
accommodating the problem. Economic growth has occurred in fact and per capita income has risen in
many areas, even densely settled ones, despite the numerous political, social, and administrative obstacles attendant
upon early development. Indeed, the increases in per
capita income found in a fair number of underdeveloped
areas over the past decade compare favorably with the
trends in most Western nations during their own early
periods of development. The race between people and
product may not always be so successful in the long run,
but at least the areas in question seem capable of winning
a kind of breathing space for themselves, during which
both rapidly increasing numbers and rising per capita
product can be reconciled. Moreover, it may be that the
forces making for reduced fertility are gathering strength
and that the present is yet another temporary "lull," much
as in the West a century ago and in Eastern and Southern
Europe about a half century ago. There are indications of
a widespread desire for lower fertility among important
segments of the population in many underdeveloped areas.
Such desires may become effective behavior in the fairly
near future, as governments become increasingly committed to explicit birth-control programs, as new cheap and
effective methods of contraception become available for
the first time, or as economic modernization itself gains
momentum. Taiwan, India, Pakistan, Malaya, and possibly
Egypt and mainland China may be early cases in point in
significant areas. On the side of mortality again, declining
death rates and the reduction of debilitating disease may
have significant favorable effects on worker productivity,
while increasing numbers of survivors among the total

number of children born may help undermine the values supporting uncontrolled childbearing.

It may also be that a fertility downtrend in the under-developed areas, when and if it occurs, would be more rapid than precedent would suggest. This has typically been the case for latecomers to the transition process, such as Germany in the West, Eastern and Southern Europe after the West, and again Japan during this century. The last is the outstanding example of a non-Western, non-European culture which has gone through something like a full transition sequence. Unfortunately we know very little about Japanese vital trends during the formative years of development, between 1870 and 1920. But we do know that fertility was already declining by 1920, continued to fall within the interwar years, and has plummeted down-ward since the war. Today Japan's fertility ranks well be-low Western levels and her mortality not much above.

These comments, to be sure, represent hopes rather than confirmed expectations. At the most, one can be a qualified non-pessimist at the moment. One final conclu-sion, however, is sure. Whether the underdeveloped areas embark upon a transition to lower fertility—and if they do, the time and speed with which the process would occur—will have a dominant effect upon the future well-being and security of the great majority of the world's population.

Suggestions for Further Reading

C. P. Blacker. "Stages in Population Growth." *Eugenics Review*, Vol. 39, No. 3 (Oct. 1947), pp. 88–102.

A five-stage classification of long-run population changes.

F. W. Notestein. "The Economics of Population and Food Supplies." *Proceedings of the Eighth International Con-ference of Agricultural Economists*. London: Oxford University Press, 1953, pp. 15–31.

A stock-taking of transition doctrines and experience by one of the early students of the subject.

G. J. Stolnitz. "Interrelations between Economic Development, Levels of Living and Demographic Trends," in D. Bogue, editor, *Applications of Demography: The Population Situation in the United States in 1975.* Oxford: Scripps Foundation and University of Chicago, 1957, pp. 5–13.

A critical review of some major evidence on the timing of past transition movements.

I. B. Taeuber. "Japan's Demographic Transition Re-examined." *Population Studies,* Vol. 14, No. 1 (July 1960), pp. 28–39.

Some aspects of the main non-Western transition experience on record.

L. van Nort and B. P. Karon. "Demographic Transition Re-examined." *American Sociological Review,* Vol. 20, No. 5 (Oct. 1955), pp. 523–27.

An analytical review of the possibility of developing a theory of demographic transitions.

Chapter 3

HOW A POPULATION AGES
OR GROWS YOUNGER

Ansley J. Coale

The age of the whole human population could, I suppose, be measured from the moment the species originated, and the age of a national population could be measured from the country's "birthday." The age (in this sense) of the human population has been estimated as at least 100,000 and no more than a million years, and the age of national populations ranges from several thousand years for Egypt or China to a year or so for some of the emerging nations of Africa.

In this chapter, however, when we speak of the age of a population we refer to the age of its members, and to be precise we should use the term *age distribution* of a population—how many persons there are at each age—rather than the age of a population. The only way a single age can be given for a group of persons is by using some sort of average. A *young* population, then, is one that contains a large proportion of young persons, and has a low average age, while an *old* population has a high average age and a large proportion of old people.

The ages of various national populations in the world today are very different, and in many countries the present age distribution differs markedly from the past.

The oldest populations in the world are found in Northwestern Europe. In France, England and Sweden, for example, 12 per cent of the population is over sixty-five, and half of the population in these countries is over thirty-three, thirty-six, and thirty-seven respectively. The youngest populations are found in the underdeveloped countries —those that have not incorporated modern industrial technology in their economies—the populations of Asia, Africa and Latin America. Half of the population of Pakistan is under eighteen years, of the Congo under twenty years, and of Brazil under nineteen years. The proportion over sixty-five in Brazil is less than one fourth what it is in France. The proportion of children under fifteen is twice as great in Pakistan as in England. Paradoxically enough, the oldest nations—China, India and Egypt—have very young populations.

The highly industrialized countries all have older populations than the underdeveloped countries, and also older populations than they did fifty to a hundred years ago. Since 1900 the median age has risen in England from twenty-four to thirty-six, in the United States from twenty-three to thirty, in Japan from twenty-three to twenty-six, and in Russia from twenty-one to twenty-seven. In the underdeveloped countries, however, the age distributions have changed only slightly, and they have, if anything, become slightly younger. In Taiwan, for example, the median age has declined from twenty-one to eighteen since 1915.

What accounts for these differences and these trends in the age distribution of populations? One obvious factor to consider is migration. A famous spa has an old population because old people come there for the cure, and university towns like Princeton have young populations because young people come there to study. But the age distribution of most national populations is not much affected by migration, especially today when almost everywhere international migration is restricted.

Whether a national population is young or old is mainly determined by the number of children women bear. When women bear many children, the population is young; when they bear few, the population is old.

The effect of fertility (as the rate of childbearing can be called) on the age distribution is clearest when a population continuously subject to high fertility is compared to one continuously subject to low fertility. The high-fertility population has a larger proportion of children relative to adults of parental age as a direct consequence of the greater frequency of births. Moreover, by virtue of high fertility a generation ago, today's parents are numerous relative to *their* parents, and hence the proportion of old people is small. Conversely, the population experiencing a prolonged period of low fertility has few children relative to its current parents, who in turn are not numerous relative to *their* parents. Prolonged high fertility produces a large proportion of children, and a small proportion of the aged—a population with a low average age. On the other hand, prolonged low fertility produces a small proportion of children and a large proportion of the aged—a high average age.

It is the small number of children born per woman that explains the high average age now found in industrialized western Europe, and the high birth rate of the underdeveloped countries that accounts for their young populations. The increase in average age and the swollen proportion of old people in the industrialized countries are the product of the history of falling birth rates that all such countries have experienced.

Most of us would probably guess that populations have become older because the death rate has been reduced, and hence people live longer on the average. Just what is the role of mortality in determining the age distribution of a population? The answer is surprising—mortality affects the age distribution much less than does fertility, and in the opposite direction from what most of us would think. Prolongation of life by reducing death rates has the perverse effect of making the population somewhat younger. Consider the effect of the reduction in death rates in the United States, where the average duration of life has risen from about forty-five years under the mortality conditions of 1900 to about seventy years today. Had the risks of death prevailing in 1900 continued unchanged, and the other variables—rates of immigration, and rates of childbearing per mother—followed the course they actually did, the average age of the population today would be greater than it is: the proportion of children would be less and the proportion of persons over sixty-five would be greater than they are. The reduction of the death rate has produced, in other words, a younger American population.

These statements seem scarcely credible.

Does not a reduction in the death rate increase the average age of death? Are there not more old people as a result of reduced mortality than there would be with the former high death rates? How then can it be said that a reduction in the death rate makes a population younger?

It is true that as death rates fall, the average age at which people die is increased. But the average age of a population is the average age of living persons, not their average age at death. It is also true, as we all immediately realize, that as death rates fall the number of old persons in a population increases. What we do not so readily realize is that reduced mortality increases the number of *young* persons as well. More persons survive from birth to ages 1, 10, 20, and 40, as well as more living to old age. Because more persons survive to be parents, more births occur.

The reason that the reduced death rates, which prolong man's life, make the population younger is that typical improvements in health and medicine produce the greatest increases in survivorship among the young rather than the old.

There is one kind of reduction in death rates that would not affect the age distribution of the population at all, that would lead to the same proportion of population at every age as if mortality had not changed. This particular form of reduced mortality is one that increases the chance of surviving one year by a certain amount—say one tenth of one per cent—at every age. The result would be one tenth of a per cent more persons at age 1, 5, 10, 60, and 80—at every age—than there would have been had death rates been unaltered. Because there would be one tenth per cent more parents, there would also be one tenth per cent more births. Therefore the next year's population would be one tenth per cent larger than it would otherwise have been, but the proportion of children, of young adults, of the middle-aged, and of the aged would not be altered —there would be one tenth per cent more of each.

Reductions in mortality of this singular sort that would not affect the age of the population at all are not found in actual human experience. However, there has been a tendency for persons at all ages to share some of the increased chances of survival, and the effect of reduced death rates on the age distribution has consequently been small—much smaller than the effect of reduced birth rates, in countries where both fertility and mortality have changed markedly.

As the average duration of life has risen from lower levels to sixty-five or seventy years, the most conspicuous advances in survivorship seem always to have occurred in infancy and early childhood. It is for this reason that reduced mortality has had the effect of producing a younger population, although the effect has usually been obscured by the much more powerful force of a falling birth rate that has occurred at the same time. Thus the population of the United States has actually become *older* since 1900, because of falling fertility; but falling mortality (with its tendency to produce a younger population) has prevented it from becoming older still.

The younger-population effect of reduced mortality is not an inevitable feature of all increases in length of life. The countries with the greatest average duration of life have by now about exhausted the possibility of increasing survivorship in a way that makes for a younger population. In Sweden today 95 per cent survive from birth to age thirty, compared to 67 per cent in 1870. At best, survivorship to age thirty in Sweden could approach 100 per cent. No important increase in population at younger ages would result. If there are further major gains in the chances of prolonged life in Sweden, they must occur at older ages, and if they occur, will make the population older.

Every individual inexorably gets older as time passes. How old he gets depends on how long he avoids death.

President Eisenhower remarked after his retirement that he was glad to be old, because at his age, if he were not old, he would be dead.

Populations, on the other hand, can get older or younger. They get older primarily as the result of declining fertility, and younger primarily as the result of rising fertility.

The most highly industrialized countries have all experienced a decline of fertility of about 50 per cent since their preindustrial phase, and they all have older populations than they used to have. In France and the United States, for example, the number of children each woman bore declined for more than a century, reaching a minimum just before World War II. In each country during this period the population became progressively older. In fact, the "aging" of the population continued for a time after fertility had passed its minimum. Between 1800 and 1950 the median age of the French population rose from twenty-five to thirty-five years, and in the United States in the same interval the median age increased from sixteen to thirty. In both countries there has been a substantial recovery in fertility during the past twenty-five years from the low point reached in the 1930s. This rise in fertility has produced the first decrease in median age recorded in the statistics of either nation. Between 1950 and 1960 the median age in France fell from 35 to 33, and in the United States from 30.2 to 29.6.

This reversal in the trend toward an older population in the United States has been accompanied by a more pronounced reversal in the way proportions of children were changing. The long-term decline in fertility in the United States meant that the proportion of children to adults steadily shrank from about .85 children (under fifteen) per adult (over fifteen) in 1800 to .33 per adult in 1940. By 1960 the proportion had rebounded to .45 children per adult. In fact, the increase in the *number* of children in the population between 1950 and 1960—more than 15 million—was greater than the increase between 1900 and 1950.

The abrupt reversal of the long-term trend toward an

older population has meant the first increase in the relative burden of child dependency in the history of the United States. The very productive American economy can certainly afford to support this burden, but it has not been painless. The extremely rapid increase in the number of children in the past decade has required the construction of many new schools and the training of many teachers. In some communities where foresight, willingness to pay increased taxes, or resources were inadequate, schools have been overcrowded and the quality of instruction has suffered.

The countries that have not undergone intensive industrialization have experienced no major changes in fertility, no trends of sustained decline and recovery such as occurred in France and the United States. Rather they have experienced a largely unbroken sequence of high birth rates. There has been in consequence little change in the age composition of underdeveloped areas. All have 40 per cent or more under age fifteen, only 2 to 4 per cent over sixty-five, and a median age of twenty years or less.

The age distributions of the industrialized countries on the one hand and of the preindustrial countries on the other are ironically mismatched with what each sort of country seems best equipped to accommodate. As we have noted before, the contrast in age of population is striking. In Pakistan or Mexico nearly one person of every two a visitor might encounter would be a child, and only two or three of every hundred would be old (over sixty-five); while in England only one in four would be a child and about one in eight would be old. In the industrialized countries where the proportion of the aged is so large, the importance of the family in the predominantly urban environment has diminished, and consequently the role of respected old patriarch or matriarch has nearly vanished. The wealthy industrial countries can readily afford to support a sizable component of old people but have not in fact always done so adequately. The aging of their populations has been accompanied by a weakening or a disappearance of the traditional claims of the aged on their descendants for material support and, perhaps more tragically, by a weakening or disappearance of a recognized and accepted position for old people in the family.

In the underdeveloped countries, on the other hand, the relatively few old people are accorded traditional respect and whatever economic support their families have to offer, and hence the aged are less subject to special economic and social deprivation.

Because of extremely young age distributions, adults in the impoverished underdeveloped countries must support a disproportionately large dependent-child population—twice as great a burden of dependency per adult in the working ages of fifteen to sixty-five as in typical industrialized countries—a burden these poor countries can scarcely afford. The enormous proportion of children makes it extraordinarily difficult, where incomes are extremely low, to provide adequate shelter, nourishment, and education for the young.

Moreover, the preindustrial countries can expect no relief from dependency as a result of the spectacular drop in death rates now occurring. Unless fertility declines, this drop in mortality will only make the populations younger, adding to the already extreme burden of dependent children.

In sum, it is the industrialized countries that, better able to afford a high burden of child dependency, have only half the proportion of children found in underdeveloped areas, and that, having abandoned the institutions giving a meaningful role to the aged, have four times the proportion of the elderly found in preindustrial countries.

The last question considered in this brief survey of the age of populations is the past trend in age distribution from man's origin to the present, and what alternative trends may possibly develop in the future.

The human population as a whole has always been and is now a young population, consisting of at least 40 per cent children, and having a median age of no more than about twenty years, because the over-all human birth rate has always been about 40 per 1000 or higher. It is almost certain that until perhaps two hundred years ago all sizable national or regional populations likewise were young, with about the same age characteristics as the population of the world.

These statements can be made with confidence, even though no reliable records of the age distribution of the world, or of world birth rates, or even records of many national populations exist for most of man's history. We can be confident that the world's population has always been young because until the last two centuries it was not possible for any population to achieve low mortality for any sustained period, and any population with a low birth rate would therefore have become extinct.

It is simply not possible for a population to have a birth rate much below its death rate for a prolonged period, as can be shown by the following example. The population of the world has grown from about one-quarter billion to about three billion since the time of Julius Caesar—it has been multiplied by about twelve. But the average annual rate of increase has been very little—about 1 per 1000 per year. If the world birth rate has averaged 40 per 1000 (a reasonable guess) the world death rate by logical necessity has averaged 39 per 1000. A world birth rate only two points lower (38 instead of 40 per 1000) would have led to an annual *decrease* of 1 per 1000, and the current population would be only one twelfth instead of twelve times the population of Caesar's day. A birth rate of 35—that of England or the United States in 1880—would have reduced the 250 million of two thousand years ago to less than one hundred thousand today.

The industrialized countries have been able to reduce their birth rates without having their populations shrink drastically because they first reduced their death rates. Beginning in the late eighteenth century some countries made preliminary steps in the improvement in living conditions and sanitation that has continued until today, and in the latter half of the nineteenth century there began the remarkable development of modern medicine and public health that so greatly extended the average duration of life in the industrially more advanced countries.

In the past few decades modern medical techniques and public health methods have been introduced into the underdeveloped countries, causing an extraordinary drop in death rates, and since birth rates have not changed, the growth of world population has sharply accelerated so that it is now 2 per cent per year.

Just as it is not possible for a population to maintain for long a birth rate much below its death rate, because such a population would shrink to extinction, it is not possible to maintain for long a birth rate much *above* a death rate, because then the population would grow to a physically impossible size. For example, had the current 2 per cent rate of growth existed since the time of Caesar, the population of the world would have been multiplied by about 135 quadrillion instead of by twelve, and there would be more than 30,000 times the entire world's current population on each square mile of land area on the earth. Starting with today's three billion persons, it would take only about 650 years for a 2 per cent rate of increase to produce one person per square foot, and about twice that long to produce a total that would outweigh the earth.

In short, the present combination of a high world birth rate and a moderate and rapidly falling death rate can only be temporary. The only combinations that can long continue are birth and death rates with the same average levels.

If man chooses to continue the high birth rate that he has always had, the human population will remain a young one—but in the long run it can remain young only by returning to the high death rate and short average life it has always had. Sustained geometric increase is impossible.

If, on the other hand, mankind can avoid nuclear war, and bring the fruits of modern technology, including prolonged life, to all parts of the world, the human population must become an old one, because only a low birth rate is compatible in the long run with a low death rate, and a low birth rate produces an old population. In fact, if the expectation of life at birth of seventy years—now achieved or exceeded in many industrialized countries—becomes universal, the average number of children born per woman must decline to about two from five or more in the under-developed areas, slightly more than three in the United States, and some two and a half in Europe. Such a decline in fertility would give the whole world as old a population as any country has had to date—only about 21 per cent under fifteen, at least 15 per cent over sixty-five, and as many persons over thirty-six as under.

A world population with the age composition of a health resort is a mildly depressing prospect. Such a population would presumably be cautious, conservative, and full of regard for the past. A young, vigorous, forward-looking population perhaps appears more attractive, but in the long run the world can keep its youth only by tolerating premature death.

We find at the end, then, that although the birth rate determines how old a population is, the death rate determines what the average birth rate in the long run must be. If prolonged life produces by its direct effects a younger population, it is nevertheless compatible only with an older population.

SUGGESTIONS FOR FURTHER READING

L. Dublin and A. Lotka. "On the True Rate of Natural Increase." *Journal of the American Statistical Association.* Vol. 20, No. 151, September 1925, pp. 305–39.

A classic article in which the interrelations of fertility, mortality, growth, and age distributions were presented with the ingenious invention of a new concept, "the stable age distribution."

United Nations. "The Cause of the Aging of Populations: Declining Mortality, or Declining Fertility?" *Population Bulletin* No. 4, December 1954, pp. 30–38.

Ansley J. Coale. "How the Age Distribution of a Human Population is Determined." *Cold Springs Harbor Sym-*

posium on Quantitative Biology. Vol. 22, 1957, pp. 83–88.

Two short articles, the second somewhat technical, explaining the respective roles of fertility and mortality in shaping age distributions.

Ansley J. Coale. "Population and Economic Development," in *The Population Dilemma,* edited by Philip M. Hauser. Englewood Cliffs: Prentice-Hall, 1963, pp. 46–69.

Includes a discussion of the significance of age distributions for economic development.

Chapter 4

POPULATION AND ECONOMIC GROWTH

Joseph J. Spengler

The study of the interaction of population and economic growth involves answering two questions. First, "How does population respond to income growth?" and, conversely, "How does economic growth respond to population growth?"

Turning first to population growth as affected by income, this may best be examined both analytically and historically, using Western Europe as an example. Around 1800 its average income was much above that found in many of today's underdeveloped countries, reflecting several centuries of slow economic and sociopolitical improvement. Its population was relatively dense only in a few parts. Its mortality remained high, generally above that found in today's underdeveloped world. Its crude natality, restrained by prudent institutional checks and often in the low 30s by 1840 or earlier, was appreciably below the rates of 40–50 found in much of today's world. Yet it did not begin generally to fall until in and after the 1870s. Even so, its population grew only about 1 per cent per year when that much, or less than half as fast as population in today's underdeveloped world.

Various conditions, few of which are present in most underdeveloped countries, co-operated to prevent Europe's natality and natural increase from rising and absorbing most of its income and savings as the industrial revolution continued to augment its national product. Political and other non-economic changes modified the tastes of populations and made them less favorable to high fertility. The knowledge of contraception increased, as well as the inclination to practice it. The economic changes which were responsible for the high rate of increase in national income tended to hold natality down and eventually to depress it. There was an increase in urbanization which is relatively unfavorable to natality. As family income rose and family consumption patterns changed, demand for improvement in the quality of children rose and thus prevented income increase from stimulating fertility appreciably. More products came into existence and were made available at prices sufficiently low to make them competitive with the reproduction and rearing of children. The relative prices of some of the elements entering into the reproduction and rearing of children rose. Eventually, as the employment of children became subject to regulation and systems of individual and collective social security were established, the utility of children diminished. Finally, as incomes rose and individuals began to purchase new kinds of goods and services, they found it necessary also to buy unanticipated complements to these goods and services, with the result that at times their expenditures upon these newer products and complements thereto increased faster than average incomes. Whatever the causal agencies at work, income increase did not produce offsetting population growth, though the changes bringing about income increases often augmented the population capacities of the countries affected.

Under certain conditions, then, income growth stimulates natality, whereas under other conditions this potentially stimulating influence may be more than offset.

Until recently much of the reduction in mortality was directly or indirectly associated with improvements in economic conditions. Then it became possible to introduce death-control methods from advanced into poor and underdeveloped countries, with the result that mortality was markedly reduced, although average income had risen very little. Even in advanced countries, after life expectancy has been raised into the seventies, it becomes increasingly difficult to reduce mortality further, though average income continues to rise. In much of the world, therefore, mortality is less sensitive to changes in per capita income than it was formerly, though under some conditions it will continue to be sensitive to variations in economic circumstances.

Because the relationship between population growth and income growth is affected by many variables, one may not set down a hard and fast statement of this relationship. Both natality and mortality may respond to changes in income, though not necessarily so. Migrants tend to move to places where incomes are relatively high. Furthermore, changes that make for growth of income generally tend to increase the capacity of countries to support population at given levels of living. There is quite a high correlation between rate of growth of population and rate of growth of national income, though the relation does not apply universally. Also there is quite a low correlation between rate of growth of population and rate of growth of per capita income. Thus the view is reinforced that one cannot tell just how these two types of growth are interrelated unless one also takes into account the impact of other relevant variables.

How a country's national income responds to an increase in its population is the second question to be examined. It was noted above that increase in population and increase in national income, by country, are positively associated, either when growth of income and growth of population have common causes, or when growth of a country's labor force makes for increase in its national product. Also, the statistical relationship between rate of growth of population and rate of growth of income per capita may be affected by a variety of factors.

The second part of this discussion can be subdivided into two kinds of population growth: an increase in density, and an increase in numbers as such. First, what are the possible economic effects of an increase in over-all population density—an increase, that is, in the ratio of a country's population to its territory? The manner in which a country's population is distributed over its territory will be disregarded, for such distribution, while reflective of a country's past history, is governed predominantly by technological changes which modify a nation's occupational structure, decrease the relative importance of its primary industries, and increase the proportion of its population situated in urban communities. Changes in this distribution flow largely from efforts to improve the location of economic activities as methods of production change, transport and communication are bettered, and the relative importance of agriculture and other primary activities diminishes.

Adam Smith supplied us with the main key to an understanding of the effects of an increase in population density. He said that division of labor is limited by the extent of the market. For, as the population of a country becomes larger and the ratio of population to territory rises, it becomes possible to develop division of labor and specialization more fully; it also becomes possible for each individual to remain in communication with a larger number of individuals and sources of information, at least up to some limiting point fixed by his capacity for communication. It becomes possible finally to realize more fully the economies of large-scale production when over-all density is greater and there are more customers and more income available for the purchase of the output of large-scale enterprise.

There are limits, of course, to the extensibility of division of labor and specialization. These are set largely by technological conditions which determine roughly how subdivisible any task or function is and how large plants and companies may become and yet remain optimally efficient. If it is possible to produce as efficiently in small plants as in large plants, the limits to the extensibility of division of labor are reached sooner than if large plants are better suited than small plants to minimize the input cost of output. Similarly, when tasks and functions can no longer be further subdivided, the limit to this source of division of labor has been reached. The limits to division of labor thus assume two somewhat distinct forms. There is the kind of limit just mentioned. There is also the limit set by the way firms fit and complement each other in the market as suppliers and as sources of demand. If a good fit is not achieved, many firms will be working at under or over capacity, with the result that unit costs will be higher than they might be. It is easier to achieve a good fit with smaller than with larger firms. In general, whatever renders small firms as efficient as large firms serves, directly and indirectly, to make full realization of the benefits of division of labor accessible to relatively small as compared with relatively large populations.

This latter point is subject to some qualification. Whatever be a nation's technological alternatives, cost minimization will depend not only on these alternatives but also on the comparative prices at which labor and other agents of production are to be had. Furthermore, since men differ greatly in entrepreneurial ability, these differences will produce differences in the size of business firms though they need not necessarily make for enlargement of plants when smaller plants are about as efficient as larger plants. If a society is quite dynamic, and plants must therefore be kept adaptable to changing circumstances, plant size in keeping with adaptability may be preferred. Finally, changes in the optimum scale of particular functions may cause some redistribution of functions among plants. In general, however, there is limit to the extensibility of division of labor and specialization through enlargement of a country's population and purchasing power.

It is also essential, when discussing division of labor with respect to a country's economy, to allow for its trading relations with other countries and its participation in international division of labor. For if a country elects to participate fully in international division of labor, it can achieve all the benefits of specialization with a smaller population than if it participates only partially. If such a country should elect not to participate in international trade and division of labor, it might require a larger population to maximize its internal division of labor. By so doing, however, it would make its average income lower than it would have been, given a smaller population and full participation in international division of labor.

It has been assumed that the only limit to the degree to which division of labor should be carried is that determined by technological conditions and the structure of prices. This must be qualified. If a country is short of agricultural land and natural resources, this shortage may make it inadvisable for it to maximize its division of labor, because it may lose more through rising raw-material costs than it gains through increased division of labor. This is the way Malthus and some of his contemporaries reasoned, for they lived in an age in which agriculture was both the dominant industry and an industry subject to diminishing returns. This is also the way later economists reasoned when the agricultural base of society began to be replaced by a mineral base in the late nineteenth century; they anticipated rising raw-material costs as a result of classical diminishing returns and the exhaustion of more accessible supplies. Indeed, as late as 1920 the great English economist Alfred Marshall said that "if the growth of population should continue for very long even at a quarter of its present rate," diminishing returns, long suspended, would again become operative and make land the most important form of material property.

Up to now, Marshall's prediction has not been realized. While the real cost of some raw materials has increased, that of others has not. Moreover, in parts of the world the input cost of produce has fallen, and even in much of the poverty-ridden underdeveloped world it remains possible to overcome various present shortages and meet food requirements through domestic efforts. Improvements in agricultural and mineral technology have, in recent decades, overcome many earlier difficulties. Furthermore, while the per capita consumption of produce and raw materials generally has risen, it has risen less rapidly than per capita income, because as incomes have risen, men have spent ever larger portions on goods and services into which agricultural products and raw materials enter in only a very minor degree.

It would be foolhardy, however, to attempt to draw much comfort from recent trends. Consumption and costs have risen no more than they have because average consumption of food and other raw materials has remained low in most of the world. Indeed, should per capita consumption of produce and raw materials in underdeveloped countries rise to the Northwest European level, aggregate consumption would considerably more than double. And should the world's population continue to grow at the current rate, it will have doubled by the year 2000 and have risen to perhaps fourteen times the present level by the year 2100. The pressure upon raw-material sources will be so intensified, given population growth of these proportions, that their costs almost certainly will rise markedly. While technological improvements will probably partially countervail this tendency toward increasing costs, these improvements may not be evenly distributed over the world. At present, in fact, it is the well-to-do nations that enjoy the greatest technological advantages. "To them that have, it shall be given" seems to apply here.

In view of what has been said, it may be presumed that improvements in division of labor consequent upon increase in over-all population density are realizable only in certain parts of the world. Intensive study might identify these parts with precision. Among them probably may be included Canada, Australia, and parts of the Soviet Union, Africa, and Latin America. The answer depends in part upon the content of the standard of life people seek. If, as average incomes rise, the demand rises for land-oriented recreation and accommodation and space generally, land shortage will set limits to how much division of labor is preferred. The same thing will happen if the per capita demand for raw materials rises notably. If, on the contrary, little store is set by space and land and raw materials, greater division of labor may be preferred.

Economists and others sometimes use the term "optimum" to describe the preferred population size for a country, given its international trading relations. They thus imply that when this optimum size is exceeded, more people are disadvantaged than are advantaged. What constitutes such optimum size depends, of course, upon what people want, upon their preferred standards of life. If the objective is the highest possible per capita income, it will be one size, generally one smaller than the populations found in many if not most countries. If this objective includes, for example, three or more children per family, the optimum will be larger, but it will presently be exceeded, and in such measure that the desired number of children will have to be reduced and made more compatible with other components of the desired standard of life. If the objective is partly political, the optimum probably will be larger than if it is entirely economic.

Objections are sometimes made that the concept of optimum is not useful because up to now it has not proven possible to define an optimum empirically and in keeping with possible changes that may modify it, or to regulate numbers in such ways as to make actual populations correspond to optima. Some have held, however, that when an actual population exceeds the optimum in size, it encounters resistance to further growth if the population in question is able to practice contraception effectively. Perhaps the major value of the optimum concept consists in the balancing of the advantages and the disadvantages of increase in population density which is associated with use of the concept.

The second part of examining the question of how national income responds to population growth emphasizes growth of population as such and not changes in density which accompany growth.

Population growth imposes two kinds of cost on a people. First, it absorbs resources that might otherwise be devoted to consumption or to capital formation. Second, it renders a population's age composition less favorable to production under more likely combinations of mortality and fertility.

Population growth tends to reduce the rate of saving. It does not affect all saving, of course, since the capital formed by corporate and other enterprise is not reduced in consequence of population growth and may even be stimulated somewhat. It does not materially affect the rate of saving of other childless savers unless the government taxes these savers for the support of increments to the population. It does, however, affect the rate of saving of families within which children are being reproduced and reared. For, with income given, the consumption requirements of children absorb income that might otherwise be saved. The savings absorbed that are relevant, of course, are the savings absorbed by *population increase;* for the savings absorbed by *population replacement* are not properly viewed as potential savings but as costs of population maintenance. There is a minor qualification to this: in so far as adult members of families work more and hence earn more in order to meet family expenses, their net savings will be reduced in lesser measure or not at all.

Population growth absorbs resources that might otherwise be used to increase physical and personal capital per head. Provision must be made for industrial, public, and private capital wherewith to equip the annual increment to the population. Provision must also be made for the education and training of population increments as well as for other costs attendant upon the reproduction and rearing of these increments.

How much capital is thus absorbed is not easy to estimate, at least on an internationally comparable basis. One probably does not miss it far when one puts at around 4 per cent of the national income the amount needed to equip increments to a population growing 1 per cent per year. Such an estimate corresponds fairly closely to American experience as well as to Canadian. It may not differ greatly from the real cost of increasing the populations of underdeveloped countries by increments essentially *identical* with those already in existence. The cost would be much higher, of course, if, as is likely, the underdeveloped countries would want to add to their populations increments *superior* to those in existence.

Suppose that the population of an underdeveloped country is averaging one hundred dollars per year and is growing 2 per cent per year; then, given the 4 per cent rule suggested above, this growth absorbs resources equal to eight dollars per capita or to 8 per cent of the national income, which is not greatly different from the rate at which many underdeveloped countries are forming capital. How much faster would this country's average income increase if its population were stationary and this 8 per cent of national income were used instead to equip the existing population and facilitate the adoption of improved methods of production? Any answer would be a guess, since it would depend on the current productivity of capital and the range of improved methods available for exploitation. Suppose, however, that the yield on capital averages about 15 per cent. Then the return on the eight dollars absorbed per capita would be about one dollar and twenty cents; this corresponds to over 1 per cent of the national income. So if per capita income had been rising 1–2 per cent per year previously, it might rise 2–3 per cent per year with a stationary population.

Certain advantages are associated with population growth, provided there is enough capital available to keep everyone at work. This, of course, is seldom the case in densely populated underdeveloped countries, and may not be the case even in those in which the population is not yet so dense. The economy is more flexible. It is somewhat easier to maintain balance among occupations and to adjust to changes in tastes or technology which cause the demand for labor to fall in some areas and occupations. Businessmen may be somewhat more optimistic and disposed to invest if they expect demands to increase as a result of population growth as well as because of increases in per capita income. It is also said that there is less likelihood that unemployment will develop because planned investments fall short of planned savings, in part because provision must be made for a growing population and in part because enterprisers may be disposed to introduce improved methods more rapidly. That these advantages are real is indisputable, but that they are worth the costs of population growth in most countries is doubtful.

The second possible cost of population growth is a reduction in the fraction of the population of working age. If this happens and the fraction of the population of working age is reduced 1 to 5 or more per cent, *potential* per capita productivity is reduced in like proportion. What actually happens, of course, depends also on what, if any, accompanying changes are made in the length of the work week, the relative number of women in the labor force, and age at retirement. It is certainly true that if the aggregate demand for labor is relatively high, it usually can be met more easily when the fraction of the population of working age is high. Another cost which varies with age structure, that of educating the young, can be passed over, at least in so far as this cost varies inversely with that of caring for unproductive older persons.

To summarize, increase in population and population density apparently remains a source of net economic advantage in but few countries, elsewhere serving to reduce the potential rate of growth of average income. In not so many decades environmental limitations will probably halt population growth if it has not been brought under effective voluntary control. Should population growth not soon be halted, capacity for economic growth, as yet very inadequately developed in much of the world, could become incapable of freeing all or even most of mankind from the bondage of extreme poverty.

Suggestions for Further Reading

Ansley J. Coale, editor. *Demographic and Economic Change in Developed Countries.* Princeton: Princeton University Press, 1960.

Philip M. Hauser and Otis Dudley Duncan, editors. *The Study of Population.* Chicago: University of Chicago Press, 1959. See chapters 22, 25, 26, 29, and 32.

Joseph J. Spengler and Otis Dudley Duncan, editors. *Population Theory and Policy.* Glencoe: Free Press, 1956.

Ansley J. Coale and Edgar M. Hoover. *Population Growth and Economic Development in Low-income Countries.* Princeton: Princeton University Press, 1958.

Harvey Leibenstein. *Economic Backwardness and Economic Growth.* New York: John Wiley and Sons, 1957.

Chapter 5

WORLD URBANIZATION: TRENDS AND PROSPECTS

Amos H. Hawley

It is because cities have had, and still have, such a crucial importance in the rise and fall of civilizations that they command our attention and excite our curiosity. Indeed, city and civilization are different aspects of the same thing. If by civilization we mean a highly developed and widely diffused culture, then for each civilization there must be a center at which knowledge, ideas and experiences are accumulated, elaborated and organized into a more or less thematically coherent mode of life and in which, too, are created the instrumentalities for projecting that mode of life over the surrounding territory. For a center to exert such an effect, it must represent a permanent settlement, situated at an intersection of routes of travel, the residents of which are emancipated from agriculture and therefore free to cultivate their special abilities, to converse with travelers from near and far, and to reflect on the implication of what they glean from those conversations.

The earliest known centers of that order made their appearance around 3500 B.C., in the Euphrates Valley. Cities spread from that region eastward into the Indus Valley and as far as southern China and westward across the plains of Mesopotamia and the Valley of the Nile. They followed the diffusion of techniques for increasing the productivity of stable agriculture—e.g., irrigation, metallurgy, the animal-drawn plow, the wheeled cart. But the cities of that early period and for millennia following were feeble prototypes of those that were later to appear. Their sizes and their capabilities for the elaboration of urban life were restricted by the meager surplus product yielded by agriculture. While no figures are available, it seems probable that the proportion of a regional population that could be supported in non-agricultural activities—i.e., in cities—seldom exceeded 3 or 4 per cent and only in a few favored localities might it have risen to 5 or 6 per cent.

In the 1000 years before Christ, cities began to dot the shores of the Mediterranean Sea. Colonies sent out from old centers in Asia Minor and Greece later became sources of further colonization. Networks of trading relationships between the new towns and the mother cities sprang up, stimulating the growth of urban population, accumulations of wealth and a flowering of culture. Miletus, Athens, Alexandria, Carthage, and Syracuse, to mention only a few, rose to commanding heights as urban centers. Their populations grew to twenty, thirty or more thousand and in one or two instances approached one hundred thousand. The proportions such figures constituted of the total populations in their dominions is a matter for guesswork. They must have been very small, in view of what is known about the inefficiency of cultivation in that era.

Urban development in the ancient period reached its highest point in the Roman Empire, especially during the first through the third centuries A.D. As the empire expanded, it opened avenues of trade and increased the volume of administration to be performed. The mounting flux of activity added to the growth of existing cities in the Mediterranean Basin and led to the creation of new ones along the inland watercourses and at the sites of frontier outposts. At the heart of the imperial system, of course, stood the towering metropolis of Rome, the residence of perhaps as many as 350,000 people at its zenith. In the Roman, as in earlier periods, unfortunately, history gives a disproportionate share of attention to cities. Consequently we are led to an exaggerated impression of their numerical importance. It is possible that in Italy urban population might have been as much as 15 per cent of the total. But it should be remembered that the Italian population had long since outgrown the productive capacity of the lands and had come to rely on North Africa and other provinces for much of its food supply. Elsewhere in the empire the proportions living in urban places were doubtlessly far below that in Italy.

With decline of the empire in the fifth century and afterward, trade and the intercourse between regions subsided. Everywhere in the West cities languished; many of them reverted to country towns, while others were evacuated or destroyed in the havoc caused by repeated barbarian invasions. Urban life all but disappeared in Europe for a period lasting several hundreds of years, though it persisted in its ancient pattern in the Eastern Empire until late in the medieval period.

The revival of trade in Europe, beginning in the tenth century, initiated a resurgence of city development. Places that had been flourishing centers before the dissolution of the Roman Empire responded to the quickening influences of trade and traffic; in other places, mainly at the sites of well-located burghs and cathedrals, the seeds of new cities germinated. The urban awakening was gradual and cumulative. For a long period lasting into the seventeenth century, the context in which urban development progressed consisted of a small-scale handicraft economy which supplied a long-distance trade in luxury items and a highly localized exchange of a limited variety of ordinary consumer goods. The great majority of people were unaffected by the events taking place. Political parochialism, laborious transportation and the weight of an agrarian tradition imposed severe limits on city growth. A mere handful of places attained or surpassed populations of 25,000. Rural population constituted over 90 per cent of the total.

For urbanization to advance beyond a rudimentary level, several currents of change must be set in motion. In the first place, there must be substantial improvements in food production, thereby releasing increasing numbers of people to engage in non-agricultural industries. Trade in services as well as in goods must expand and diversify, for trade is the means of providing an urban population with sustenance. More than that, trade establishes lines of communication and dissolves cultural differences. But without a growth of manufacturing there is little to trade. This is not to say that every urban place must have an equivalent amount of manufacturing industry in its complement of activities; rather every urban place must have access through trade to manufacturing industry wherever it is located. Both production and exchange depend on an accumulation of capital. So also does the improvement of transportation, without which the increased volume of food and manufactured goods cannot be effectively moved from producer to consumer. Finally, a centralization of political power is essential. Only thus is it possible to achieve and maintain over adjoining areas a dependable coinage, a standard set of weights and measures, freedom and safety on the roads and other uniformities required for regular and frequent exchanges.

All of this had been in the making for some time and was becoming visible in seventeenth- and eighteenth-century Europe. That was a period of both accelerating change and consolidation of the effects of change. An emergent technology was becoming manifest, novel not only for its mechanical features but for its economic and political innovations as well. It would soon so diminish distances and shorten processes of all kinds that widely scattered people could be drawn into larger and more complex systems than had ever been known previously. By the end of the period Europe stood at the threshold of a profound reorganization of its social structure, a reorganization that would be dramatized in a massive urbanization of its population.

At the beginning of the nineteenth century, according to the best evidence available, less than 2 per cent of the world's population lived in cities of 100,000 or more inhabitants. There were only twenty-two known places of that size in the world. Not more than 2½ per cent lived in cities of 20,000 or more population. Europe, at that time, was not much more urbanized than the rest of the world. The proportions of populations living in cities of 10,000 or more people were less than 5 per cent in Austria and

Germany, 6 per cent in Sweden, 10 per cent in France and approximately 21 per cent in England. The United States, destined to become one of the foremost urban nations, had a mere 4 per cent of its people in cities of 2500 or more inhabitants.

Near the close of the preceding century, around the time Thomas Malthus expounded his dismal theory of population and poverty, the rural countryside had come to resemble a population reservoir filled to overflowing. That was due mainly to a long-run decline in mortality which began after 1750 as a result of increases in the abundance and the stability of the food supply. The continuing fall of the death rate not only permitted more people to survive each year, it added progressively to the number of people in the economically active ages of life. Rural overpopulation was further aggravated by reduced manpower requirements in agriculture brought about by more extensive farming and by increased productivity per farm worker. Vast numbers of people, therefore, were available, in fact were poised to take advantage of alternative opportunities. Only a slight inducement was needed to release streams of migrants pouring into cities. Thence came the manpower needed to staff the rapidly expanding urban structure.

During the ensuing one hundred years urban population in Europe doubled and tripled. By the last decade of that century England, where economic changes began earliest and proceeded most rapidly, had over 61 per cent of its people living in cities of 10,000 or more. In France the proportion in places of the same size had reached 26 per cent, and in Germany, Austria and Sweden cities of 10,000 or more population claimed over 15 per cent of each state's population by the end of the century. Similar experiences occurred elsewhere in Northwestern Europe, notably in the Low Countries. The number of European cities with 100,000 or more population increased from twenty-two, in 1800, to 120, in 1895; in the same period their proportion of the total population advanced from less than 3 per cent to 10 per cent. Such figures, of course, do not represent the total magnitude of urbanization; many places of less than 10,000 people were properly classifiable as urban places. Nor do they measure the extent to which urban organization had penetrated the daily affairs of the rural population.

The swarming of population to cities was not without its social costs, as in fact is no major social change. Although the efficiency of cities as centers of economic organization was advancing rapidly, their effectiveness as centers of social life lagged a half century or more in arrears. The mounting numbers of newcomers crowded into inadequate housing arrayed along narrow, poorly drained streets. The congestion worsened an already dangerous sanitary situation. Neither the knowledge nor the incentive for the protection of public health had advanced much beyond that of medieval days. Moreover, civil disorder was endemic. The preponderance of young males in the migrant streams provided an additional source of turbulence to an already chaotic situation. Separated from the informal sanctions of family and village, compelled to live in squalor, crowded with strangers and subjected to unpredictable employment opportunities, the new urban population was a breeding ground for crime and violence. Municipal administration was unprepared for the problems facing it. Few services and few controls were provided. Standards for working conditions and safety in industrial establishments were virtually unknown; more than that, the concept of the public interest was hardly enough developed to thrust itself into so private a domain as business enterprise. Hence occupational hazards joined unsanitary conditions to preserve high mortality rates in cities while they were falling elsewhere. The situation might have been much more serious had it not been possible to drain off some of the excess population to overseas settlements in the New World. Later, urban death rates also yielded to the influences making for decline, though they have retained a small margin of excess over rural rates to the present day.

There were ameliorating influences in the early indus-

trial city, and they eventually led to reforms of many sorts.
But a long time would pass before Western man would
learn how to live in cities; his education is not yet completed. Midway through the protracted process of accommodation to the new circumstances of life, one important
lesson was learned. That had to do with man's adjustment
of his rate of reproduction to the exigencies of the urban
context. Thus, following a period of accelerating population
growth and some hundred years after the death rate
started its fall, the European birth rate entered upon a
long-term decline. Specifically, the decline of fertility resulted from the substitution of the business enterprise for
the family as the basic producing unit of society. With the
shift of that function away from the family, the having
of children ceased to be economically imperative; it became a matter of personal preference. Thereafter the rate
of population growth in Europe began to subside.

Through the course of history to the end of the nineteenth century, then, the center of gravity of urban development had moved westward and northward. In the
process it had been transformed from a pattern of widely
scattered centers of modest size designed to dominate the
hinterlands politically and militarily but having rather
tenuous economic and social relations with them. It became one of a multiplicity of interrelated cities constituting
at least the bare structure of a system that soon would em-
brace every aspect of the political, economic, and social
lives of the citizens of national states. The new pattern was
built on the strength of machine technology, extensive
specialization, economic rationalism and the cultivation of
mass markets. The economy was necessarily expansive,
constantly reaching out for new resources and enlarged
markets. In whatever direction it extended itself, the in-
dustrial-commercial economy provoked or threatened to
provoke fundamental changes in the societies that were
touched.

Urbanization spread from the northwesternmost corner
of Europe outward in all directions, as adjacent territories
were brought successively within the orbit of expanding

European influence. City growth reached its peak in England and the Low Countries during the first half of the nineteenth century; it attained its crest in central and southern Europe and in North America during the latter half of that century. In Africa, Asia and Latin America sharply accelerating rates of city growth seem to be largely a twentieth-century phenomenon.

Many parts of those areas, though possessing old urban traditions of their own, had also had recent introductions to European urbanization, for Western imperialism had fostered the rise of huge entrepôt cities in colonial holdings throughout the Old World. But these monolithic cities—such as Bombay, Calcutta, Singapore, Manila, Jakarta, Hong Kong and many lesser ones—stood apart from their environs and exerted little influence on them. Yet the colonial metropolises fitted into a framework of world urbanization which is still very much in evidence. That is, major cities have clung to coastal rims and to the banks of navigable streams to reap the obvious advantages of low-cost transportation for bulk cargoes. Nor were the colonial cities entirely unique in their relative independence of hinterlands. In general, cities until recently had many more interchanges with one another than with their respective localities. Hence they tended to resemble one another more than they did their cultural settings. It is only with the maturation of urban organization in entire societies that the attention of major cities has turned inward, so to speak, to establish close and manifold linkages with inland regions.

In the Old World and in Latin America, which together include most of the developing nations, city growth is proceeding at a rapid pace. Unfortunately the data for the measurement of the trend are uneven in both availability and quality. Furthermore, the definition of an urban place differs widely among the many nations. Growth in urban places of 100,000 or more population, however, is reported with fair uniformity. Using that, then, as at least a partial measure of urban growth, we find that large cities have been increasing at about 5 per cent per annum over the past ten years, which is about twice the average general growth rate in their areas. The modal rate of large city growth is around 7 per cent, though the rates range above 12 per cent annually in Kenya, Leopoldville Congo, Columbia, Ecuador and Algeria, or four to six times the growth rates of their respective total populations.

The full import of these events is not immediately apparent. Is urbanization in developing areas the same phenomenon as that which occurred in Europe? Does it bear the same relationship to economic and cultural change in the one place that it did in the other? Such questions are easier to answer in retrospect than in prospect. It would be unwise, therefore, to try to summarize the relationships among trends in more than tentative terms. Moreover, summarization, inescapable in a talk as short as this, glosses over important differences. The areas of rapid urbanization today are, in fact, quite heterogeneous.

Given that reservation, it is noteworthy that the rate of urban increase shows no consistent relationship with measures of economic change such as the growth of manufacturing industry, capital accumulation or gains in agricultural productivity. Some of the highest rates are found in areas which Professor Rostow describes as being at the "take-off" stage of economic growth; but others with high rates of urbanization still have far to go before reaching that stage. In any case, short-run observations are apt to be very misleading. Yet some significance must attach to the fact that the rate of large city growth is inversely related to the per cent that manufacturing product is of total domestic output, to per capita income and to the average per capita caloric content available in the food supply. By the same token, urbanization rates vary directly with proportions of the economically active population engaged in primary production.

There is more than a trace of suggestion in these observations that urbanization has begun in a great many, if not all, developing countries well before any appreciable economic growth has occurred. Indeed many of the developing nations are still too poorly integrated to support a viable national economy. For example, in countries with annual per capita incomes of less than 125 dollars, which are also countries with very high urban growth rates, the amount of domestic mail delivered annually is but eight pieces per person. That may be compared with forty-seven pieces of domestic mail per person in countries with per capita incomes of 375 dollars or more and 258 pieces of mail in the advanced nations of the West. The poorest of the new nations have but two telephones per 1000 population, while the better-off have forty-nine and the advanced nations 253. Or again, the most undeveloped nations have newspaper circulations that average twenty-three per 1000 population, the somewhat more developed nations distribute 140 newspapers per 1000 population, and in the most advanced nations circulation frequencies amount to 322 per 1000 population.

While it is possible that small gains in economic growth may produce relatively large increases in urban population in the initial phases of large-scale economic and social reorganization, it seems more than likely that other factors have also contributed to the current trends. One of these, in many of the new nations, has been the substitution of national for foreign personnel in governmental and other administrative positions, coupled with a great expansion of governmental functions. Another and perhaps more significant circumstance is a rapid decline in the general death rate, repeating the European experience, though due in this instance to a systematic diffusion of Western sanitary and medical knowledge. In consequence, the rural populations of developing countries, which were in many cases already living at or near subsistence levels, have suddenly been swollen with excess numbers. The large, bustling cities doubtlessly have seemed to offer an escape from the crowded countryside. Floods of refugees from rural poverty and to some extent from internal disorders incidental to the modernization process have inundated cities. But the movement is premature. Only a very small fraction of the newcomers manage to gain a foothold in the urban system. The great mass hang on the edges of

cities in hope and despair. They must live by their wits or
on the charity of the occasional kinsman who finds employment. The precariousness of life is heightened by in-
fluxes of still more people. For population growth in most
new nations is racing ahead, unimpeded as yet by declining birth rates.

Although the great numbers of people aggregated in
and around large cities pose serious health and civil problems, they also constitute an abundant supply of cheap
labor. As capital becomes available, the huge pool of unemployed might prove to be a rich resource from which to
feed the manpower needs of expanding industry. Much of
that labor supply is untrained, however, not only tech-
nically but also in the discipline of a rational economy and
in the regimen of urban life. Perhaps another generation
or more must pass before former rural dwellers can participate effectively in a modern economy.

Urban growth in the new nations is reminiscent in several respects of that which occurred in Europe a hundred
years or more earlier. There is a similar excessive migration from hinterlands overcrowded as a result of the widening margin of births over deaths, a similar burden of
social costs induced by population resettlement, and a
similar inability of cities to absorb the displaced rural
people. But there is one important difference. No large
empty spaces remain in the world, such as there were in
preceding centuries. Hence there is no opportunity to re-
lieve the rigors of the transition by substantial emigrations
abroad. In the modern world each nation must solve its
demographic problems within its own boundaries. Consequently, to accomplish with minimum cost a broad-scale
population redistribution requires that two major changes
occur almost simultaneously: there must be a drastic reorganization of agriculture to increase output and to bring
agriculturalists into the consumer-goods market, and there
must be an equally abrupt multiplication of urban employment opportunities. Whether that can be done without a centrally managed economy and stringent population controls remains to be seen.

A second difference lies in the rate and character of the urbanization process. Events are occurring in the new nations in a matter of a few decades which in the European experience were spread over two centuries or more. The European transition to an industrial economy, though hectic enough at the time, was sufficiently gradual to permit the laying of a firm foundation in the habits of the people, in the building of transportation systems, housing and other necessary social overhead, as well as in capital accumulation and industrial investment. Advances followed upon one another in a more or less orderly fashion as the implications of mechanical technology were unfolded. The new nations seem bent on collapsing all of that into a brief interval of time. One wonders about the consequences of skipping stages, such as the domestic-industry stage, of leaping over great distances and great historical disparities by airplane before learning to travel on the ground within a gradually widening universe of discourse, and of setting out to adopt alien forms of organization without having had experience in the preliminary steps of their evolution. Success in this bold venture will quite probably disclose new and unexpected patterns of social change.

The world settlement pattern has altered markedly since the beginning of the nineteenth century. What was then about 2½ per cent of the population living in places of 20,000 or more has become, in 1960, almost 25 per cent. No major continental area now has less than 13 per cent of its population in such places. The 1440-odd urban places of 100,000 or more people now hold 16 per cent of the world's people instead of the less than 2 per cent in 1800. The proportions vary from 11 per cent in Asia to over 50 per cent in Oceania.

That the developing nations will continue in the path of urbanization is scarcely questionable. They have been brought too fully into the community of nations to remain in limbo between traditional and modern social orders. Nor can they return to their earlier conditions. They are caught up in an irreversible and inexorable movement. To what extent they will become urbanized one can only guess. Certainly it will vary with the forms taken by the different economies. It seems unlikely, however, that any nation in the future will need over 25 or 30 per cent of its population in primary production, if indeed that much, in contrast to the 50 to 75 per cent many of them now have. But as indicated previously, urbanization is not confined to cities. It is a mode of life which envelops an entire population regardless of place of residence or occupational category.

While urban aggregation has been spreading to all parts of the world, the process has been changing its character in Europe and North America. The predominantly centripetal form of the movement, which prevailed down to the present, gave way in the twentieth century to a dispersion of urban agglomerations over steadily enlarging local areas. Quick and highly flexible means of transportation and communication, as represented by the motor vehicle, cheap electric power, the telephone, the radio and television, have so reduced the frictions of space that dense, compact cities are no longer necessary. Accordingly a sprawling metropolitan area is replacing the city as the significant urban unit in the West. A repetition of that change in other parts of the world will be delayed until rising levels of living make comparable facilities for movement available to the masses of populations.

Suggestions for Further Reading

Lewis Mumford. *The City in History.* New York: Harcourt, Brace and World, Inc., 1961.

Urban history as viewed by a humanist and architect-planner.

Henri Pirenne. *Medieval Cities: Their Origins and the Revival of Trade.* Translated from the French by Frank D. Halsey. Princeton: Princeton University Press, 1939.

An authoritative study of the emergence of the European city from the feudal town.

Roy Turner, editor. *India's Urban Future.* Berkeley and Los Angeles: University of California Press, 1962.

A symposium on the problems and implications of urbanization in one of the world's largest new nations.

UNESCO. *Social Implications of Industrialization and Urbanization in Africa South of the Sahara.* Paris: United Nations, 1956.

Reports and supplies commentary on a large number of field studies of the urban experiences of native peoples in Africa.

Adna Ferrin Weber. *The Growth of Cities in the Nineteenth Century.* Ithaca: Cornell University Press, 1963.

An incomparable quantitative study of the rise of modern cities.

Chapter 6

TAKING AN INVENTORY OF
180 MILLION PEOPLE:
THE U. S. CENSUS

Conrad Taeuber

In April 1960 the United States took its eighteenth decennial population census. It established the official population totals for every state, county, municipality, and each of the smaller divisions of government. It also supplied a vast amount of information about the geographic distribution of the population. From it we know how many men and women we have, how many children of school age, how many professional workers, and how many unskilled workers. It gives information about the incomes of persons and of families, the size of families, and the migration of the people. Because similar censuses have been taken at ten-year intervals in the past, the 1960 census also provides a valuable tool for the measurement of many changes that are taking place in the United States. A census is not only a snapshot of the present, but a good means of comparing with the past, and it gives important clues to some of the developments that may be expected in the future.

The United States census is not the oldest census, for counts of the population go back to the beginning of human history. Governments have long felt a need to know something about their people, whether it was to gauge the potential of military manpower, the possibilities of further growth or of additional revenue, or the need for certain public services or provisions. The need to provide enough food has always been an important reason governments wish to know how many people there are.

The United States census, however, is the oldest regular continuous census of population. The founding fathers provided that a census was to be taken within three years of the establishment of the new country and every ten years thereafter.

The basic purpose of the census was to meet a problem that the founding fathers foresaw clearly. They had provided that in the House of Representatives, the number of representatives from each state should be based on the population of that state. Clearly the states could be expected to grow at different rates, and it was equally clear that new states would be added as settlement moved away from the Atlantic coast into the vast and largely unknown areas to the west. Following each census, the number of representatives from each of the states was to be determined on the basis of the population of that state.

Providing the basis for determining representation of the states in the House of Representatives is still a major purpose of the census. Following the census in April 1960, in accordance with the law, the Census Bureau reported to the President in November 1960 the official population count for each state. The Congress had previously determined that the total size of the House of Representatives should be continued at 435 members, as it had been since 1910. The Congress had also determined the method to be used in computing each state's share. As a result of the 1960 census, nearly half of the states changed their number of representatives—sixteen of them lost and nine gained. The largest gain was that of California, which increased its total by eight members. Pennsylvania, which lost three members, was the largest loser.

The President of the United States transmitted this information to the Congress shortly after it reconvened in January 1961. At the next elections to the Congress, in 1962, the number of representatives elected from each state was the new number as it had been determined by the 1960 census.

Although apportionment, as we call it, was a major reason for the establishment of the census on a regular decennial basis, this is by no means the only purpose that is served by the census. That first census, in 1790, was very

simple. Even then it was considered useful to determine
the total number of households as well as persons, and to
find out how many men and women there were. It also
asked for the number of boys under sixteen, as well as
men sixteen and over, presumably because men might be
called upon in the case of a need for military manpower.
At that time slavery was still legal, and it was necessary to
count the number of slaves, in part because a slave counted
as three fifths of a person in determining the number· of
persons for purposes of legislative apportionment. Not all
Negroes were slaves, however, and the census counted
how many of them were slave and how many free.

Secretary of State Thomas Jefferson had hardly completed his report to the President concerning the approximately four million persons who had been counted in the
1790 census when voices were raised to the effect that the
nation needed more information about its people than had
been included in that census. This expression of the need
for more information about the nation and its people has
continued to the present day. It has led to changes in
content from one census to the next, with questions being
added as the need for them was demonstrated and questions being dropped when they were no longer necessary.

By the time of the third census, in 1810, the government wished to have additional information about the
growth of its manufactures. Now there is a census of manufactures every five years. By 1840 questions about agriculture were added, and now there is a census of agriculture every five years. Questions on housing were included
from time to time, and since 1940 a census of housing has
been taken at the same time as the census of population.

A census of business was established in 1929 and this
census is now taken once every five years. A number of
other smaller censuses have also been established on a
regular basis to provide information on important elements
in the economy. Preparations are now under way for the
first census of transportation.

In the census of 1790, the federal marshals were simply
instructed to count the population and were told what

items of information to secure. The marshals then posted the information which they had assembled in a public place for all to see, and to give persons who had not yet been included the opportunity to have their information added to the returns for the appropriate district. The returns were summarized by hand for publication. Several censuses were taken before it was felt necessary to provide printed questionnaires to the enumerators, and it was 1850 before it was considered necessary to provide space for entering the details about each individual rather than simply securing the information for each household.

As the nation grew, as the needs for information about the population grew, and as the techniques for census taking were developed, it became increasingly clear to the government agencies charged with the taking of the census that improved accuracy and greater speed in reporting the results were necessary. In the census of 1890, it was possible to make use of a newly developed procedure for punching of cards to record the data about each person. This was the invention of a former Census Bureau employee named Herman Hollerith. James Powers, another Census Bureau employee, had worked on the same problem and had developed a similar approach. The contributions of these men to the handling of masses of data by governments and by private business is well known. This was the beginning of the mechanical sorting and counting machines that later led to the development of the modern computer for such work. The search for methods to improve accuracy and speed in the release of the returns has been a continuing concern of the Bureau of the Census. There is already some planning for improvements which might be put into effect in 1970.

Planning for the 1960 census can be said to have begun immediately after the 1950 census had been taken. In the course of the processing of the 1950 census returns and in the evaluation of the methods and results of the 1950 census, a number of suggestions for improvement and for further study were developed. Steps were taken to test some of these through actual field trials.

The determination of the questions to be asked and the
form in which the results are to be issued is left to the
Director of the Census, acting on behalf of the Secretary of
Commerce. Certain questions, such as those on age and
sex, have been a part of the census since the beginning.
Questions such as those on education, occupation, income,
and migration had been so widely used that it could be
taken for granted that they would be continued. There
are others about which some doubts might be raised in
view of the changing conditions, and there were many
suggestions for new questions.

The question was raised, for instance, whether it might
not be appropriate to devote less attention in the census to
the foreign-born population than had been considered
necessary during the period of heavy foreign immigration.
Because the proportion of aliens is very small, the question
on citizenship was dropped, except in New York State
which still required it for the apportionment of the state
legislature. The growing concern with metropolitan-area
problems led to including questions about how people
travel to and from their place of work. It was decided to
try to obtain more accurate returns relating to age by
asking for the month and year of birth instead of the traditional question on age at last birthday. Although the censuses in the past had collected some information about
religious organizations, the United States census has never
included a question asking the individual about his religious affiliation, preference, or belief. Many other countries include such a question in their census as a matter of
course, and there was substantial support for a similar
query in the 1960 census. However, it was not included.

Studies were made of the census experience of other
countries as well as of our own. Considerable attention
was given to the uses that had been made of data from
earlier censuses, in order to help in evaluating the changing
needs for census results.

The federal government is by no means the only user.
State and municipal governments, private business interests, health, welfare and educational authorities and a host

of others rely on the census to provide essential information for many purposes. The powers and duties of municipalities are generally defined in state laws which use official population figures as one of the criteria. The population totals are also an important element in the distribution of large amounts of money from the federal government to the state governments, and from the state organizations to the local governments. As part of the preparations for the 1960 census, efforts were made to secure the views of users of census reports. The earliest consisted of a number of meetings held in all parts of the country to give users a chance to meet with Census Bureau officials to consider joint problems. These meetings were usually arranged in cooperation with private statistical and business organizations. The meetings provided an opportunity for detailed examination of problems that had been encountered in the use of the data from past censuses or the needs for new items or new modes of presentation. Many suggestions for improvements were made. Although the views expressed were not unanimous, there were two suggestions which resulted from virtually every such meeting. All of them emphasized the need for the publication of more statistics for small areas, including areas within the larger cities, and the need for greater timeliness in the publication of results.

The Census Bureau maintains close working relations with the national and regional professional associations that have an interest in census data. During the years of planning for the 1960 census, members of the Bureau staff took advantage of many occasions to discuss proposals for the next census with members of such organizations, particularly at their annual meetings. Some of the organizations established special committees to formulate and report the views of their members concerning the forthcoming census, and to work with the Bureau in census planning.

The American Statistical Association, the American Marketing Association, and the Population Association of America maintain permanent committees to advise the

Bureau of the Census on matters of policy and on other
matters of primary concern to the membership of these
professional organizations. In addition, three special advisory groups were established to consult with the Census
Bureau staff about the 1960 census. One was a Technical
Advisory Committee, consisting of nineteen persons who
were known as experts in the field of population. They
included university professors, private research workers
from business and non-profit groups, and statisticians in
federal, state and local governmental agencies. This committee held eighteen meetings at which it reviewed all
aspects of the census plans. Because of the interest of the
federal government agencies in the census, the Bureau of
the Budget was asked to appoint an advisory group, including representatives of the federal agencies which had
a direct interest in the census. To secure wide public participation in the planning of the census, a Council of Census Users was established, including representatives of
some seventy national private organizations; plans for the
census were discussed with them and their suggestions
solicited.

Many individuals sent letters to the Census Bureau, or
to their representatives in Congress, expressing views on
proposals and asking for consideration of their particular
needs for census data.

The census of the United States is the responsibility of
the federal government, and it is carried out by the U. S.
Bureau of the Census. The Bureau has the responsibility
for determining the questions to be asked, for recruiting,
training and supervising the persons that do the census
work, and for the tabulation and publication of the results.
It bears the full costs of the census. In taking the census, it
cannot follow the practice that is used in some countries,
of delegating some of the work to provincial or state governments and, through them, to individual local governments. Local government officials and schoolteachers are
not under the supervision of the federal government, and
therefore are not automatically available as census enumerators. State and local governments cooperate, but the

final responsibility for the work rests completely with the federal government.

It has been the practice in the United States to recruit temporary personnel for the census. For census purposes, the country is divided into enumeration districts, which have a population of about 700 persons and preferably not more than 1000. Enumeration districts should have boundaries which can be readily identified, and their boundaries must take into account the boundaries of municipalities, counties and states, as well as some local political units, such as wards, and the statistical areas for which the Census Bureau intends to publish results. Enumeration districts were outlined in advance of the census, often with the assistance of local groups. Maps showing the boundaries of each such district were prepared by the Census Bureau.

The enumeration district became the work unit, both for the collection of the information and for the later steps in the tabulation of the data. Each enumerator was given one, or more, enumeration districts as his or her area of responsibility. About 160,000 enumerators were engaged in the 1960 census. The enumerator generally was a resident of the district which was assigned to her. (Most of the enumerators were women.) In addition, there was a crew leader for each sixteen enumerators; the crew leaders in turn reported to 400 temporary field supervisors, who reported to the Washington headquarters through the Census Bureau's seventeen permanent regional offices. Altogether some 180,000 persons were recruited for the 1960 census, some of them for as little as two weeks and some for as much as two years.

The recruitment of such an army of enumerators is not easy. The work requires the full time of the individual for a short period, and much of the enumeration must be done in the evening when people are more likely to be at home. The rate of pay is not high. In many of the rural areas it is necessary to drive an automobile. It is a source of real national pride that enough public-spirited persons could be found to take on these assignments and to carry them through to completion.

Prospective enumerators were required to meet certain minimum essentials. They were mature persons, in good health, citizens of the United States, high school graduates, and of good reputation in their local community. Each of them was required to take a written test that was designed to test the ability to understand and follow instructions such as those which would be given as part of the census training and the ability to read maps such as those which the enumerator would need to use as part of the census work. Only those persons who satisfactorily completed these written tests were appointed as enumerators. After a person had been appointed, there was still a period of training before the actual work of enumeration could begin. Many of these persons who had not sat in a schoolroom for many years found it strange that they were back in school for four mornings or afternoons, being instructed in the methods and requirements of census taking and learning the rules under which this census was to be taken. There were a few who did not successfully complete this training and they were dropped from the rolls.

The census is a big national undertaking in which there is much interest. For months prior to the census date, magazines, newspapers, radio and television had been bringing information about the census to the public, and at the time of the census there was also a substantial advertising campaign, made possible through the voluntary work of the advertising industry. The appointment of an enumerator, crew leader or district supervisor was news in the area affected, and in many communities there was an active campaign for the hiring of enumerators. Thus in many ways people were informed about the census. During the last week in March the mail carriers delivered the Advance Census Report form to all homes. This form contained only a few questions about each of the individuals in the household and about the home in which they lived. The householder was asked to fill this in and to have it ready for the enumerator who would call within a few days. When the enumerator called, she asked for the Advance Census Report form and reviewed the entries which had been made on it. If everything was in order, she then transferred the information to a special form called a "Fosdic" form, which could be read by the electronic equipment. If the form was not ready, or was incomplete, she proceeded to ask for the necessary information.

Special arrangements were made to secure information about persons who were not living in households, such as those in institutions. The night before the census date, questionnaires were given to all persons in hotels and motels. Special arrangements also were made to include in the count those persons who were not likely to be counted in the regular enumeration. One night was set aside for a special enumeration of missions, flophouses, and other places where homeless people are likely to be found. Every effort was made to include not only the people who have regular living arrangements, but also those people who do not. Members of the armed forces, as well as civilian government employees who were out of the country on the census date were counted under special arrangements. In the 1960 census, for the first time, provision was made to have a special count of other U. S. citizens living overseas. They were not included in the total population of the United States, but a special report giving information about this group is included in the census publications.

Two major questions are asked about the work of each enumerator. Did the enumerator include all persons who should have been included in that enumeration district, and were the entries on the questionnaires correct? If each enumerator missed only one household in her enumeration district, the population count would be short by about half a million persons. Experience has shown that despite the training, some enumerators misunderstand some of the instructions or fail to carry them out properly and thus contribute to errors in the census results. Since most of the errors are made by a small proportion of all enumerators, it becomes particularly important to identify these persons early and retrain or replace them.

It was the responsibility of the crew leaders to guard against errors. Each crew leader was expected to familiarize himself with the enumeration districts under his charge and to identify any possible problem spots in advance. Moreover, in each of the districts he had made a list of fifteen to twenty-five housing units, starting at a specified point and proceeding in the order in which the enumerators were to do their work. Within the first days of each enumerator's work, the crew leader reviewed it with her. If she had failed to include any of the units which he had previously listed, or if there were errors or omissions in the reports, steps were taken to make sure that the enumerator worked more carefully in the future. If her work was entirely unacceptable she was to be removed from the rolls at this point, or, if additional training seemed likely to be profitable, she was given that training and told to report for a second review of her work after a few days. Each enumerator's work was given a final check by the crew leader before the work in a district was considered to be complete. Regular progress reports were made from enumerators to crew leaders and from crew leaders to district supervisors, and on up to Washington.

As the enumerator went from house to house, she left a longer form at one household out of every four. This form called for additional information, such as the occupation and industry of each working person; the amount of schooling each person had received; the country or state in which he was born, the place where he lived five years before, the place where he worked, and how he went to and from his work; the income received during the previous year; the method of heating the home and the fuel used for heating, cooking, and heating of hot water; the possession of an automobile; air conditioning and certain other household equipment; and a number of related questions. This form was to be filled in and returned to the census office by mail.

About one third of the enumerators were continued in this second stage of the census work. They were given additional training, particularly on the definitions that related to the items in the household form, and then were given the forms that had come in by mail. They had the responsibility of making sure that there was a household form for each household or person for whom one was required and that the entries on the form were complete and consistent. To carry out this work they went back to the households or used the telephone as needed. Their work was also checked by their crew leaders. They transferred the information which had come in to another set of Fosdic forms, which were shipped to headquarters.

This procedure was used for about four fifths of the population. In some areas, where distances between households are greater, it would have been too expensive to have enumerators go back to that fraction of the households that might need to be visited a second time if they failed to return completed household questionnaires. In those areas the enumerator secured the information for the household questionnaires from the sample household as soon as she had found that a particular household had been drawn in the sample.

This arrangement of having part of the information come from all of the population and part from only one fourth of the population was designed to save time and money, for obviously it meant less effort in field collection, fewer pieces of paper to handle in the office, and fewer items to count.

Counting up the information obtained for 180,000,000 persons is not a simple task. Totals must be available for each of some 18,000 incorporated places, for some 35,000 townships and similar political units, for about 3100 counties and for each of the fifty states. In addition, in the larger cities, arrangements were made to provide statistics for small areas known as census tracts, which were designed for statistical purposes. There were about 23,000 of these. In the larger cities, also, some statistics were to be presented for the 750,000 city blocks. In order to get all this information tabulated and printed in good time, it was decided to make use of modern electronic computers.

The Fosdic forms played an important role in this work. This term, FOSDIC, is an acrostic for Film Optical

Sensing Device for Input to Computers, a machine that had
never been used before. Built especially for the 1960 census, it has the ability to read marks that have been made
in specified places on the form and then to translate what
it has read into magnetic tape which the electronic computers can read. Most of the entries on the forms that the
enumerator turned in were made by blacking in little circles. Thus, instead of writing "male" or "female" on the
questionnaire, the enumerator simply marked one of the
little circles that appeared opposite the words "male" or
"female." However, replies to questions about a person's
work or the country in which he was born were written on
the form. Since the machine did not read words, it was
necessary to have some persons translate the words into
code marks that the machine could read.

When this had been done, the questionnaires were photographed on microfilm. This film was passed through
the Fosdic machine, which transferred the information to
computer tape in a language that the electronic computer
could read.

The job of writing instructions for the computer was
much more difficult than that of writing instructions for
the enumerators. The computer has an enormous ability to
do work and does what it is told to do. It does it very
rapidly and very accurately, but if what it is told to do is
not right, the results will be wrong. In ordinary clerical
work the supervisor is always there. A clerk can ask
whether the instructions really mean what they seem to
mean, and the supervisor can suddenly say, "Oh, I didn't
mean it that way at all; I mean it this other way." Or the
clerk can suspend the work while she gets an answer to an
unforeseen question. This is much more difficult when one
is working with these giant computers, and so every effort
must be made to give the computer complete instructions
for every case that might arise in dealing with replies to
many questions about the circumstances under which
some 180,000,000 people are living.

But this was finally done and several million instructions
were written for the computers. When the computer was
finished with its task, the results were in the form of mag-

netic tape, which cannot be read by the human eye. But this tape was turned over to another new machine—a high-speed printer, which could take the magnetic tape and print out the tables that were to be published. At this point human beings again entered the picture. They reviewed the results to make sure the instructions had been carried out. They also inserted page numbers, and some titles and headings, and made sure everything was ready for final printing. The Government Printing Office arranged to have them photographed, to have plates prepared from the photographs, and to have the printing done from the plates.

If you had only one copy of each of the reports resulting from the census, you would need a shelf over 15 feet long, for you would have about 100,000 pages of reports, containing over a billion numbers. From this you could learn a great deal about the people of the United States, or about any place within the United States. You would find there the answers to many questions which government, business, and other private persons need to ask about their communities, and you would also find the basis on which many public as well as private actions are based. If after a few years you could look at the census volumes on the shelves of many users of the census results, you would find many well-worn volumes.

From the census of 1960 we learned that the population had increased by about 18 per cent in ten years, to a total of almost 180 million persons. The population living on farms had decreased greatly; the population in many large cities also had decreased, and the greatest increase had taken place in suburbs around large cities and in medium-size cities. Half the people had moved to a different house or apartment in the preceding five years, housing in general was much better than in 1950, and more families had electrical appliances and other conveniences. We learned, in addition, that half the young men who had recently completed their schooling had finished a little more than twelve years of school; that college graduates earn about $3800 per year more than graduates of elementary school; that married men living with their wives earned about two and a half times as much as men living alone; that one in five married women who had children under six years old at home was in the labor force; and that 77 per cent of all married couples with one member over sixty years old owned the homes in which they lived.

Quality control is an important part of any statistical operation, and the Bureau has been much concerned with the quality of the results it secures. Steps are taken to assure a high quality of performance in all stages of the work. In addition, the Bureau has conducted a series of studies during and after the census to evaluate the census results. Information concerning possible errors or misinterpretations is useful not only in helping improve the next census, but also in giving the user some help in determining what interpretation he can make of the data. Some households are interviewed a second time, and if there are differences between the two responses an effort is made to learn why these differences exist. Census records are also matched against records from other sources, and an effort is made to explain any differences that may exist. The results of these several studies are made available in order to assist persons who will be using these census reports.

The questions to be asked in any census are those which are especially useful to the nation, and they will differ from time to time as conditions change. However, in many respects the needs of nations for information about their people are similar, and there is much that is similar in the censuses of different countries. The similarities as well as the differences are important. The United States has cooperated with the United Nations and its agencies in the development of its census plans, in order to make sure that in important respects the results of the United States census can be compared with those of the censuses taken in other countries.

SUGGESTIONS FOR FURTHER READING

U. S. Bureau of the Census. *The 1950 Censuses—How They Were Taken.* Procedural Studies of the 1950 Censuses, No. 2. Washington, 1955.

U. S. Bureau of the Census. *Procedural Report on the 1960 Censuses of Population and Housing*. Bureau of the Census Working Paper, No. 16. Washington, 1963.

U. S. Bureau of the Census. *Principal Data-Collection Forms and Procedures*. U. S. Censuses of Population and Housing, 1960. Washington, 1961.

U. S. Bureau of the Census. *Processing the Data*. U. S. Censuses of Population and Housing, 1960. Washington, 1962.

Carroll D. Wright and William C. Hunt. *History and Growth of the United States Census*. Prepared for the Senate Committee on the Census. Washington, 1900. Covers census history from 1790–1890.

Chapter 7

LONGEVITY AND MORTALITY IN THE AMERICAN POPULATION

Mortimer Spiegelman

The historical record of the longevity and mortality of the American population parallels closely that of the peoples of several countries of Western Europe and, viewed in a broad sense, reflects a parallel economic, social, and scientific development. A crude life table indicates that the average length of life in Massachusetts and New Hampshire was about thirty-five years in the late eighteenth century, when the United States was just emerging as a nation. This figure is practically at the level of that reported for Sweden at about the same time. By the middle of the nineteenth century, the average length of life reached about forty years in Massachusetts, very close to that for England and Wales near the same period. Although these figures point to some improvement in longevity and mortality for the United States in its early years, the path was by no means smooth; severe outbreaks of yellow fever, smallpox, and cholera were not uncommon. Whatever the advances in sanitation and medicine were over this period, their contributions to the improved health record were undoubtedly small. The principal factors were social and economic progress, and then only in an indirect manner through changes they brought by improvement in the environment. Their role, though difficult to assess at any time, has since continued.

The second half of the nineteenth century witnessed the birth and growth of the public health movement in the United States, with initial emphasis on sanitation and preventive measures against the common infections. By 1900 the average length of life reached forty-seven years, a gain

of seven years in a half century. During the following decades up to the outbreak of World War II, the public
health movement intensified throughout the country and
medical progress brought in new preventive and therapeutic measures. At the same time, rapid social and economic
progress gave rise to a high standard of living with an improved environment at home and at work, better education,
an appreciation of personal cleanliness, and an abundant
and varied food supply of high quality. Under those circumstances, the average length of life in the United States
rose to sixty-three years by 1940; this was sixteen years
more than in 1900.

Notwithstanding the absorption of a substantial proportion of medical and nursing personnel into the armed
forces during World War II, the longevity record of the
American population improved and advances continued
up through 1954, when the average length of life reached
69.6 years. This level was maintained for several years and
then rose slowly to an average length of 70.0 years in 1962.
Thus, in the period of a little over two decades since 1940,
the average length of life increased by seven years.

The recent successes in prolonging the average lifetime
had beginnings shortly before World War II with the development of new chemotherapeutic agents. Since World
War II, new therapeutic agents, such as the antibiotics and
hormones, and a host of other advances in medicine and
surgery have brought remedy or relief to many afflicted by
illness and have also saved lives.

Several distinct factors may be recognized in the improving postwar longevity record for the United States.
First, there are not only the advances in the scope and
quality of health goods and services, but also the growth
in their quantity; typical is the increase in the construction
of medical-care and public-health facilities. Second, the
health services are being provided by medical and allied
personnel whose training and equipment are undergoing
constant improvement, although already at an advanced
stage, and who are benefiting by a ready exchange of ideas
through modern means of communication. Third, the fi-

nancing of the costs of medical care to its consumers has been greatly eased by the rapid growth of voluntary health insurance among the self-supporting and by the development of public welfare programs for the indigent. Fourth, the population of the United States has become very health-conscious as a result of health education programs and publicity given to advances in the medical sciences. As a fifth determinant, reference is made again to economic progress. Some of its impact has already been cited. Equally significant is the fundamental role economic progress has played by providing an increasing flow of wealth into the development of health programs and by releasing manpower for health research and services as a result of industrial and agricultural efficiencies.

From the broad picture of health progress, attention will now be turned to some of its details. In the United States, the longevity record for females has always been better than that for males. Thus in 1962 the average length of life for females was 73.4 years while that for males was 66.8 years, a margin of 6.6 years in favor of females. However, not only do females have the better record for longevity, but they have also made the greater gains. For example, from 1940 to 1962 the average length of life of females rose by 8.2 years, compared with 6.0 years for males.

Health progress can also be considered in terms of mortality, which is obviously the counterpart to longevity. It is typical that mortality starts at a relatively high rate in the first year of life, drops rapidly to a low point at about age ten, then rises gradually with increasing age to about mid-life—about forty-five years—and afterward rises sharply with advancing age to the terminal years—about age 110. The mortality rates for the United States in 1962 were less than 2 per 1000 at each age from one to thirty-four years and less than 1 per 1000 at each age from two to eighteen years. These rates rose to about 8 per 1000 at age fifty and to 27 per 1000 at age sixty-five.

In general, the relative reductions in mortality for the United States have been greatest at the early ages, amounting to as much as 66 per cent at ages one to four years in the period from 1940 to 1962. At ages five to thirty-four years, the mortality rates were cut over half and at ages fifty-five to eighty-four years the reductions amounted to under 20 per cent. Thus mortality in the United States has become increasingly a problem of the older ages. When the mortality rates according to age are examined for each year from 1940 to 1962, and separately for males and females, it appears that most of the reduction occurred before 1954 and that, since then, the improvement for males has been at much the slower pace. An understanding of these mortality changes over the years is provided, to some extent, by an examination of data regarding causes of death.

The outstanding feature in mortality reduction so far during this century is the control achieved over the infectious diseases. In 1900 the three leading causes of death —pneumonia and influenza, tuberculosis, and diarrhea and enteritis—accounted for almost one third of the total mortality. In the current situation (1962), and at a much lower mortality level, only pneumonia and influenza still ranks among the first ten causes of death; tuberculosis and diarrhea and enteritis rank much lower. In their place, as leading causes of death, are the chronic diseases and accidents. In 1962 diseases of the heart alone accounted for 39 per cent of the deaths from all causes, cancer for 16 per cent, cerebral hemorrhage for 11 per cent, and accidents for almost 6 per cent.

The recent picture regarding causes of death varies strikingly with age. Accidents head the list of causes of death for both males and females at ages one to twenty-four years. Pneumonia and influenza together rank second at ages one to four years, but they are outranked by cancer at ages five to twenty-four years. Accident fatalities maintain their lead among males at ages twenty-five to forty-four years, with cancer in first place for females. For each sex at this stage of life, heart disease is in second place among the causes of death. At ages forty-five and over, diseases of the heart rank first as a cause of death for both

males and females. Second place is taken by cancer for
males at ages forty-five and over, and for females at ages
forty-five to sixty-four. However, among females at ages
sixty-five and over, cerebral hemorrhage ranks second to
diseases of the heart.

A brief review of recent trends of mortality from the
leading causes of death provides some understanding of
the more rapid improvement in the health record for females compared with males. In the case of diseases of the
heart, the mortality rates for females have been decreasing
gradually, while those for males have shown little change.
Mortality rates from cancer have tended upward for males,
while those for females have shown either slight change or
have actually decreased. For both cerebral hemorrhage
and accidents, each sex benefited by a decrease in mortality, but the reductions were more rapid for females than
for males.

The infant mortality rate—that is, deaths under one year
of age per 1000 live births—was 25.3 in both 1961 and
1962. This level is about half the rate in 1940, namely
47 per 1000 live births, and just one fourth of the rate in
1915, when such data first became available. However, as
in the case of mortality in general, the pace of reduction
in infant mortality has slackened appreciably since 1954.
A more spectacular picture is provided by the improvement
in maternal mortality—that is, the number of deaths from
conditions associated with pregnancy and childbirth per
10,000 live births. This rate was 3.5 per 10,000 live births
in 1962, less than one tenth of the rate for 1940, and nearly
one twentieth of that for 1915. Contrary to the situation
for infant mortality and for mortality in general, maternal
mortality has continued to improve since 1954.

In the United States, as in other countries, for each sex
and throughout adult life the married have the advantage
of lower mortality than the unmarried. This is generally
attributed not only to the selection of healthier lives
through marriage, but also to a self-selection on the part of
the unhealthy to stay out of marriage. Not to be overlooked
is the better care that may be expected in married life not

only in times of illness, but also to lessen its chances of
occurrence. In the case of the widowed, the higher mortality experienced may be a consequence of the poorer circumstances in which, as a class, they find themselves.

Using 1950 records, a study was made of the mortality
of American males classified according to broad occupational groupings. The poorest mortality record was established by both white and non-white laborers, and the best
record by farmers in the case of white males and by man-
agers and proprietors in the case of non-white males. There
was a wide range in mortality between the extremes. The
ratio of mortality for the least-favored occupational category to that for the most-favored category was 1.5 for
white males and over 2 for non-white males. These variations in mortality among occupational groups arise largely
from environmental influences. There is some evidence,
from insurance sources, that the range of variation in mortality between the most-favored and least-favored occupational categories has been narrowing.

The level of longevity and mortality varies appreciably
within the United States, with the best records in the essentially rural states of the West North Central region, where
living conditions are generally at a high level. The poorest
records are found in the regions of the South and Southwest, where living conditions are at lower levels than in the
rest of the country for large segments of the population.
However, when these longevity and mortality records are
examined for the interval from 1930 to 1950, it is found
that the states with the poorer records have been making
the more rapid gains. As a result of this difference in longevity and mortality trends, the margin between the most-
favored and least-favored areas has narrowed appreciably.

There are few countries—and none of comparable size
—with a longevity record surpassing that of the United
States. The most populated country with a better record is
England and Wales, where the average length of life in
1961 for males was 68.0 years; this is 1.0 year more than
for males in the United States. Females in England and
Wales had an average length of life of 73.8 years, only

.2 of a year greater than for females in the United States.
However, by age forty the average remaining lifetimes are
practically identical in the two countries. Outstanding records for longevity have been traditional in the Scandinavian countries and the Netherlands. For example, in 1960,
males in Sweden had an average length of life of 71.2
years, an advantage of 4.6 years over males in the United
States. In the case of females, Sweden had a much smaller
margin over the United States, its average being 74.9 years
and the advantage amounting to only 1.8 years.

With mortality before mid-life at very low levels in the
United States, the other English-speaking countries, and the
industrialized countries of Western Europe, attention has
been concentrated on the situation at the older ages. It
has been found that mortality in mid-life and later in the
United States is lower than in England and Wales and other
English-speaking countries in many instances, but not as
low as in the Scandinavian countries and the Netherlands.
However, the rate of decline in mortality in mid-life and
later during the last quarter-century has been about the
same for the United States as for these other favorably situated countries.

A recent comparison of some interest shows that the
average length of life for the Commonwealth of Puerto Rico
is practically at the level of that for the United States.
When the mortality rates for the two areas are examined
according to age, it is found that the advantage of Puerto
Rico is confined solely to mid-life and later. Before mid-life,
mortality is appreciably higher in Puerto Rico, a situation
due in large measure to the widespread prevalence of infectious conditions, such as diarrhea and enteritis and tuberculosis. The inference drawn from this comparison is
that the survivors to mid-life in Puerto Rico represent the
hardy stock that escaped or warded off the debilitating infections of their earlier years, while the weaker element
succumbed to them. Accordingly, the average length of life
is hardly a suitable measure of the health status of a community or nation in all circumstances. Only surface indications regarding health status are provided by comparisons

of areas with records for high longevity. However, where the average length of life is low, a poor situation is clearly evident.

As is the case within the United States, there are indications that the range of variation in longevity and mortality among the countries of the world is narrowing. This was effected not only by the rapid growth of medical and public health knowledge, but also by advances in communication, which quickly disseminated such knowledge, and by the resources put into their application. Especially noteworthy are the results produced by the concentrated efforts in the postwar period toward the control of the infectious and parasitic diseases in the less industrialized countries. A good example is furnished by Ceylon, where the death rate per 1000 population within a decade was brought down from an average of 16.5 in 1945–49 to only 9.9 in 1955–59. Over the same interval, in the United States, where the infectious and parasitic diseases were already largely under control, the general death rate declined somewhat from 10.1 to 9.4 per 1000 population.

In order to form some opinion of the probable course of longevity and mortality for the United States over the next few decades, the records of the recent past are studied in detail. Particular attention is given to the individual states and countries that have established superior records, since what they have already accomplished should be attainable by the nation as a whole. Equally important is the rate of medical progress. As far as the United States is concerned, the level of mortality before mid-life but after infancy is already so low that further reductions at this stage of life as a result of medical progress will produce little gain in longevity. The problem is more complex in mid-life and later where the chronic diseases predominate in the mortality picture. Since the chronic conditions are still largely of obscure origin, medical progress will reduce mortality at the higher ages largely through therapeutic accomplishments in both medicine and surgery. Thus, in contrast to the past, when preventive measures were the principal factor in gains in longevity and reductions in mortality, future benefits will come largely by prolonging the lifetimes of the physically impaired.

In view of the uncertainty in any prognostication, it has become customary to offer projections of longevity and mortality in terms of a range rather than any one set of figures. Thus it is expected that the average length of life in the United States by the year 2000 will reach between sixty-nine and seventy-four years for males and between seventy-five and seventy-nine years for females. Compared with 1960, these figures indicate gains of between two and seven years for males and between two and six years for females. The range of estimates for the year 2000 is wide and will very likely encompass the actual figures.

Gains in longevity and reductions in mortality carry implications in many directions. The role of these trends in the growth of population is commonly recognized. Also apparent are the increased numbers of people brought into the older age brackets by the rising chances of survival. For example, the chances of surviving from birth to attain age sixty-five were only 41 per 100 according to mortality at the beginning of the century; with current (1962) mortality, these chances are 71 per 100. Whether or not this increase in numbers at the higher ages carries with it a rise in the proportion of total population at this stage of life depends upon the course of the birth rate and migration.

For all of United States history, males have always outnumbered females—until 1946, when this situation was reversed, very largely as a result of the more rapid gains in longevity of females compared with males. This excess of females is particularly marked at the older ages.

Improved longevity has also had a profound effect on family life. Most important, it has increased appreciably the average length of married life and thereby diminished very greatly the problems and burdens of orphanhood for dependent children. However, as a result of the increasingly greater chances of survival for women, the likelihood that they will outlive their husbands has gone up, with a consequent rise in the probability of wives becoming widows. Still another product of the increasing differential between the sexes in chances of survival is a rise in the expected number of years by which wives will outlive their husbands.

SUGGESTIONS FOR FURTHER READING

L. I. Dublin, A. J. Lotka, and M. Spiegelman. *Length of Life.* New York: Ronald Press, 1949.

This book traces and interprets the progress made in health and longevity from earliest times, with emphasis on social and scientific influences.

United Nations. "With Special Reference to the Situation and Recent Trends of Mortality in the World." *Population Bulletin* No. 6, New York: United Nations, 1963.

This source reviews regional variations of mortality, characteristics of the decline in mortality, and variations in mortality by causes of death.

M. Spiegelman. *Introduction to Demography.* Chicago: Society of Actuaries, 1955.

Chapter 4 discusses measures and characteristics of mortality, and Chapter 5 describes methods used in the construction of life tables.

M. Spiegelman. "Recent Trends in Mortality at the Older Ages in Countries of Low Mortality." *Proceedings of the International Population Conference.* New York, 1961.

This brief paper, together with the lengthier paper presented by the author at the World Population Conference in Rome in 1954, reviews the international mortality situation in the industrialized countries since about 1930.

I. M. Moriyama. "Change in Mortality Trends in the United States." *Vital and Health Statistics.* U. S. Public Health Service Publication No. 1000, Series 3, No. 1, Washington, 1963.

This is a comprehensive study of the recent leveling off of mortality rates, and identification of disease factors responsible for the change in the trend of over-all death rates. An assessment is made of prospects for changes in the future.

Chapter 8

THE FERTILITY OF
THE AMERICAN POPULATION

Charles F. Westoff

Today most of the attention of persons concerned with population is focused justifiably on the developing areas of the world where rapid population growth threatens to outpace economic growth. Much less attention has been directed toward the less ominous but equally interesting phenomenon of the American "population explosion." The United States population today is growing at about the same intrinsic rate of natural increase as the world as a whole—that is, at nearly 2 per cent per year. At this rate the population would double every thirty-five years. The U. S. rate of growth actually is closer to that of the newly developing areas than to that of most other countries of Western civilization. This similarity in growth rates is deceptive, however. In the large populations located in the developing areas, the rapidly accelerating rate of growth has been brought about by sharp declines in mortality, while in the United States the higher growth rates of the last two decades result from an unparalleled rise in fertility. Thus, although the demographic appearance is the same, the underlying reality is quite different indeed.

To place recent American fertility in perspective, we must first examine the historical trend of the birth rate and the factors apparently responsible for this trend. Then we can take a better look at recent developments and future prospects.

Demographic data for early American history are not easily available. However, there is some evidence that American fertility during colonial days was among the world's highest. The average married woman had about eight children. In those days, high infant and general mortality rates claimed perhaps half of these children before they reached marriageable ages. Nevertheless, despite this higher mortality, the size of families was much greater than now. The birth rate, estimated at about 55 per 1000 population, contributed to such a high rate of natural increase that as early as 1660 the white population of America was probably predominantly native-born. This high fertility was attributed by contemporary observers to the abundance of land and the economic opportunity offered by the untapped resources of virtually an entire continent. It was also a response to social factors supporting a norm of high fertility—for example, the traditional religious values of the early American versions of European Protestant sects and the generally low status of the female. The typical life history of the colonial woman encompassed little or no formal education, early marriage, and conformity to the frequently onerous domestic roles of housekeeper, cook, and mother.

During the nineteenth and early twentieth centuries there was an almost uninterrupted decline in American fertility, culminating in the all-time low of the early 1930s. Although temporal variations in birth rates can frequently be explained in purely demographic terms such as changes in age composition or marriage rates, there is no doubt that the chief factor responsible for the long-term decline in the birth rate was a reduction in the number of children born to married women of each age. This decline brought fertility to its lowest level with the women born in 1906–10, whose childbearing occurred mainly in the depression decade of the thirties and in the war years. By the time they completed their childbearing period in the early 1950s, they had produced an average of 2.3 children.

What caused the decline in fertility in the United States? It was not a phenomenon unique to the United States, but a pattern that had begun in France and England and spread throughout western Europe. Although our evidence is indirect, we can at least enumerate several plausible explanations pertinent for all of these populations. All were undergoing radical transformations of their social and economic systems, so that the family was surrendering many of its traditional functions such as economic and educational activities to organized agencies of the factory and the school. It was a period of spreading industrialization with an accompanying decline of agriculture as the dominant economic activity and with a related redistribution of population from rural to urban areas. These social and economic changes brought with them new secular values which gradually undermined the hold of early Protestant belief systems. Rising levels of education and mobility and changes in the status of women involved more and more people in a life outside of their immediate family and local community. The resulting secularization implied a relaxation and frequently a repudiation of traditional values surrounding marriage, family, religion, and the authority of older generations. The substitutes were more materialistic values of individual success and a growing emphasis on "rational" criteria of behavior. In short, this was a period in history when the individual, cut loose from the ancient ties of land and kin, was introduced to a new world holding out the promise of material success judged by impersonal standards of performance and competition.

Against such a background—only briefly sketched here —a reduction in family size is understandable. A "rationalization" of reproduction was a logical consequence of the new social and ideological climate. Of course, technological innovations in the manufacture of contraceptive techniques played a vital role, although folk methods of contraception, known for centuries, took the lead. The emerging small-family norm appeared first in the more educated, white-collar classes of the urban population, resulting in the frequently observed pattern of differential fertility summarized in the oft-quoted adage "The rich get richer and the poor get children." As far as we know, this differential pattern of decline has been characteristic of all Western societies.

The main picture of American fertility has been this

long trend toward the small families of two and three children. This has been largely obscured, however, by the more recent dramatic changes in fertility in the post-World War II era. Although in the immediate postwar years most Western countries briefly experienced a sharp increase both in the birth rate and in the marriage rate, the United States and a few other countries such as Canada, Australia and New Zealand have continued to experience higher fertility long after completing their short-term demographic compensation for the postponed marriages and births and long after other Western countries had returned to prewar fertility levels. The higher fertility of the United States population for the past fifteen years has been a fascinating, as well as puzzling phenomenon. The *demographic* components of the fertility resurgence must first be carefully examined before advancing any speculations about its social origins.

Contrary to popular assumption, the increase in the average number of children per couple is not the primary cause of the high fertility levels of the past fifteen years. More important has been an increase in the proportion marrying, as well as a trend toward marrying at younger ages. Not only does the United States have one of the highest marriage rates in the West, but the low average age at first marriage (around twenty for women and twenty-two to twenty-three for men) is virtually unparalleled among industrialized nations. And earlier marriage means earlier childbearing. It has become increasingly clear that change in the timing of births has played a major role. Part of this timing change is the making up of births postponed during the war. Another aspect of timing change involved the advancing or borrowing of births from future years as a result of earlier marriage, earlier childbearing in marriage and a closer spacing of births. In other words, women have been marrying at younger ages and having their babies sooner and closer together as well as having more children on the average.

But it is also true that more children are being born per married woman than for many decades in the past. The

trend toward larger families appeared first in the reproductive performance of women born in the second decade of
the century, and examination of the early fertility of subsequent cohorts discloses a continuation of this reversal of
the long-term historical decline. This increase in average
number of children per woman in no way implies a return
to the large families of seven or eight children per woman
that characterized early American history. The proportion
of such large families has continued to decline. The dominant pattern has been a rather moderate family size of
two to four children. This has resulted from a reduction in
the proportions of both childless and one-child families as
well as from the continued decline in the proportion of
larger families. The reason that fewer couples have no
children or an only child is that very few couples *want*
fewer than two children and there have been continued
improvements in the treatment of sterility. Nevertheless it
is estimated that one third of all American couples in the
reproductive ages suffer from physiological impairments
to reproduction ranging from complete sterility to inability
to conceive at a normal rate. This includes women who are
chronically unable to carry a pregnancy to term. However, there is no evidence that impaired fecundity is more
prevalent than in other countries or earlier times.

There has also been an upward shift within the two- to
four-child range. The average number of children per
married woman is very likely to exceed three children, as
women now in their thirties complete childbearing. One of
the interesting statistical aspects of this process (started
long before the war) has been a continuous reduction in
the variance of family size—that is, couples are becoming
more alike in the number of children they have as well as
in other more commonly observed aspects of mass consumption. This consensus on two to four children should
not be misconstrued to imply that there is no demographic
significance to the range—there is an enormous difference
between two and four children in the implication for rates
of population growth. Nor is it true that all group differ-

ences in fertility have disappeared as a result of this growing consensus.

We have seen that the baby boom in the United States
is a rather complex admixture of changes in the marriage
rate, age at marriage, the spacing of births and, finally, of
a modest increase in the number of children per family.
That there has not been any real return to large families
is consistent with the observation that there is no evidence
of any return to the family of the numerous functions it
lost during the long history of industrialization. But there
is evidence of considerable interest in children and home
with the development of suburbia and the great increase
in home ownership. The role of housekeeper and mother,
now surrounded with the latest home-appliance conveniences, has been idealized in postwar fiction and advertise-
ments. During the prewar decades it was the career girl
who was more likely to be the heroine.

These are probably reflections of more basic social
changes, some of which we can enumerate. With wartime
employment and postwar demand for consumer goods,
economic prosperity returned after a prolonged depression.
Although this happened in many other countries that did
not experience the extended fertility revival that we have
in the United States, the availability of credit for home
mortgages and other purchases was probably carried further here than anywhere else. In the United States also
(as in many other countries) profound ideological and
structural changes were taking place. Beginning in the
1930s federal legislation ran counter to the whole ideology
of laissez-faire economics and individual self-reliance. Such
innovations as social security benefits on retirement, unemployment and disability compensation, minimum-wage
laws, federal insurance on bank deposits, subsidization of
agricultural production, the principle of government responsibility for full employment, federal housing legislation, and the like, combined to legitimize the new ideology
of a right to minimal protection from economic need. The
rapid growth of labor unions and the increasingly security-
conscious content of their contracts with industry also con-

tributed to the new ideology. The substitution of a system of institutional security for individual responsibility was further advanced by industrial retirement pensions, group medical insurance plans, disability insurance, and many other contractual welfare provisions.

One consequence of these developments has been to remove one of the primary reasons for postponement of marriage—the economic. The implication for marital fertility is that the return of economic security relieved many couples of anxieties formerly conducive to the effective practice of family planning and higher rates of consciously planned pregnancies. In short, an earlier climate unfavorable to earlier and higher fertility was effectively modified.

Other changes in the organization of economic activity, the amount of leisure time available and the mass development of suburbs have also combined to stabilize family-work relationships and to re-establish the community and neighborhood as a primary group.

These explanations are all speculations at best and perhaps what we are attempting to explain is no more than a readjustment to the abnormally low fertility of the 1930s. But it seems to have some of the markings of genuine changes in reproductive behavior.

One of the prominent features of American fertility behavior is that the family size achieved by each successive cohort probably increasingly reflects the desires and plans of the parents. Almost all American couples who do not have sterility problems sooner or later employ some form of fertility control during their marriage.

Data on the family-planning practices of couples are derived from special surveys. Curiously most of these studies have revealed a high proportion of unplanned or accidental pregnancies—perhaps as high as 50 per cent of all pregnancies. If one accepted this at face value, one could easily be led to believe that family-planning practiced by American couples is very ineffective. Close examination suggests another conclusion however. Most of the pregnancies reported as accidental turn out to be first and second pregnancies. Recent research indicates that couples tend to be quite casual in their practice of contraception early in marriage. Following the achievement of the *number* of children desired, however, the effectiveness of family planning seems to improve markedly. Although research bearing on this point is limited, such improvement would appear to be the result primarily of an increase in the regularity of use of whatever method of family planning is employed, rather than a change in methods or several other possible explanations that have been investigated. This improvement in regularity of practice presumably results from the increased motivation to control fertility after the last child wanted has been born. One implication of this relationship—and again there is only very limited evidence—is that the particular method of family planning is less important in determining effectiveness than is the motivation with which it is practiced.

This relationship between family-planning effectiveness and desired family size should not be overemphasized however. There certainly are numerous families in the United States that are larger than the parents ever intended. This problem is especially acute at low income or educational levels, but again the problem of motivation rather than only information about methods appears vital. The assumption that all low-income populations will reduce their fertility if only they are provided with some acceptable form of family planning has long since been abandoned by most scholars in this field.

The negative relationship between socioeconomic status and fertility, so pronounced during earlier times when fertility was declining rapidly, has diminished considerably in the period of the baby boom. Although the lowest classes on the economic and educational scales still have the highest fertility, the lowest fertility is no longer found in the highest classes but rather somewhere in the middle. Not only has the linearity of the association disappeared, but the magnitude of the relationship is now very low. This is a generalization that appears to hold for most countries in Western civilization. The consensus on the two- to four-child family has obliterated much of the socioeconomic differential in fertility. This contraction of group differences has resulted from the continued diffusion of a small-family norm in the lower classes in combination with a sharp increase in the fertility of the college-educated, middle, and upper-income white-collar classes. A very significant proportion of the baby boom can be attributed to the resurgence of fertility among those classes of the population previously in the vanguard of the fertility decline.

The rural-urban factor has also diminished in importance for fertility. Once a strong influence for higher fertility, the traditional rural culture has been transformed by technological and economic changes, and only 9 per cent of American population was still living on farms in 1960. Nevertheless there is still a wide difference in fertility between farm and urban population, with current fertility running about 25 per cent higher in the farm area. There is also some evidence that a rural background continues to exert an influence for higher fertility in the industrial classes of urban areas for a generation or so after migration. But there is little doubt that we are close to the end of the important rural-urban differential in fertility.

It would be erroneous to conclude that Americans are now all alike in their fertility behavior or that group differences as such have all disappeared with only individual differences remaining. There are two other group characteristics that do make an important difference in fertility and show little sign of diminishing—race and religion.

Prior to World War II, the fertility of the non-white population was also declining, although in the mid 1930s it was still about 30 per cent higher than the fertility of the white population. Moreover, the non-white birth rate in urban areas was reaching very low levels comparable with and occasionally lower than that of the urban white population. So the over-all difference was being sustained largely by the very high fertility of the rural Negro population. With cityward migration accelerating rapidly in the 1940s, it appeared that even this differential had a

limited future. It has therefore come as something of a
surprise that non-white fertility increased more rapidly
than white fertility during the baby boom. Whereas the
fertility of the white population by 1960 had increased by
about 50 per cent from its low in the 1930s, non-white
fertility increased by about 70 per cent. The reasons for
this are by no means clear, although several theories exist.
Whatever the reasons, the Negro population of this country is increasing at a true rate of 2.7 per cent per year—
among the highest growth rates in the world. (The annual
true rate of natural increase in the white population is
about 1.9 per cent.) Of course the Negro population in the
United States, despite some similarities, lacks most of the
fundamental characteristics of the populations of the developing areas in the world. This implies that its current
rate of growth is more elastic than that of the typical traditional society just beginning the modernization process.

Information on religion is not available in American
official statistics. Our information on the reproductive behavior of the different religious groups is drawn almost
entirely from recent, privately supported university research. It is for this reason that we have hardly any information on time trends in the religious differential.

It is only the Catholic religion in the United States that
has any real bearing *per se* on fertility. When we refer to
Protestant and Jewish fertility we are really talking more
about non-religious factors such as income, education, residence and other characteristics that may be jointly associated with Protestant or Jewish religious affiliation and
fertility. This is not entirely true, of course, since the be-
liefs of various fundamentalist sects among Protestants and
Jews do have some direct bearing on fertility and in many
other sects a new moral ethic of responsible parenthood
seems to be emerging.

Actually there was less of a difference in the past than
one might expect between Catholic and non-Catholic fertility. Sample survey data collected in 1957 suggested perhaps as little as a 10 per cent difference for women born
early in this century, while Jewish women were reproduc-

ing at a rate of 25 per cent below the national average. Another survey, however, that collected data on expected family size for younger women (those presently in their twenties) indicates a much larger difference, with Catholic women expecting nearly a third more children than Protestant women. This general impression has been clearly confirmed in more recent studies as well. It seems quite clear that Catholics have contributed disproportionately to the baby boom in this country.

The Catholic population, located primarily in the largest metropolitan areas, is of course distinct in practicing a religion which prohibits the practice of any form of birth control other than periodic continence or, as it is more popularly described, the rhythm or safe-period method. It should be noted that the Catholic Church apparently is becoming increasingly sensitive to the modern "population problem" and seems steadily to be liberalizing its point of view. One of the interesting recent research findings on Catholic fertility in the United States is that Catholic couples *desire* larger families than non-Catholics, an attitude that is not due to any misapprehension that the Catholic Church explicitly favors large families. Although some forms of idealization of larger families undoubtedly occurs at informal levels, the social mechanisms supporting the high-fertility norm have not yet been studied systematically. One such support is a Catholic education, particularly the Catholic college, which seems to encourage familistic orientations, especially among young women, in contrast to the general secularizing influence of higher education.

We have now covered the main features of fertility in America—the long-term historical trend to the small family, the modification of this trend and a resurgence of fertility in the past two decades, internal group variations in fertility and the change in these differentials. In closing we should take a brief look into the future.

Will American couples continue the pattern of fertility established in the 1950s? Or can we expect a reversion to prewar levels? Those who follow closely the monthly *Vital*

Statistics Reports have observed some evidence of a slight decline in fertility during the recent past. Whether this will continue or not is uncertain. The most promising approach to the forecasting of fertility is the one first utilized in consumer-preference studies. Instead of asking women whether they are planning to purchase a refrigerator or automobile over the next so many months, annual surveys now ask these women to estimate their fertility over the next few years. The most extensive research of this nature does suggest a slight downward trend in fertility, with women born at the beginning of World War II expecting fewer births than their older sisters born during the depression. But demographers know best of all what a tricky business such forecasting can be. With this new direct approach to the women themselves, however, it may be some consolation to be able to blame the women for changing their minds.

SUGGESTIONS FOR FURTHER READING

Ansley J. Coale and Melvin Zelnik. *New Estimates of Fertility and Population in the United States*. Princeton: Princeton University Press, 1963.

   Presents an annual series of estimates of births, birth rates and fertility rates for the United States from 1855 to the present.

Ronald Freedman. "The Sociology of Human Fertility." *Current Sociology*. Vol. 10–11, No. 2, 1961–62.

   A review of important trends and issues in research on the sociology of fertility, including an extensive bibliography of international references.

Ronald Freedman, P. K. Whelpton, and Arthur A. Campbell. *Family Planning, Sterility and Population Growth*. New York: McGraw-Hill, 1959.

   Presents the results of a 1955 national sample survey of married women aimed at estimating their future fertility as well as describing fecundity impairments and differential fertility.

Wilson H. Grabill, Clyde V. Kiser, and P. K. Whelpton.

The Fertility of American Women. New York: John Wiley & Sons, 1958.

Traces the history of reproduction in the United States from colonial times through the baby boom.

Charles F. Westoff, Robert G. Potter, Jr., and Philip C. Sagi. *The Third Child.* Princeton: Princeton University Press, 1963.

Reports the most recent results of a study of social and psychological factors affecting American fertility.

Chapter 9

INTERNAL MIGRATION AND POPULATION REDISTRIBUTION IN THE UNITED STATES

Everett S. Lee

FACTORS IN THE REDISTRIBUTION OF POPULATION

Internal migration is but one of the elements in the redistribution of population within a country, but for the United States it has been by all odds the most important. Because of the way in which redistribution has taken place and because of the rapidity of the process, the consequences are pronounced in this country and are quite different from those found elsewhere. Some of the effects, as we shall see, may be counted as good, others are doubtful, and some are definitely bad. Whatever the valuation of the effects, they serve to distinguish the American people from their immigrant forebears and the American culture from the European heritage.

Other factors in the redistribution of population are differentials in fertility and mortality and the relative attractiveness of various areas to migrants from abroad. Some sections of this country have had an especial appeal to Europeans, but since World War I immigration has been so greatly reduced that its effect on population distribution has become negligible. Earlier, when America was the goal for millions, the immigrants who concentrated themselves in northern cities sometimes accentuated and sometimes diminished the over-all redistribution of population. Differential mortality has never had a striking effect on population distribution, since death rates do not vary enough from region to region. The contrary is true of differentials in fertility, but states with high birth rates have generally had high rates of out-migration with the one partially offsetting the other. However, internal migration is left as the major force in altering the internal population balance and redistributing our population.

The Great Movements

The redistribution of population that has taken place through migration can be described very generally as consisting of three broad movements. First and greatest was the migration from east to west which consolidated the country and dispelled threats to American sovereignty. Even as the West was being populated, the second movement, that to the cities, set in, transforming us from a nation of farmers into an industrial power. The third great movement was the migration from the South to the North, a movement which of late has taken on special significance because it has become primarily a migration of Negroes. All three movements continue today.

At the beginning of the nineteenth century our population was hemmed in by the Appalachian Mountains and distributed in a narrow band along the Atlantic coast. From there settlement spread over a thousand-mile front for twenty-five hundred miles into the West. Millions of people were involved and no movement of comparable size and rapidity has taken place anywhere else in the world. The frontier is said to have disappeared about 1890, when settlement became continuous from coast to coast, but the westward movement continues almost unabated. The West is still the fastest-growing region in the country, and California has probably surpassed New York as the largest state. From 1950 to 1960 the population of the West increased by nearly 40 per cent, as against 15 per cent for each of the other three regions. California alone grew by over five million persons during the decade, and accounted for nearly a fifth of the increase for the entire United States.

The redistribution between rural and urban areas has been just as striking and no less important. At our first census, in 1790, only 5 per cent of the population lived in places of 2500 or more inhabitants, and it took a half century for that figure to double. But as the pace of industrialization quickened, the redistribution of population accelerated. By 1870 the urban proportion had reached a quarter, and by 1920 half of the population fell in that category. Today 70 per cent of the population is urban, and most of the remainder live in non-farm areas. Only 8 per cent remain on the farm, almost a complete reversal of the situation at the time we gained independence. Because urban fertility has remained consistently below rural fertility, the faster growth of towns and cities depended upon migration, partly from abroad to be sure, but for the most part upon migration from the countryside.

The movement from the South to the North has not involved as many persons, but the consequences have nevertheless been momentous. Long a region of high fertility and low industrialization, the South has remained a region of out-migration. Though there has been much westward migration from the South, the prime goals for Southern out-migrants have been the not too distant centers of the Northeast and the North Central States.

The urbanization of population continues, but there has been a shift in the main currents of population redistribution. It can no longer be described as a combination of movements from the East to the West and from the South to the North. Rather it is a movement from the interior of the country toward the peripheries. In each of the last two decades about half of the three thousand counties in the United States lost population. In general, these were interior counties and their losses were balanced by large gains along the Atlantic and Gulf coasts, in the areas bordering on the Great Lakes, and along the Pacific coast. Such southern areas as the state of Florida and eastern Texas are now rapidly growing areas. In the gaining areas there has been an increasing concentration of industry, while the economic base of the agricultural interior continues to be eroded.

Not all segments of the population were simultaneously or equally affected by the redistribution of population. The

Negro, in particular, shared little in interregional movements before World War I. In 1790 about 90 per cent of the Negro population was in the South, and in 1910 the proportion had hardly changed. At that time little more than a quarter of the Negro population was urban, as compared with nearly half the white population. Since then the redistribution of Negro population has proceeded much more rapidly than that of whites. By 1960 Negroes were even more urban than whites, and only five out of every nine Negroes remained in the South. This represents by far the most rapid redistribution of any major segment of the population. Partly for this reason, it has been attended by many problems.

THE VOLUME OF INTERNAL MIGRATION

It is clear that a great volume of internal migration has been and continues to be a necessity in the United States. Otherwise our development, political and otherwise, would have been seriously affected, and our economy could not operate with its present efficiency. Ours was long an undeveloped country with millions of fertile acres awaiting the plow. Indeed, we had so much land in relation to population that until the turn of this century there was much that was free for the taking. Discoveries of important mineral deposits have been made repeatedly in faraway places, and factories are placed in remote areas with complete confidence that an adequate labor supply can be attracted.

Indeed, migration is a part of the American way of life. We are nearly all only a few generations removed from immigrant ancestors, whether they landed at Plymouth Rock or at Ellis Island, and the tradition of leaving the homeland persists in a volume of internal migration that can only be described as enormous. In postwar years more than thirty million people moved from one house to another in each twelve-month period. Within this group of movers we classify the ten million who moved from one county to another as migrants. Of these, six million moved from one state to another. Relating these figures to population, we find that one in five Americans changes his place of residence each year, one in fourteen migrates from one county to another, and one in thirty from one state to another.

Astounding though they are, these figures understate the volume of movement. They do not include the moves made by persons who die during the year or who return to the place of origin, and only one move is counted for each person. Yet within a single year many thousands of persons make more than one move, and there are records of persons who changed residence four times and even more in a single year. Such cases, of course, are exceptional, but it is estimated that the number of moves and migrations obtained from our current population statistics falls short of the actual number by perhaps a quarter.

Furthermore, the rates just given are averages for both sexes and for all ages combined, and are far below the peak rates for young adults. At the ages of maximum migration, twenty to twenty-four, one in six males moves from one county to another, and one in ten changes state of residence. High rates of migration, though perhaps seldom as extreme as these, have been the rule rather than the exception throughout our history. It is only since 1947 that annual rates can be calculated, but estimates made independently by Henry S. Shryock of the United States Bureau of the Census and myself indicate that the present high rate of population redistribution through migration has continued for at least a century. We are a nation of migrants, and we always have been.

DISTANCE OF MIGRATION

Not only is the volume of migration great, but the distance covered in a single move is often considerable. Migration from New York to California, for example, is not uncommon, though this is a distance of over twenty-five hundred miles, more than that from Oslo to Rome or from Paris to Moscow. In appraising migration within the

United States, we must keep in mind the size of the country and the included units by which migration is assessed. Excluding the outlying states of Alaska and Hawaii and the territories and possessions, the United States is still much larger than the whole of Europe outside the Soviet Union. Our largest states are larger than any of the countries of Europe, and there is a California county which is larger than Denmark, Austria, Belgium, or the Netherlands.

It is true, of course, that distance is a limiting factor in migration. Long-distance migration is expensive as well as disruptive of family ties and associations. Therefore as distance increases from a given area, the number of migrants from that locale tends to diminish. Nevertheless half the persons who leave a county migrate to a different state, and half of these pass through neighboring states to reach more distant areas. Successive moves may then remove the migrant even farther from the place of origin; for example, we know that much of the movement from the east to the west coast was accomplished in stages, with each move taking the migrant farther west. And, though our regions are fairly sharply defined (the South, for example, differs greatly from the Northeast in physical and cultural setting), three fifths of the persons living outside the state in which they were born have migrated to a different region. It is also clear that as the distance of migration increases, so does the selectivity of the process.

SELECTIVITY OF MIGRATION

Indeed, the selectivity of migration is almost as important as the volume of migration. Migrants are by no means a cross section of the population. Like immigrants from abroad, internal migrants are typically young adults in the ages of greatest productivity and of greatest reproductivity. In general, rates of migration are quite high for very young children; they fall during the school years, then rise to a peak in the early twenties, remain at a high level until about age thirty, then decline sharply with age. For young children the rates are high because they are moving with parents who are themselves in the ages of high mobility, and the decline in rates during middle age represents increasing economic and social establishment as well as advancing age *per se*.

In long-distance migration, males predominate, but for shorter moves there is little difference in male and female rates. However, since marriage is often attended by migration, females tend to migrate at somewhat younger ages than males simply because they marry younger. The dissolution of marriage, as well as its formation, is associated with migration and, as perhaps might be expected, divorced persons and persons separated from their spouses are among the most migratory of people.

The amount of education also has an effect upon the propensity to migrate. In general, the highest rates of migration are for the best-educated, and as education decreases so does migration. Again the relationship becomes stronger as the distance of migration increases. Where long distances are involved, the rates for the college-educated are often twice those of any other educational group. Partly this is because the better-educated have more knowledge of different parts of the country, but another reason is that higher education is characteristic of persons in occupations where migration is common.

Among the various occupational groups there are extreme differences in the incidence of migration. Most migratory are professional and semiprofessional workers for whom rates may be two or three times those for farm owners, ordinarily the least migratory group. Farm laborers, however, have much higher rates of migration than do farm owners, particularly in recent years as increased farm mechanization has removed much of the need for farm labor. And among professional as well as agricultural workers, there are groups with low rates. Often these are persons for whom state licenses or certifications are necessary; these are seldom transferable from one state to another. An established list of clients is probably as great a deterrent to migration as ownership of a farm or a store.

Not only are relatively high proportions of migrants highly educated and well placed on the occupational scale, the fragmentary studies that exist even suggest that they are more intelligent as well. Nevertheless we cannot agree with E. A. Ross, who likened New England of a generation ago to a fished-out millpond in which only carps and suckers were left, that migration acts to drain away the most promising citizens from areas of out-migration to the benefit of receiving areas. Looking at the other side of the coin, we find that high rates of migration characterize groups at both the top and bottom of the socioeconomic ladder; it is in the middle that rates tend to be lowest. Thus, laborers as well as professional men have high rates of migration, and the unemployed are more likely to be found among migrants than among non-migrants. Rates of mental disease also seem higher for migrants than for non-migrants. It would therefore appear that both success and failure may be accompanied by migration, and the gains to receiving areas through the in-migration of highly educated persons of professional and managerial status must be balanced against the receipt of the unskilled, the uneducated, and the disturbed.

It has been suggested that the kind of selection that occurs depends upon the balance of "push" and "pull" factors which impel the migration. For example, among farm laborers the pull of higher but uncertain wages in the city has perhaps been a lesser factor than the push of declining opportunities in the countryside, but for highly skilled technicians it has largely been a matter of weighing a good situation against a possibly better one elsewhere. Thus engineers have been able to choose among many jobs in all parts of the country. For such people, the choice is not always an economic one—it may rest upon such factors as climate, the quality of the public schools, or the possibilities of the "good life." Such considerations have become so important that employers increasingly place their establishments in places thought to appeal to the kind of employees they need. Thus research laboratories cluster around Boston, and electronics factories are built in California.

MIGRATION AND THE STATE OF THE ECONOMY

While American rates of internal migration, as judged by the standards of any other Western country, are always high, they vary considerably from time to time and from place to place, depending upon political events and economic opportunities. Dorothy Swaine Thomas has classified each of the decades from 1880 through 1950 as periods of either high or low economic activity and has compared rates of net migration for these intervals. Inasmuch as there was a pattern of alternating high and low decades, it was possible to compare rates of migration in the decades of high economic growth with preceding or following decades of low economic growth. The comparisons were made separately for males and females and for a number of age groups. In almost every comparison, migration rates were higher during the decades of intensified economic activity.

Not only is migration diminished in depressed periods but there is some evidence that the direction of migration and the selection of migrants may differ from those observed in prosperous periods. During the worst years of the great depression of the 1930s there was probably a net movement back to the farm, contrary to all recent experience. Even in the mildly depressed year, 1949–50, there were reversals of the usual migration streams. In prosperous periods rates of migration for young males rise to high levels but are lowered considerably by lessened economic activity. On the other hand, the migration of older persons and of females seems less affected.

Even when some areas are booming, others are depressed; it is this difference in opportunity that spurs migration. But for many people in depressed areas the need for migration comes too late. After families have been formed and after an occupation has been pursued for many years, the willingness to migrate lessens. Even now in the coal fields of West Virginia, as on the farms of the South, older people without steady jobs remain to eke out a living from part-time work or go on relief. The young depart but the middle-aged remain. It is this reluctance to leave a place in which it is no longer economically advantageous to stay that has led some observers to declare that there is too little migration in this country. In a dynamic economy even a little stability of population can sometimes be vexing.

THE STABILITY OF POPULATION

But there is more stability of population than the rates of migration would indicate. If the rates cited here were probabilities that applied with equal force to all members of the population, there would soon be a nearly complete reshuffling of our people. On the average, a man would change his residence about thirteen times in the course of a lifetime, and he would migrate from one county to another about five times and from one state to another at least twice. Everywhere a good part of the population would be made up of recent arrivals and there would be few old residents to maintain traditions and create sectional distinctions. However, it can be shown that while some people continually move from one place to another, many are quite stable and remain within the state or even the county of birth.

In each of the years between 1955 and 1960, one in five persons changed residence as usual, but only about half were living in a different house at the end of the period from that at the beginning. Not one in three but only one in six were living in a different county in 1960 than in 1955, and the one in twelve living in a different state falls equally short of the expected one in six. For this five-year period, at least, there was a surprising stability of population in the face of such high rates of mobility. On the other hand, much of the total movement must be attributed to a relatively small part of the population.

Looked at from the point of view of state and region of

birth, the stability of population is more impressive. Little more than a quarter of the 1960 population was living outside the state of birth and only about one in seven resided outside the region in which he was born. About 90 per cent of the persons living in the Northeast, the North Central States, and the South were born in the region of residence, but in the West the proportion was only 60 per cent. Thus, despite high mobility, there is enough stability of population to assure the continuance of sectionalism.

The proportion remaining in the state of birth changes with age, however. Whereas 90 per cent of the children under five were still in the state of birth in 1960, the proportion had fallen to 80 per cent by ages fifteen to nineteen, and 70 per cent by ages twenty to twenty-four. Thereafter change was slow, and nearly two thirds remained in the state of birth throughout the older ages. Largely because of heavy out-migration from the South, the proportion remaining in the state of birth was somewhat lower for Negroes than for whites.

Such averages, however, do not describe the population of any particular state. Some states have attracted many in-migrants while keeping most of their own citizens. Others have lost population to other states but have attracted few in-migrants. And, incongruously, there are states which have lost high proportions of their own natives but have nevertheless been attractive to migrants from other states. Thus some states have populations which are largely immigrant, others have populations that are predominantly in-state born, and others have varying balances of in-migrants and out-migrants. In this respect the variation by race is considerable.

Mississippi is a state that has lost heavily through out-migration with little replacement through in-migration. About a third of the whites born in Mississippi were living in other states in 1960, and at ages thirty to thirty-four the proportion was close to a half. Even so, the out-migration of Negroes was much more pronounced. Four out of nine of the Negroes born in Mississippi had left by 1960, and at ages thirty to thirty-four only a third were left. At the same time there was so little in-migration that nearly 90 per cent of the whites and 95 per cent of the Negroes living in Mississippi had been born in the state.

The opposite situation is found in California. Nearly nine tenths of the persons born in California were still living there in 1960 and the proportion varied little with age, the youngest children being only a little more likely to still be in the state than the oldest adults. But fewer than four out of nine of the native Americans living in California had been born there, and this is a figure that is heavily weighted by young children. Only a third of the adult native population had been born in the state, and at ages fifty and above the proportion was less than a fifth.

Nevada is the prime example of a state that has been more or less deserted by the persons born there but has nevertheless been attractive to persons from other states. Even before the age of five almost a third of the children born in Nevada have left the state, by age ten the proportion is greater than half, and by age thirty it is nearly 90 per cent. By contrast, a quarter of the children under five who were living in Nevada were born in other states, and this proportion increases with age so that at age seventy-five nearly three quarters of the native American population were born elsewhere. This is a phenomenon that is repeated on a lesser scale in other states. In Pennsylvania, for example, the losses of native whites through out-migration have varied from about 100,000 to over 600,000 in each of the decades since 1870. Up to World War I these losses were largely compensated by migration from abroad, but since then the rising tide of Negro in-migration has provided a partial replacement.

THE CORRELATES OF MIGRATION

Though, as we have seen, there is a considerable degree of spatial stability in our population, it is probably true that nowhere else is there a people with fixed abodes who migrate so freely over long distances. The correlates of this phenomenon are many, but we are just beginning to study them carefully. Present attempts to set them forth must therefore be labeled as speculations rather than findings. On the positive side it has been argued that it is through migration that our population can adjust readily to the increasingly rapid rate of economic change, and that migration is an important factor in promoting a sense of national unity. Both individualism and democracy are said to be promoted by migration.

These things seem highly desirable. Individualism and equalitarianism have long been American goals, and the exaltation of national over local allegiances is imperative. But high rates of migration bring with them many problems as well. Family ties are broken and perhaps a sense of indifference toward immediate surroundings is engendered. Often it is easier to move away from a bad situation than to correct it, and migrants may have a tendency to look for temporary expedients rather than long-run solutions for local problems.

Whatever the correlates are, they deserve study and comparisons with other countries. As their economies develop, many countries are coming to resemble the United States more and more, and they are marked by increasing rates of migration. Our situation will soon be not so different from that of other countries.

Suggestions for Further Reading

Conrad and Irene Taeuber. *The Changing Population of the United States.* New York: John Wiley & Sons, 1958.
    This work contains a good general discussion of internal migration in the United States.
Dorothy Swaine Thomas. *Research Memorandum on Migration Differentials.* New York: Social Science Research Council Bulletin 43, 1938.
    Although out of date and soon to be reissued in revised form, this monograph is still the best statement of what is known of the differences between migrants and non-migrants. Among the differentials treated are age, sex, physical and mental health, and intelligence.

Everett S. Lee, *et al. Population Redistribution and Economic Growth, United States, 1870–1950.* Vol. I. Methodological Considerations and Reference Tables. Philadelphia: American Philosophical Society, 1958.

The first of a series, this volume presents more information on trends in interstate migration by age, sex, race, and nativity of whites than is elsewhere available, along with series on industrial development and income distribution.

Clyde V. Kiser. *Sea Island to City: A Study of St. Helena Islanders in Harlem and Other Urban Centers.* Columbia University Studies in History, Economics and Public Law, No. 368. New York: Columbia University Press, 1932.

A classic study of the migration of Negroes from the South and their adjustment to northern cities.

Ronald Freedman. *Recent Migration to Chicago.* Chicago: University of Chicago Press, 1950.

An important study of migration to our second largest city. More than a study of migration, it is a study of ecological relationships within the city and is one of the best treatments of migration and social disorganization.

Benjamin Malzberg and Everett S. Lee. *Migration and Mental Disease.* New York: Social Science Research Council, 1956.

An investigation into the relationship between migration and mental disease. Its thesis that migrants have higher rates of mental disorder than non-migrants has been challenged but is generally supported by other investigators.

Chapter 10

THE GROWTH OF
THE AMERICAN POPULATION

Rupert B. Vance

As of April 1, 1963, the population of the United States
was estimated at 188,643,000 people—a far cry from the
3,929,000 population reported in the first census, taken in
1790. This represents an increase of 4,700 per cent in the
population in 173 years.

An electric population chart on display in the main lobby
of the Department of Commerce in the nation's capital
shows what this means in terms of population growth.
When this essay was written, the mechanism of the re-
corder was set to show an average of:

> 1 birth every 7½ seconds
> 1 death every 18½ seconds
> 1 in-migrant every 1½ minutes
> 1 out-migrant every 23 minutes

Taken together, these components were giving the United
States a net gain of one person added to the population
every eleven seconds.

Such a growth trend can be best explained by citing the
unique features of American demographic history. In the
United States the idea of population has had all of the
dynamic implications of its verb to populate—the process
of peopling a new country. Economic and political expansion have proved to be of prime importance in the nation's history. As a young nation, the United States developed one of the highest rates of population increase
known in the world, and as it grew it became the world's
most extensive experiment in both international and internal migration. It is the opening up of a new continent and

the growth of a developing economy that explain the increase of the American population.

Fertility is, and has been, the crux of American population growth. In the dangerous period of early settlement, high birth rates compensated for the high death rates of a newly settled country. With access to free lands and Western homesteads the population grew rapidly, and as death rates came down, fertility rates for a time remained among the highest in the world—some eight children per family in the colonial period. Aided by increasing foreign immigration, this trend hastened the settlement of a new continent. The population more than doubled each generation, a fact Robert Malthus was able to cite in support of his population doctrines.

With fertility so high, there was but one possible trend—downward. The decline in fertility began early and continued without interruption, until 1940. In terms of the family, it can be said that the decline in fertility amounted to the decrease of about one child per generation until the outbreak of World War II.

The smaller-family system began among the well-to-do, in the urban middle-classes, and among the educated, and it spread from them to the city working class and to the rural families living in the hinterlands. These differences in the size of families by different social classes are apparent in the earliest studies made of the American population. Since these differences ran contrary to the social and economic status of the population, they have made the task of democracy more difficult in the attempt to realize the doctrine of equal opportunity. Old-established families have consistently had fewer children than rural families and the newer immigrants; the small farmer and the Negro population have had larger families than the middle class. While the American people do not accept eugenics and do not emphasize heredity, American demographers have generally spoken of the heavy burden this differential reproduction places on the American educational system. With the gradual passage of the heavy demand for rough and unskilled labor and the rising demand for educated workers, demographers have advocated a reversal of the differential: that is, larger families for those best able to look after their children and smaller families for those less able to provide opportunities for advancement.

This trend seems to have put in its appearance with the most recent phenomenon in American demography, the so-called baby boom. This reversal of the falling birth rate occurred at the outbreak of World War II. From 1940 to 1960 the population increased by 47.7 million persons, a number almost as large as the total population recorded by the census of 1880. The new fertility was unexpected by the general public—in fact it was not predicted by demographers. But it can be explained as a phenomenon of the new prosperity and expected social security. Moreover it occurred among a people well aware of the means of how to limit family size, and perfectly capable of reducing the birth rate if a depression should strike again. Birth rates which fell as low as 18 in 1933 rose to 25 per 1000 and since then have fluctuated, going down to some 22.4 per 1000 in 1962. The baby boom is a phenomenon of the middle class, of the well educated, and is especially found among the young married set with age-specific birth rates for women aged twenty to twenty-four that are the highest in our history. There is no return to the large-size family of the past, but with the present mortality rates an average size of between three to four children per family will give the country an extremely rapid population increase. Since this is an urban middle-class phenomenon, we can point out that the rural birth rate is still decreasing and the baby boom thus serves to decrease population differentials. If rural and lower-class fertility continue to decline, the birth rate may even out among all of America's classes. The one exception to this at the present is the birth rate of the Negro, which has remained high, and as Negro mortality decreases the Negro rate of increase goes higher. Especially important here is the great decrease in childlessness, seen also in the white population. Also, for the first time in history, the birth rate of the South has approached that of the rest of the nation at approximately 23 per 1000 population.

Certain demographic factors are known to favor this type of population increase: namely, an equal balance of the sexes, a young population, and along with this a greater popularity of marriage at young ages. All of these conditions are found in the United States. Because of large-scale immigration, discussed later, the sex ratio has been predominantly masculine in the United States since early settlement. By mid-century, however, the effect of foreign immigration had passed its crest and for the first time in history the American population became more feminine than masculine. Women in the United States now live an average of almost six years longer than men and this excess of females is found in the older age groups, especially the widowed. Below thirty the sex balance is still masculine; and since there are enough husbands to go around, marriage rates remain high.

Two types of natural dependents exist, the very young and the very old. Both are supported by the working force —that is, the population in the mature ages of twenty-one to sixty-five. As the birth rate fell, the ratio of children to be supported by the workers decreased and the country was able to spend more on child welfare, public health, and education. For some time this situation remained, until the aging population served to increase the burden of support of the elders. Spending on child welfare, of course, increased the efficiency of the oncoming workers, and the United States has benefited from this transition. At the present, groups reaching sixty-five and over are increasing, while the effect of the present baby boom has served to increase the proportion of younger dependents. So far, however, these trends have not served to unbalance the budget, and population increase continues.

It is an open question whether fertility will remain at the present high level of the baby boom. Certainly this seems dependent on continued prosperity, with the possibility of young marriages and continued education for those aspiring to middle-class status. The type of urban life now developed in suburban areas denies the view once held that city life means a fertility low enough to threaten population replacements. Continued prosperity—the affluent society, to use Professor Galbraith's term—seems as much committed to something like the three- to four-child family as to the automobile—both classed as consumer durables by certain imaginative economists. The proportion of deliberately childless couples has shriveled to a very small number, while adoption by sterile couples is a growing trend. It may come as a surprise to certain groups to learn that competitive, mobile America, bent on success, has now a higher birth rate than Catholic countries like Spain, Portugal and Italy. This is likely to continue in the United States as long as prosperity continues. If prosperity fails, the majority of American families, it has been said, are as well equipped with the knowledge to turn off the stream of births as one would turn off the water at the tap.

We have tended to outrun our story in that one of the great contributions to American population increase has been foreign immigration. The United States early became the world's prime example of international migration. In the golden age of migration almost all who wanted to migrate could go and no one would stop them—neither the country they left, nor the country they sought. In the swarming of Europe up until World War I some 60,000,000 went overseas; over 40,000,000 came to the United States and possibly 37,000,000 of these stayed. In time, the subject of foreign immigration finally became one of controversy, and the stream was thinned by laws setting up quotas that made distinctions favoring northern and western Europeans over those from southern and eastern Europe.

Now that the country is settled and its economy has reached maturity, the course of immigration is much better understood by American demographers. The great overseas migration delivered free on board these shores a labor supply reared and educated at Europe's expense. In military power and in economic development these immigrants and their offspring must have hastened the maturity of the

United States by at least fifty years. That they should become good Americans was accepted as a matter of course.
When the process proved slow and ethnic groups became
involved in the slum life and the machine politics of our
fast-growing cities, these ethnic groups were blamed as a
matter of course. When economic development passed the
need for unskilled labor and the flow was cut off, the immigrant then began his remarkable climb up the social ladder,
pretty much in terms of the American dream of equality,
based on the date of his arrival and the nearness of his culture to that of the original colonial stock. Today the treatment of immigration in American history has changed from
counting the disabilities the United States suffered at the
hands of its immigrants to recounting the hardships they
underwent in the Atlantic passage and their new community life. These hardships were many, from the trip by
steerage where the immigrant family was simply sold space
between decks on which to sleep, to the lack of prestige
the immigrant suffered in speaking a foreign tongue, belonging to unskilled occupations and to separate churches,
and in facing unequal treatment in communities which
boasted of their equality. That this has passed in the main
was indicated by the election of a fourth-generation immigrant of Catholic faith to the Presidency of the United
States. This has been a symbol to many people of immigrant stock of what social mobility means in the United
States. Those who have not participated equally in this
advance have been distinguished by color differences, a
phenomenon which is still not rightly understood in the
settlement of America and the development of American
ideals.

Just what the immigration movement has meant in its
net addition to the American population has been difficult
to estimate. The figure is large, larger than some have
thought, and the degree of its success is stated when we
say that this major movement seems to be practically over.
The rise in the nation's birth rate means that immigration
from heaven is likely to take the place of immigrants from
abroad. And now that European fertility has declined and

industrialization has spread throughout the continent, the pressure to migrate to America has fallen to a new low level. Except for wars and rumors of war, this need would, no doubt, prove to be very small indeed. It now appears that the problem of refugees and displaced persons has been solved in most European countries, and Western Europe has attained an economic growth rate higher than the United States has been able to develop in recent times.

The United States has also served as an experiment in internal migration. The very pattern of settlement in which the eastern seaboard was colonized and furnished population increase meant that the country would develop a tremendous westward movement. This westward movement, set first on occupying the frontier, has been a main historical trend in the United States. In the period when land was prime wealth and agriculture the leading occupation, the homestead policy drew settlers farther west in their covered wagons. Isolated at the beginning, they lived in the subsistence economy of the frontier. When the railroads were built they could send their products east and buy finished goods with the proceeds. With the development of industry and commerce, Western areas grew to a parity with the East, developing great city areas like Chicago. The great rural urban migrations built up these cities and drained the rural areas where agriculture had developed problems of overproduction of food and fiber. The use of machinery on farms and the spread of scientific agriculture enabled fewer farmers to feed more city dwellers and to send the farmers' sons, no longer needed, to become the factory and white-collar workers of the new cities. With World War I the Negro joined this stream of migrants, and now a larger proportion of the Negro population lives in cities than of the white population. Withal, the great majority of American people are urban, mostly living in metropolitan areas. The new migration now is a movement out of the inner city into its fringes. Every large American city is surrounded by rings of suburbs, composed of people who have moved out to take advantage of what they hoped would be country living. These suburban dwellers continue to work in the cities, however, and create the necessity for quick transportation. These commuters regularly fill the highways, buses and commuter trains on their daily journey to and from work.

So great is this trend that in certain parts of the country the suburban dweller who moves out in search of green trees and grass finds that he has run out of open country. Real estate developers, creating new housing projects, now find that the suburbs of one metropolitan area back into the suburbs of the next. Two such areas of almost continuous settlement have developed in the United States. From Boston south to Washington one is hardly ever out of sight of continuous urban settlement. From the New Jersey coast west to Chicago a similar development has grown up, with a trend toward the formation of one enormous, more or less integrated, urban strip. Only a country with agricultural surpluses and land in plentiful supply could afford to be so heedless in its disposition of land resources. Undoubtedly the time will come when the United States will be unable to gobble up land so recklessly, as in the creation of its profusion of clover-leaf approaches to four-lane highway systems. At present, however, settlement and transportation demands continue to take land out of agricultural use.

In common with the rest of the world, the United States has experienced great declines in mortality. Accordingly, much of the nation's population increase was due to the fact that while the rate of births was going down, the death rate went down much faster. In 1800 Americans lived, on the average, to be about only thirty-five years of age. By the 1960s they were living at least twice as long—seventy years and more. The decline in the death rate has been practically continuous from 1900 to the present, going down from 17.2 deaths per 1000 to around nine. To illustrate what this means for any modern nation, it can be stated that the effect is practically the same as if death had been abolished before age forty. This can be emphasized by pointing out the great changes in the causes of death among the population. Sixty years ago the major killers were found among the infectious and contagious diseases which killed children and young adults: tuberculosis, pneumonia and influenza, and the great killers of childhood, diphtheria, enteritis, down to such diseases as measles, mumps and scarlet fever. Today the major causes of death are degenerative and chronic diseases of a maturing population—that is, heart disease, cancer, cerebral hemorrhage, nephritis, diabetes. Much has been done in the control of chronic diseases, but as these are the diseases which cause death as man nears the end of the life span, we shall have to wait until science can come forward to change the process of aging to expect greater progress. It has been pointed out that except for cancer and diabetes, these diseases are bound together in a syndrome that may be called the hypertension complex. In this situation the strain on the circulatory system meets the tensions of American life to create characteristic symptoms in the bustle of American population.

It has been suggested that the best way to determine the major killers which affect the population is to calculate the remaining years of life lost to the people by each cause of death. In this country a non-medical cause, accidents, also related to the hurry and bustle of American life, is shown to cause more lost years than many major causes of death. The campaign against industrial accidents has met success but practically nothing has yet been done to reduce the terrific incidence of automobile deaths on the highways. With this one exception, medical science, public health, sanitation and organization of medical care is so arranged that the death rate continues on its decline even after the population has reached a life expectancy of seventy years.

The question was raised, during the depression period, as to whether the growth rate of the American population would fall below the replacement level. Since this question has been answered in the negative, it may be well to raise another question: Is the United States likely to become overpopulated? Realizing all the difficulties that this question brings up, the answer also seems to be "No." In the first place, there is still room for physical as well as economic expansion in terms of American resources, manufacturing and finance. In the second place, it seems likely that the knowledge the American people have of family limitation and their inclination to use it will reach all but the poorest and least educated. So far, in line with those who fear the effects of differential reproduction, the United States has relied mainly on public welfare and social security payments to help equalize opportunity. The final view is, then, that population growth has helped to settle and develop this country and while the American people are committed to such growth, as the baby boom shows, they are also able to check population growth if the need should arise.

In the summing up, pivotal aspects of population growth, major factors in the settlement of the continent, include the interplay of agriculture and industry; of the frontier and urbanization; of regionalism and nationalism. All are necessary to interpret the balance that has developed between population growth and economic development in this country. The United States began as an agricultural enterprise, thirteen colonies of farms and plantations. For a long time land was the main source of wealth, and the country pressed westward as it converted the free lands of the frontier to homesteads, farms, and ranches. Back East there rose the growth of cities as seaports and commercial capitals, but urbanization waited upon the coming of industry, manufacturing and transportation. This beginning is well represented by the English mechanic, Samuel Slater. Migrating to Rhode Island with the plans of textile machinery memorized, he founded the American textile industry and a family fortune in the early nineteenth century.

Given the wide domain of the United States, the differences between agriculture and industry and between open country and growing cities helped to develop major regions which came to show difference in many things besides population density and growth. The Northeast was the first to become urban and industrial; its high birth rates fell and it attracted foreign immigrants to satisfy the new demands for industrial labor. The South remained agricultural longer, devoted to the production of staple crops—like cotton, rice, and sugar cane; it depended on slave labor and developed fewer cities. As population moved westward, mining and the growing of livestock were found best suited to large, subhumid areas of dry plains and mountains. While these sections of the West remain the most sparsely settled area in the country, the Pacific coast section is growing rapidly, even where rainfall is lacking.

The Northeast will long remain the most urban and most populous part of the country, but certain trends are bringing the different regions closer to the national average. Thus the South is increasing its trend toward cities and manufacturing; and in pushing population out of agriculture, its birth rate is lowered. The Pacific coast is growing faster than any other part of the country and bids fair to duplicate the commercial and industrial structure of the Northeast. At present rates California will soon exceed the state of New York in total population. Along with this convergence in development, an important trend leads to a greater equality of per capita income between the regions. Along with the trend toward equalizing fertility among these large sections, there is a better hope of regional-national integration. Finally, internal migration also serves as an economic equalizer for the whole country as workers move from low-income to high-income areas. In addition business concerns move industrial plants and capital from fully developed areas of lessening profits to less-developed areas of growing profits. America is still seeking, in its over-all population policy, the stabilization of agricultural production at a level high enough to retain a stable proportion of the people on the land. This goal is not yet in sight, for agricultural technology has not yet played its full part. Nevertheless as the urban population—all customers of the farms—continues to grow, the possibility of balance draws closer. In the end, the lesson of American economic and population growth may prove to be one of convergence. This means that regions tend to draw near to similar trend

lines of development, that birth rates as between socioeconomic classes approach nearer equality. In view of the
American hope of equality, this is a consummation greatly
to be desired.

SUGGESTIONS FOR FURTHER READING

Conrad and Irene B. Taeuber. *The Changing Population
of the United States*. New York: John Wiley & Sons,
1958.

This volume, issued as one of the 1950 census monographs, is the best single survey of the changing size,
structure, and characteristics of the American population.

Donald J. Bogue. *The Population of the United States*.
Glencoe: The Free Press, 1959.

This is one of the most comprehensive collections of
statistics about many aspects of the American population, with insightful comments, summaries, and inter-
pretations.

U. S. Bureau of the Census. *Historical Statistics of the
United States: Colonial Times to 1957*. Washington,
1960.

A major reference for historical statistical series on
many demographic, social, and economic aspects of the
American population.

William Petersen. *Population*. New York: Macmillan, 1961.
Part I, "The Population of the United States," pp. 18–
306.

This rather large section of a general text in population surveys many aspects of population of the United
States.

Dennis H. Wrong. *Population and Society*. New York:
Random House, 1961.

This small paperback book contains a survey of population trends as well as numerous references to the
American population.

Chapter 11

POPULATION TRENDS IN NEWLY DEVELOPING COUNTRIES

Nathan Keyfitz

To secure a perspective on population changes, we can start by looking back to the time, at the turn of the twentieth century, when the world contained just over one and a half billion people. At that moment, which is within the memory of men now alive, there was a fairly clear division between the developed peoples of Europe and America, who numbered 500 millions, and the rest of the world, over 1000 millions in number. The rest of the world mostly lived in Asia and were, by one formula or another, under the rule of Europeans. Africa and Latin America together contained fewer than 200 million people.

In the sixty-three years of the twentieth century which have so far gone by, drastic changes have occurred. These are not only in numbers, which are the main interest of this discussion, but in the very language which is used for describing the situation. Colonial rulers and so-called natives alike have disappeared; so have backward peoples, the white man's burden, and the *mission civilisatrice*. The relation of the Europeans to the people of other continents, which was once seen by the former as a responsibility of the more advanced for the tutelage of the retarded, and by the latter as thinly veiled exploitation, has changed into a formal relation of complete equality. All sit as equal members of the United Nations; with a few exceptions all have set up the governmental and diplomatic apparatus of independent states. One could not today use the language of 1900 in describing world population or politics. Some progress has been made away from the more patent kinds of inequality and toward a degree of respect for human rights over the last sixty-three years.

The first change, in the matter of numbers, is that world population has just about doubled. It is hard to be exact in this statement, because we do not know how many human beings there were at the turn of the century or, even now, how many there are today, despite tremendous attempts which have been made to secure data. But it seems that some time in 1960 or 1961 we passed the 3000 million mark. It is roughly correct to say that the countries which were colonies or otherwise subordinate members of the world system in 1900 and are known as the "underdeveloped" countries of today have doubled their numbers to about 2000 million, while those which bore the white man's burden are now the "developed" countries with a population of about 1000 million.

It is well to see something of the changes in the distribution of population which have been occurring at the same time as the last doubling of the total. In 1900 Europe had a larger proportion of the world population than it had ever had before, and probably more than it is likely to have again. Europeans reached the peak of their relative numbers at the same time as they exercised political dominion over most of the world. Asia grew from 900,000,-000 to 1,700,000,000 people; it did not quite double, and its proportion of world population dropped slightly.

The most spectacular gains were made by Latin America, which we can define as consisting of all the people on the mainland and islands extending from the United States to the South Pole. These numbered only 63,000,000 in 1900; today they number nearly 225,000,000. Countries which were of modest size have become very large indeed. Brazil took a census at the end of the year 1900 and counted 17,300,000 people. Another count, made in 1960, numbered 69,700,000. From 17 million to 70 million during this century, which is to say during a single lifetime, suggests a change in the very nature of the national community.

One way of thinking about these figures is to compare

them with the populations of European countries when these were underdeveloped. The first census of England and Wales was taken in 1801, when the industrial revolution was well under way; it counted 8,900,000 persons. The French census of the same date showed about 30 millions; France was far and away the most populous country of Western Europe. In the course of its enormous industrial development of the nineteenth century, England's population grew rapidly; at the end of the century there were 33,000,000 people, a nearly fourfold increase. And if England had not quite 9,000,000 people in the time of its industrial revolution, it had even fewer in earlier periods of its history. The world-wide conquests in the reign of Elizabeth I, like its heights of literary achievement, were accomplished by an England of five or six million people. Its total population, the proportion who were able to read and write, the number who lived in cities, were all of about the same order as Cambodia today. Compared with Elizabethan England, present-day Ceylon and Peru are not only very large, but are also highly literate and urban.

The earlier phases of the industrial revolution seem to have been accomplished everywhere by tiny groups of enterprisers. As these accumulated capital and set up more and more workshops, their enterprises needed more and more workers, and the offer of wages brought these workers into existence. At least this is the way the classical economists saw the matter, and the description seems essentially correct. Without capital, labor is not usable. Before capital was accumulated, people stayed in the countryside and lived in traditional fashion in a moneyless, costless economy of subsistence agriculture; but even there it was well that there were not too many of them, lest by requiring the use of less fertile lands they lower average income. The reproductive powers of the human race are such that people quickly appear once the conditions for their employment exist, which is to say when enterprise armed with capital comes on the scene. The history of nineteenth-century Europe at least exemplifies this. And when the human factor is no longer needed in such large numbers, as at the present time, it ceases to appear; most European countries are increasing at less than 1 per cent per year. The United States and Canada, which still seem to offer more space and opportunity, are growing a little faster while Japan, like Europe, has a low birth rate. I do not mean to imply that these changes in Europe, America and Japan were either an automatic compliance of the supply of people with the demand for them, nor that the supply of people was deliberately planned by anyone. I leave to one side the explanation of the mechanism, and merely call attention to the fact. Our main interest now is the quite different process in the presently underdeveloped countries.

What are the reasons for the current extraordinary growth? At one level the answer must be either that births are greater than in the past or that deaths are fewer. For the world as a whole, migration has so far been zero, and for most large areas in most years it has been small.

Here we are more handicapped in respect of knowledge of the facts than in the discussion of total population; if the worst censuses are within 5 or 10 per cent of their target, the worst vital statistics may be out by 20 per cent or more. In most of the underdeveloped world, birth registrations are especially incomplete. In India about 26 births per 1000 of population are registered; in fact at least 40 births occur per 1000 of population. We know this in two ways: by field surveys which have been carried out using samples in small, well-defined areas, taking care and going to considerable expense to enumerate all the births in these sample areas; and by comparing successive censuses. Though it is probable that even the best sample surveys miss some people and that the censuses are not complete, it seems safe to take it that births are of the order of 40 per 1000. If deaths were 13 per 1000, which is about what the vital statistics show, the rate of increase would be faster than that shown by successive censuses. Let us suppose that death rates are of the order of 17 per 1000; this would make the present increase something like 2.3 per cent per year. It was actually about 2.1 per cent per year in the ten-year period between the censuses of 1951 and 1961. Ceylon has better statistics; it shows about 36 births per 1000 and 9 deaths, making a rate of increase of 2.7 per cent. Just as Ceylon's statistics are better than India's, so its death rate is probably lower. It is easier to control both deaths and the statistics of deaths in a small, compact country than in a large country.

In order to see what will happen in the future, it is useful to translate rates of increase, for example that of India which I am guessing to be about 2.3 per cent, into the length of time it will take the population to double. It happens to be very easy to do this with all the accuracy needed for our purpose. One takes the number 70, and divides the percentage rate of increase into it. This results in an error of less than one part in a hundred. Taking the formula for granted, we note that 70 divided by 2.3 gives 30, very nearly, as the number of years in which the population of India will double if the rate of 2.3 per cent is maintained. Ceylon's rate of 2.7 per cent divided into 70 gives a doubling in twenty-six years. These periods of time are very much less than the sixty-three years which the population of the underdeveloped world took to double the last time. The pace is accelerating.

Whatever acceleration is shown in Asia is exceeded in Latin America. Mexico increased by 3.1 per cent per year during the period 1950 to 1960, as we find by comparing censuses and taking a geometric average. This means a doubling in twenty-three years. But since the 1950s the rate has further increased. Mexico at the moment reports that it has a birth rate of about 46 per 1000 and a death rate of about 12; this would make its rate of natural increase 3.4 per cent, and bring the time of doubling down to twenty years. Venezuela is growing faster than Mexico; Central America, at about the same speed; Brazil, a little slower but accelerating rapidly.

The countries which have good statistics are not a representative sample—far from it. There is little doubt that the quality of statistics is highly correlated with the quality of health services. One would not, therefore, transfer results

from Ceylon and Malaya to Nepal and Laos, or from
Mexico to Ecuador, at least not as of today. But isolation
does not seem to persist long in the twentieth century.
The improvements in mortality which we find in the more
accessible countries on the coasts of all the continents will
find their way to the interiors within a very few years.

For, after all, such health methods are very simple. More
than any other one thing, they consist in spraying with
DDT to kill the anopheles mosquito, which is the carrier
of malaria. Sometimes solid areas are sprayed by plane,
sometimes only houses so that people are not infected while
they sleep. The results are felt immediately. Ceylon was
the scene of an anti-malaria campaign about the time
World War II ended. In the five years before the war her
death rate had averaged 24 per 1000; in 1946 it was 20,
and in 1947 it was 14.

Since we know that such procedures and achievements
are spreading everywhere, we can safely count on the rates
now found in the most advanced parts of the underdeveloped world soon coming to apply universally. This completes a cycle of world history—man's conflict with
bacteria, which have always been deadlier than his larger
enemies. The first victory was Jenner's invention of vaccination against smallpox; this was followed by Pasteur's
theoretical discoveries. By 1900 chlorination of water
supplies and other elements of urban sanitation had spread
through Europe and North America. The arrival of DDT
and antibiotics in the last thirty years completes the cycle.
These are applied at very little cost and have had a greater
effect on the death rate than all the elaborate and expensive apparatus of hospitals and medical insurance.

What can we say about the future in the light of such
facts as we have? A few years ago the United Nations
worked out a series of projections for the several countries
of the world which is the most complete and reliable in
existence; it arrived at a total world population of
6,900,000,000 in the year 2000. This implies a doubling in
about thirty years, which is probably longer than it will
actually take. I believe that the march of events has out-

stripped the UN projections, as it has nearly all the other projections I know of. If population growth is really accelerating, projections of the most recent rates into the future will be short. But even the United Nations gives Latin America over 600,000,000 by the end of the century, nearly the population of China today. China would have something of the order of one and one half billions on a similar, conservative scale of projection. As early as 1975 Brazil will have passed the 100,000,000 mark, and Mexico will have reached 53,000,000.

The United Nations tables permit an interesting comparison by continents. Without attempting to find out exactly how many persons of European and non-European descent there have been at various times, we simply note as a rough index of this the population of Asia, excluding the U.S.S.R., as against that of Europe plus the United States and Canada. In the year 1900, which continues to serve as a kind of bench mark in this discussion, the ratio was 1.7; there were more Asians than Europeans together by about 70 per cent. This seems to have been the low point of the index for all time. In 1800 the ratio was 3.0; it was subsequently changed by the enormous growth of Europe relative to Asia during the nineteenth century. The UN figures for 1950 show it to be unchanged from 1900— still 1.7, but thereafter it rises rapidly and reaches 3.1 in the year 2000, according to the projections. The relative expansion of Europe's population in the nineteenth century is matched by the relative expansion of Asia's in the second half of the twentieth.

If population growth—sheer numbers of people—were a race between East and West, a pacific competition like the Olympic Games in which each side could aim at demonstrating its vitality and virility by producing the larger crop of babies, there would be nothing more to say. That Europe's relative gain at the time of its industrial revolution should be reversed when Asia and other continents come to economic maturity seems perfectly reasonable.

Unfortunately the matter is much more complicated than this. The presently underdeveloped countries are be-

ginning their industrialization at a density so much greater
than that of Europe when it was in the same position that
the role of population in their growth may be very different from its role in Europe. The fourfold increase of England during the nineteenth century began with a small
population and ended up with one that was beyond the
capacity of England to feed. She lived by trading manufactured materials for food, a system which obviously could
not be adopted by every country in the world simultaneously. What will happen to an area that starts with something like ten times the density of late eighteenth-century
England? England and Wales in 1801 had 8,900,000 persons on about 58,000 square miles; Java has 65,000,000
persons on 48,000 square miles. The density in the first
case is about 140 per square mile; in the second it is about
1,350. It is interesting to note that living on an island settled at a density of 140 persons per square mile set Malthus
thinking about the shortages of foodstuffs and the tendency
of the human race to outrun its means of sustenance.
We can imagine how his exposition would have increased
in vigor by statistics of present-day underdeveloped countries.

Malthus would certainly have included in any edition
of his book that we can imagine him writing today the
careful calculations of food production made by the Food
and Agriculture Organization of the United Nations. For
the world as a whole, excluding mainland China, it finds
that for the year ending in mid-1961 the increase in food
production over the preceding year was only 1 per cent,
while the population increased a good deal more than this.
However, the preceding year had made a more important
gain over the year before it, and the net outcome for the
two years together was to keep the food curve somewhat
above that of population. This is an example of the random
component of food production that constitutes a subtle and
treacherous aspect of the population issue. Population follows a steady curve of increase, while food production is
a random variable which sometimes goes up and sometimes down in its variation around an apparent upward

trend. India's output has risen as much as 11 per cent in
one year and dropped as much as 5 per cent in another
year, all in the past decade. World food production shows
a smoother curve than the production of individual countries, but even in the grand total there have been drops in
some years and increases in other years of as much as 5
per cent. It is the function of food stocks to smooth out
such changes, but a difficulty of the present situation is
the inability of some of the countries whose population is
growing fastest to finance such stocks. It has come to be
one of the uses of foreign aid to perform the smoothing for
individual countries.

To leave the variations and come back to the trend: the
Food and Agriculture Organization shows that the index of
volume of food production rose from 77 to 117 in a period
of about twenty-five years ending in mid-1961, an increase
of just over 50 per cent. How will things stand during the
next twenty-five years if the population doubles, as is likely,
and food production does no better than it has done? The
margin is very great; if people double while food increases
by 50 per cent, then we can see without much pencil-
and-paper work that each individual will on the average eat
exactly 25 per cent less. Since in many parts of the world
people are eating none too well at present, the reduction
of 25 per cent is a serious threat against which any existing stocks would be negligible.

But objections may be made to my arithmetic, for I
have set expected future population increase against past
food increase, which is not fair. What then are the chances
of doubling food production during the next twenty-five
years? Applying in reverse the handy formula we have used
before, this means that there would have to be an average
increase of about 2.7 per cent per year. Many things can
be done. Arable soils which are not presently used can be
put under the plow. Better varieties of rice, wheat and
other crops that are already in use in some places can be
extended to other places. New varieties can be developed;
there is no reason to think that discoveries in genetics and
agronomy have come to a stop. Substitution of tractors for

horses increases the net return of agriculture by using
mineral energy instead of vegetable energy for the work
of plowing. To these things, possible with no further technical advance, can be added the application of atomic energy to distill water economically from the sea, the cheap-
ening of present methods of growing algae and other plants
without soil, etc. We must not make the mistake of Malthus and the classical economists in underestimating subsequent technical progress.

But in refusing to make the error of Malthus, we must
not go to the opposite extreme. If his mistake was a pessimism of unamiable aspect, the opposite error is an irre-
sponsible optimism that could lead to disaster on a scale
never before known. For technical advances have been
occurring in the past twenty-five years and have been applied. Huge efforts have been made in agricultural extension, in every conceivable means of persuading farmers to
use good methods and of finding good methods to recom-
mend to them. The net result has been the 50 per cent
increase which FAO reports. The process of finding and
spreading the best methods takes time. If it is carried on
at a pace which only equals the increase of population,
then the problem is unchanged except in one respect: its
scale is increased. And in the matter of population, scale is
everything. Anything that leaves the problem unchanged
except for increasing its scale is making it worse.

As a way of thinking about how scale makes a difference, consider the case of Ireland in the 1840s. Its population of about 7,000,000 was drastically affected by famine;
its people reacted by marrying at later ages and by moving to the United States, where more than a million Irish
emigrants became laborers, policemen, politicians and other
kinds of useful citizens. Suppose that somebody had been
able gradually to improve the means of growing potatoes
to keep up with the population, perhaps with the addition
of foreign aid in foodstuffs to tide over bad years, until the
population had grown to 35,000,000 with the same standard of living as in 1840. The problem would be five times
as difficult; it would now be beyond any possible solution

through migration. It would have come to resemble the problem of Java, whose 65 millions are beyond help through migration even to Sumatra, a large and relatively empty island which is only a few miles away. Their increase is well over a million a year, and the resources to move and resettle that many people are not to be had. If Indonesia were to undertake such a movement, she would have to spend on it the resources of management and capital which are the means of economic development.

The exhaustion of the land, the impossibility of raising the food that would nourish such giant populations as are now coming into existence, has a variety of social consequences. I give an example from current Indian history. India has passed laws to liberate the service castes of its villages from the customary disabilities under which they have lived from ancient times. They were under obligation to make clay pots, to shave their clients, or to do whatever service their particular caste obligation required. Their clients were in general peasant farmers. A tradition that coerces people into such personal relations is objectionable in principle, and the wretched existence of the service castes had rightly aroused the attention of Indian legislators. But in the more crowded sections of India it may well turn out that the farmers are more anxious to release their miserable servants than the latter are to be released. The growth of population has brought rural densities up to 2000 per square mile, and subdivision of land has gone to such a point that on his postage-stamp plot the farmer can raise but a small amount of food; his hungry family today has no trouble in eating all of it. They may be glad to give the service castes their freedom and henceforth cut their own hair, make their own dung cakes for fuel, and dispense with the night watchman since they have no property to guard. There may be nowhere for the onetime service castes to go but to the city to seek a job in industry. And if industry does not grow sufficiently to give them jobs, they may only join those hundreds of thousands who live and die on the sidewalks and in the squatter colonies of Calcutta and other cities. If the rural population is dense enough, and if industry does not grow rapidly, such social measures as the liberation of the service castes may be entirely futile.

To cite no more than one other of the consequences of population pressure on the land, it even makes difficult the collection of taxes. In all of the instances where development has occurred—in England, Japan, and the U.S.S.R. the process was especially obvious—it was financed in large part by taxes on the peasant. The tax was never intended to take away from him the food that he had grown for himself and his family, but rather to spur him to grow more food that would nourish the people of the cities while they built up manufacturing industries. But many administrators in the crowded countries will tell you that today this is difficult, if not impossible; to impose a tax that would spur the peasant to produce more is out of the question unless there is land to which he can apply his efforts beyond the plot he is now cultivating. This is an aspect of the fact so well known to the classical economists that if labor is the source of all value, it cannot be applied except to land; some cooperation from nature is inherent in all production.

It might be said that such a view is old-fashioned. With the advance of technology, man has liberated himself from abject dependence on nature. With modern methods he can make nearly anything synthetically, which is to say he can make it out of those natural elements which are widely distributed. Bauxite, which is found nearly everywhere, can be made into aluminum. Air can be made into fertilizers. The farmer does not need to set aside a fifth of his land to provide the oats for his plow horses, leaving only the remaining part for human food; with gasoline-driven tractors providing energy more lavishly than oats could do, the whole field is at his disposal. All this is true and is the reason why modern students are not as preoccupied with the land problem as were their predecessors. To exaggerate only slightly, if enough capital is available we do not need to worry about land until the human race is packed to the point where there is no standing room left.

The difficulty is accumulating that capital, a process whose initial phase is nowadays called economic development. To put the matter in the simplest terms, capital requires saving on the part of someone, abstention from present consumption in the interest of the construction that will permit more consumption in the future. Some of such saving in favor of the underdeveloped countries has traditionally been done by the people of the developed countries, through a system of world-wide investment, and this process continues today. If international investment is less now than it has been in the past, it is supplemented by a certain amount of saving by the developed peoples in the form of foreign aid, which differs from investment in that the donor often does not expect any interest or even the return of his capital. But neither of these forms can be quantitatively sufficient. The investment of the underdeveloped countries depends on the effort and abstention of the people of those countries themselves.

When a country is able to save a net of about 12 per cent of its income and put this effectively into new investment, it is usually launched on development. But at the same time as land scarcity makes taxation difficult, it similarly inhibits the application of labor that would result in saving. And quite aside from this obstacle, which, like the facts of the preceding paragraphs, arises out of *population density*, we note another and different handicap of the presently underdeveloped countries due to the rate of *population increase* which they show. Even if land existed in plenty, if populations were one tenth of what they now are in the crowded regions but still increasing at 3 per cent per year, the problem of providing the new members of the population with equipment would be very difficult. In a country where 3 per cent is added to the population each year, and in which two dollars or pesos or rupees of investment is required to equip a man to earn with his labor one dollar or peso or rupee of income from then on, the investment must be 6 per cent of income annually merely to put the newcomers on the same basis as the people already there. Thus a considerable amount of saving is required merely to keep the structure unchanged and prevent the increase of poverty. Six per cent is about the amount of saving that went on in colonial societies. Since the most progressive of the underdeveloped countries today probably are saving less than 10 per cent of their income, only 4 per cent is available on these assumptions to raise income per head. With 4 per cent they can at the very most raise income per head at 2 per cent per year. And my assumptions in this calculation are so generous that they would not be accepted by any respectable economist, who would insist that most investments require much more than twice the initial input of the income they permit. It would not be extreme to say that a country that saves 10 per cent of its income and is growing at 3 per cent per annum will just about be able to prevent a fall in the average income of its citizens; it will hardly be able to change its industrial structure in the direction we know as economic development. And this statement refers to a country that is not yet crowded, that still has plenty of land.

With these and other difficulties in its way, the typical underdeveloped country, or at least its elite, has begun to give attention to the birth rate. Much of the trouble stems from the fact that its births have remained at traditional levels. The development-minded elites are asking, and we may well ask too, why have births remained so high?

Through all of history human cultures have contained elements that encouraged large families. This is true at least of the cultures that have survived. There may have been other cultures in which people could let themselves off lightly in regard to raising a family, but until recently, death rates have been so high that any societies whose generative vitality was low have died out. This element within the structure of ideas that promoted large families was associated with the sense of power and progress of the group, as well as with its mere continuance. Ideas have considerable inertia, and many still think of numbers of people as having some relation to economic and political power, not realizing how far machines have made mere unequipped manpower obsolete.

In addition to the firmly embedded idea that large numbers of people are an instrument of power are some social practices by which individuals really depended materially and in the meaning of their lives on the number of children they brought into the world. Operation of the peasant holding after the owner was too old to work it required his having sons. Thus quite aside from family continuity, a kind of immortality through the passing on to one's sons of the family land, there was the practical matter of being provided for in one's old age, before modern pension systems were established.

Ideas and practices that are as ancient as man himself, or at least as old as settled agriculture, cannot change as fast as the death rate has fallen. People continue to have six, seven, eight children, just as they did when half of these died before reaching working age. The sort of rational adaptation of means to ends, taking account of the latest facts, which people of modern education are privileged to be able to make in at least a rough way in the affairs of their lives, is beyond the capacity of the peasant. He has made an adjustment that permits his survival; he has shrewdness, persistence, industriousness, but he lacks flexibility. This flexibility comes with education and with living in a modern industrial civilization. Once these are attained, there is no doubt that the birth rate will settle down to the much lower levels that the modern death rate requires. The history of all the presently industrialized countries shows this—the instance of Japan after World War II is perhaps the most striking. Within a decade her births fell from about 35 per 1000 to about 18 per 1000. The adaptation of births to deaths is a function of industrial society and is not much affected by ideology; the Soviet Union makes much of the Marxist view that population troubles are a feature of capitalist organization and will disappear with socialism; in fact her birth rate is within one or two points per thousand of that of the United States.

All this can be summed up in two sentences. With industrialization people would adapt their practices to present low death rates, and the population dilemma that has provided the occasion for this volume, and for so much study and concern, would happily disappear. But on the other hand the high birth rate is preventing industrialization by causing it to be starved of capital.

What is to be done to break the circle is a matter for the people of each country to keep thinking about until they come up with the answer that they will apply. To arrange the social framework so that individuals will limit their families to the point that the interests of the nation require is easy only in the saying. In the concrete society, developed or underdeveloped, there is such a variety of interests, so many elements of irrationality, such lack of facilities for even putting the issue to people, that any real social change requires great effort. The essential feature of the underdeveloped country has been the isolation of its peasantry; its villages were in a very real sense not within reach of any message simply through lack of the physical means of communication. They have had no newspapers, and only gradually are whole villages coming to acquire a single radio. The villagers generally do not speak the language of the distant city elite, having their own dialect or entirely separate speech. Even if they nominally speak the same language, the range of concepts of the peasants is different from those of the urban elite and those I am using in this essay. To convey the message of economic rationality, of which one aspect is family size, requires its translation into terms far more concrete than I have managed in this rather abstract argument.

One thing is sure: on the conveying of that message and the consequent solution of the population problem depends the future welfare and happiness of mankind.

SUGGESTIONS FOR FURTHER READING

Ansley J. Coale and Edgar M. Hoover. *Population Growth and Economic Development in Low-income Countries.* Princeton: Princeton University Press, 1958.

A monographic study, concentrating especially on

India, of the difficulties which population growth places on the accumulation of capital.

Kingsley Davis. *The Population of India and Pakistan.* Princeton: Princeton University Press, 1951.

Detailed historical and statistical analysis of the growth of population on the Indian subcontinent.

Thomas Malthus, Julian Huxley and Frederick Osborn. *Three Essays on Population.* New York: New American Library (Mentor Books), 1960.

Contains a handy condensed version of Malthus' theory in his own words.

Irene Taeuber. *The Population of Japan.* Princeton: Princeton University Press, 1958.

Gives in detail nearly every aspect of Japan's population, past and present.

Warren S. Thompson. *Population and Progress in the Far East.* Chicago: University of Chicago Press, 1959.

Discusses in some detail the population and related social and economic trends in East and Southeast Asia, with special attention to Japan, China, and India.

Chapter 12

POPULATION AND
FAMILY-PLANNING PROGRAMS
IN NEWLY DEVELOPING COUNTRIES

J. Mayone Stycos

For most of man's history a large and rapidly growing population has been viewed as desirable. Until recently the principal ingredient of military power was manpower, and numbers therefore enhanced the prestige and power of the lord, the prince or the leader of a clan. Moreover, until modern developments in health technology, death came early, and to compensate for high rates of mortality, societies very early tended to develop customs, if not explicit policies, that would guarantee replacement and growth through high rates of birth. Thus most societies where death rates are high are characterized by early marriage, religious exhortation to increase and multiply, and by family and community pressure on the female to have many children.

In the present century a number of European and Asiatic countries have stressed the need for large and rapidly growing populations both as an element of national power and, sometimes, as a symbol of national virility. Several nations developed family-allowance payments that subsidized additional numbers of children, and public extolling of large families frequently accompanied the economic benefits. Within the past decade the emergence of new nations in Africa and Asia has caused a resurgence of interest in measures to increase population size. A number of these nations have small populations relative to their neighbors or relative to their area. These facts, combined with feelings of nationalism unknown during colonial periods, have given them a certain amount of anxiety about building up their population size to become powerful vis-à-vis their neighbors.

Thus national policies to influence the rate of population growth are not new. What are relatively new in the world are national policies aimed at slowing or retarding the rate of growth. This is, of course, because the problem has changed. Countries undergoing economic modernization today have rates of fertility probably higher than those of Medieval Europe and have rates of mortality considerably lower. The excess of births over deaths is therefore unusually large not only in terms of rates, but because the populations of modern states are so much larger than ever before that even a modest rate of increase may mean great absolute increases in population.

Another factor that accounts for nations' relatively recent concern about population is long-range economic and social planning. Many countries only recently have been attempting to chart their future needs, resources and goals in a scientific and integrated fashion. Five-year, ten-year and longer-range plans are becoming a normal pattern for governments. When a nation today looks carefully at its needs for schools, hospitals, jobs, housing, etc. over, let us say the next twenty years, it cannot avoid the impact of the population problem because many populations will almost double in about twenty-five years' time.

Thus it is understandable that countries such as Egypt, India, Pakistan, most of the communist bloc, Puerto Rico —all of which strongly emphasize national planning—have programs that are aimed at curbing high birth rates. At the same time, nations not conspicuous for their concern for long-range economic and social planning are rarely concerned with population problems. Most Latin American countries would fall in this category, but if the Alliance for Progress is successful in its efforts to encourage Latin American nations to engage in systematic national planning, we may soon see a commensurate interest in population planning.

What kinds of programs are currently being attempted? What sort of problems do they face and what are their chances of success? Before these specific questions are answered, the general nature of the problem facing any modernizing country wishing to slow its rate of population increase will be described.

The having of children under the conditions of most societies is one of the most natural and pleasurable sequences in the world. Not to have children requires actions demanding effort or restraint—delayed marriage, continence within marriage, or contraceptive practices which at their present stage of development are troublesome. In order to undertake such actions, a married couple must be conscious of the disadvantages of having too many children or having children too rapidly. In nations where there is the possibility for advancement in life, either for one's self or one's children, we can anticipate that people will delay immediate gratifications for future rewards. But in a society where progress seems impossible for a family, where advancement may in fact depend more on luck or connections than on hard work or sacrifice—in such a society it may be by no means clear why there should be any particular advantage in having three or four children rather than six or seven. In short, it is unrealistic to expect strong motivation for family planning to develop without social change which will place economic and social penalties on large families.

Most countries which we call modernizing are taking steps that should result in some degree of social mobility—mass education, technical training programs, development of industry, progressive tax policies, community development programs, etc. Where such programs are beginning to have an effect, it is most likely that family-planning programs will speed up the process of motivation for small families by providing the means.

Relatively few nations have made the attempt, and their experience is so recent that we have little to go by. However, these and a few other, more limited experiments are sufficient to give a feeling of confidence with respect to several generalizations. A good range of examples can be provided by choosing three countries: Puerto Rico, Japan and India.

Population problems are especially severe in Latin America because death rates are generally lower than in Asia and the Middle East and birth rates are at least as high. Programs of fertility control face special obstacles in Latin America because of the predominance of the Catholic religion, which opposes most methods of birth control. Probably mainly for this reason, no Latin American nation has endorsed a policy on population limitation. However, the Commonwealth of Puerto Rico, with an essentially Latin culture and a Catholic population, has experimented with both private and government programs.

In the late 1930s, a law was passed in Puerto Rico permitting the sterilization of women in public hospitals for reasons of health or social-economic pressures, and at the same time family-planning clinics were opened throughout the urban and rural health units of the island. A full range of modern contraceptive methods was made available free of charge, dispensed by doctors and nurses in the clinics. Aside from public attacks from the Catholic Church, however, no publicity was given to these programs—i.e. while excellent facilities were provided, no attempts were made to inform the people of these facilities or to motivate them to use them. Nevertheless significant numbers of women began to use the clinics, and female sterilization proved so popular that some local politicians dispensed bed space in hospitals as rewards for patronage. The Church made its major challenge to the program in the last Puerto Rican election when a Catholic party was formed. A major explicit objective was to change the laws with respect to birth control and sterilization, but the party's candidates were overwhelmingly defeated in the elections.

What effect has the program had? The Puerto Rican birth rate has declined steadily over the past decade from about 36 to about 30 per 1000. However, a large if not major explanation of this decline lies in the heavy out-migration from the island of people in the reproductive ages, rather than in real fertility declines of resident couples. Despite the fact that large numbers of couples have taken steps to limit family size, there is a tendency to start only after having had several children and to practice birth control relatively inefficiently.

Because of the deficiencies in the government program, a private program was initiated in 1959 that attempts to distribute simple contraceptive methods to the rural population by an elaborate system of volunteer workers in rural communities. Twenty-two professional workers have recruited and supervised over 1400 volunteer workers who, in turn, contact families in their communities and supply them regularly with contraceptives. There is some reason to suspect, however, that the very success of this program has caused the government to relax its own efforts, and the effectiveness of its clinics has therefore appeared to decline.

A different context for government program is provided in the case of Japan. Following World War II, Japan's population increased alarmingly. In 1948 a law was passed permitting women to have legal abortions for economic reasons. Contraceptive services were also supplied by 800 Eugenic Protection Consultation Centers, and thirty thousand nurses, midwives, and health workers were trained in family-planning techniques. The program appears to have had dramatic results. In 1950 only one in five couples in Japan reported use of contraception. By the end of the decade, two in five reported use. Moreover, those practicing contraception started to do so earlier in their married lives than had been the case before the program. Increases in abortion were even more spectacular. By 1961 over 40 per cent of married women had had at least one abortion, and the number of annual abortions in Japan now well exceeds the number of births. Within just over a decade the birth rate of Japan was halved, and it is now below that of the United States.

Unfortunately it is difficult to know how much of this decline would have occurred without the government program, since the birth rate had begun to fall before the program was initiated, but it seems safe to say that without the program declines would have been slower. What accounts for the spectacular decline of the Japanese birth rate?

In the first place, Japanese population is one of the most literate in the world, making it unusually accessible to printed media. Second, Japanese culture is relatively free of religious or other taboos on open discussion of sexual matters. Consequently it has been possible for Japanese newspapers and magazines to carry information on birth control which would be unthinkable in Western cultures. The combination of high literacy and wide distribution of popular women's magazines has put Japan far ahead in the possibilities for dissemination of information. In various surveys in Japan it has been found that about half of married women report they learned about birth control through magazines. In such a context the provision of facilities for family planning has a much greater chance for success than in countries where even basic information must be provided.

India presents still another case, and a vitally important one. India's population of about 450 million is so huge that even a modest rate of growth would mean the addition of large numbers yearly to the population. But since the death rate has been halved in the past twenty-five years and the birth rate has declined only slightly, every year India adds about ten million people to its population. This amounts virtually to adding each year the population of a London or New York.

The factors tending to sustain high fertility in India are numerous. Average age at marriage is sixteen for females, and declines in mortality mean that more women than ever before are living through the reproductive ages. In rural areas, religious, social and economic forces result in a high value's being placed on offspring, especially males. Widespread illiteracy, low proportions of women in the labor force and the predominance of agriculture are obstacles to change in fertility patterns.

Nevertheless various surveys in India with respect to desired family size have produced results similar to those in other countries. The average villager wants three or four

children, not a dozen or an unlimited number. Over the
past decade the Indian Government has taken steps to en-
able the population to realize such goals. In the first five-
year plan, beginning in 1951, 1.3 million dollars were allocated for cautious probing and experimentation in the
field of family planning. The second five-year plan allocated about ten million and a national program was put
into effect. In 1961 the third five-year plan was initiated,
with a much more ambitious program and a budget of 57
million dollars. What kinds of measures have been taken
in these programs?

By 1960 each of India's fifteen states had family-planning boards that advised the departments of health on
family-planning matters. A central family-planning board
has the same function at the national level and a post of
director of family planning has been created within the
health ministry.

By 1960 there were over 4000 urban and rural clinics
providing free contraceptive materials and advice. A broad
program of mass communication was also developed, uti-
lizing posters, films and slides. Village leaders were also
mobilized and given basic information about family planning. In some states sterilization has been emphasized,
and a cash payment is given for those who volunteer. In
1961 about 46,000 sterilizations were reported. In the
third five-year plan, clinics are being minimized and community efforts maximized.

As far as can be ascertained, the national program has
had no effect as yet on the birth rate, and the results of a
number of studies in specific areas of India have been dis-
couraging. However, at least one major project conducted
in Singur since 1957 seems to have had positive consequences. The birth rate declined from 42 to 37 in four
years, whereas in a comparable region without the program the birth rate has shown less change. However, in
the Singur study a much more intensive program was
launched than is typical in the national scheme. For example, personal contacts by field workers, group discussions in the village, emphasis on husbands as well as

wives, and continued contact over the period were more characteristic here than in the average village covered by the national program.

To complete our rapid survey of population-control programs, a word about the situation in communist countries seems necessary. Although traditional communist ideology has tended to deny that population growth *per se* can be a problem in a socialist society, the facts of demographic change have compelled most of these nations to re-evaluate their policies. A rapid population growth as the result of declining death rates following the war has produced considerable difficulty in the achievement of per capita improvements in housing and consumer goods desired by most communist nations. Moreover, communist officials were aware that large numbers of non-legal abortions were occurring. As a result, in the past few years every European communist nation with the exception of Albania and East Germany (which has a severe manpower shortage) instituted a national program of legal abortions, often accompanied by contraceptive programs. The justification has usually been in terms of health—that abortions performed under medical supervision will reduce the threat to maternal health existing under a system of non-legal abortions.

The high incidence of abortion is indicated by recent figures compiled by Dr. Christopher Tietze, director of the National Committee on Maternal Health. In Bulgaria and Czechoslovakia in 1961, the number of legal abortions was close to half of the number of live births, and even in Poland abortions represented about a quarter of the number of live births. In Hungary legal abortions exceeded the number of live births, and in Greater Budapest there were twice as many abortions as births. Birth rates in all these countries declined markedly after the introduction of legal abortion programs, and all countries in the Eastern European bloc now have birth rates below that of the United States.

What are the implications of these examples for understanding past family-planning programs and the probable conditions for their successful development elsewhere?

First, it is clear that programs to effect a decline in high birth rates are not impossible. Nowhere, whether on a national or local basis, have efforts met with active opposition on the part of the target population. To the surprise of many, there is a basic desire for moderate-sized families wherever in the world husbands and wives are questioned in a systematic and careful fashion. Further, there is a widespread demand for information about means to limit family size.

Secondly, there is a long and complex series of steps between this basic interest in family planning and the actions necessary to bring an actual decline in the birth rate. From short-range and limited experiments and longer-range broad programs as in Puerto Rico and India we may conclude that even intensive efforts do not produce marked changes in a short period of time. However, these experiments, even when they have "failed" by the rigorous standard of affecting the birth rate, have taught us a great deal about what is needed in such programs.

Thus we know that the kind of private program by voluntary organizations typical in the United States and England is totally inadequate for modernizing countries aiming to reduce their birth rates. Even in the West such programs have had only a minor direct influence on contraceptive practices, and the conservative and amateurish character of such organizations is certain to weaken their impact in other countries. Moreover, as we have seen in the case of Puerto Rico, the very existence of private agencies may give the governments concerned an excuse for inaction. This is not to say that voluntary agencies cannot be useful, especially in the early stages of a family-planning movement; but in successful programs the efforts of voluntary groups are likely to complement, not replace or duplicate, the programs suitable for governments.

Although moral objections to abortion may be strong in the United States and in some other countries, the fact is that wherever legal abortion has been permitted it has been widely practiced, and this in part represents merely a shift from non-legal and medically dangerous abortions to abortions with little risk to the health of the mother. Surveys in Latin American cities are beginning to disclose a hitherto unrealized number of non-legal abortions, a fact of great concern to departments of health, both because of the cost in health and the high economic costs of hospitalization due to complications following the abortions. In many countries where legal abortion is an ethical possibility in terms of local values, it probably will be seriously considered and adopted in at least some cases. In others the substitution of contraceptive services would be a more likely alternative.

Another related conclusion is that the provision of facilities is not enough when a country aims for a successful program. The traditional medical approach which awaits the arrival of a patient in a clinic or office and presupposes a highly individualized doctor-patient relation is unrealistic and unlikely to reach many people in modernizing countries today. The average individual interested in family planning does not even view it as a medical or health problem but as an economic one. The successful programs are likely to involve the approach, personnel, and techniques of non-medical disciplines such as agricultural extension, adult education, community development, mass communications, applied sociology and anthropology. Where there has been success in India, we have seen that it appears to be associated with such broader techniques of education.

Even further, normal commercial channels for disseminating information and supplies have been neglected in every organized government program to date. In Western countries, commercial outlets rather than clinical have been the major sources of supply. The recent report of the Director of Family Planning in India, emphasizing such outlets, and the volunteer system employed in Puerto Rico's private association show that a non-clinical distribution system can be highly effective in rural areas. Such potential outlets exist in every country: in India existing distribution networks for tea and kerosene are available; in Africa the itinerant peddler; in Latin America the tiny retail stores in rural areas. Because of their economic inefficiency such outlets require government subsidies in order to distribute materials at feasible prices, but they would be far more economic and effective than clinical systems.

Japanese experience shows the tremendous potential of the popular press as a channel of information. All modernizing countries place heavy stress on literacy in their development programs, and it would not be long before popular newspapers and periodicals could be important carriers of information. Even at the present time urban populations can be reached by stepped-up magazine and newspaper coverage, and radio usually reaches even the most remote rural regions.

Finally, there has been a tendency to ignore males in most programs. Males are better educated, more influential in decision making within the family, more exposed to modern influences and probably more sensitive to economic pressures than are females. In Western countries declines in birth rates have been achieved primarily by male methods, and the popularity of male sterilization in India and the responsiveness of males to education in the Singur experiment all indicate that males cannot be ignored if family-planning programs are to be accepted widely.

All of this adds up to the conclusion that reducing birth rates can be done but will be an arduous task for interested governments. Because of the complexity of the problem and the length of time it takes to affect fertility, the planning and initiation of national programs cannot wait until population growth becomes acute, if the programs are to be successful parts of long-range development programs. Nations which have not yet introduced programs should not count on technological miracles to solve their population problems or push the problem into an indefinite future. Population control is entirely possible, but just like any other serious problem it takes time, money and brains. There is a shortage of all of these, and for this reason every modernizing country aiming to limit population growth probably must give careful scrutiny to its population problems well in advance of the time that crash programs may be necessary. There is some evidence that international agencies giving technical and economic assistance to modernizing countries are changing their policies to give more aid to population programs. But the basic demand as well as the eventual major responsibility must come from the countries concerned.

Suggestions for Further Reading

Ronald Freedman. "The Sociology of Human Fertility." *Current Sociology.* Vol. 10–11, No. 2, 1961–62.

Extensive essay and bibliography on fertility and fertility control research since the Second World War.

Clyde V. Kiser, editor. *Research in Family Planning.* Princeton: Princeton University Press, 1962.

Research reports on family planning programs, approaches and techniques.

Lee Rainwater. *And the Poor Get Children.* Chicago: Quadrangle Books, 1960.

Intensive social-psychological study of contraceptive behavior and attitudes among an American lower-class group.

Melvin G. Shimm, editor. *Population Control.* New York: Oceana Publications, 1961.

Articles on religious, legal and economic aspects of population control in a number of countries.

J. Mayone Stycos, editor. "Family Planning in Modernizing Societies." *Journal of Marriage and Family Living.* Vol. 25, No. 1, February 1963.

Articles on population-control programs in India, Pakistan, Japan, mainland China, Lebanon, Caribbean, Egypt, and Chile.

Chapter 13

THE POPULATION OF LATIN AMERICA

T. Lynn Smith

Many striking superlatives are being used nowadays to describe the phenomenal increase of population that is taking place throughout the world; but their use is more appropriate in connection with the changes now going on in the twenty American nations which collectively make up what is commonly known as Latin America than for any other large portion of the earth. At least since 1925 the populations of Mexico, Central America and Panama, the three island republics, and South America have been characterized by exceptionally high rates of natural increase and consequently by rapidly mounting numbers of persons. Furthermore since 1950 the rates of growth have risen to even higher levels than those attained before mid-century, and there is every reason to suppose that between 1960 and 1970, and possibly until 1980, the population of Latin America will maintain its record-breaking rates of increase.

A few statistics assist one to place the recent rates of population increase in Latin America in perspective. However, for periods before 1900 the results are clouded by a lack of census data and by the obvious inconsistencies in and unreliability of the various population estimates. By the turn of the century, though, it appears that the world's population had mounted to about 1,630 millions, of whom some 43 millions, or 2.7 per cent, were Latin Americans. Twenty years later, or just after the close of the First World War, the earth's inhabitants had increased to about 1,811 millions, whereas the population of the twenty Latin American countries had swollen to about 89 millions, or 4.9 per cent of the total. After 1920 there was a quickening of the pace at which the population of the earth was increasing, and by 1940 it reached 2,250 million; but the speed with which the Latin American peoples were multiplying rose even more rapidly, so that by 1940 they alone numbered about 123 millions, or 5.5 per cent of the world's total population. Even the mass destruction and loss of life accompanying the Second World War did not halt the increase of world population, although it slowed its rate temporarily. In the Latin American countries, though, the war did not lessen the rapid rate of growth. As a result, by 1950, when the earth had come to have about 2,510 million inhabitants, 154 million of them, or 6.1 per cent, were Latin Americans. Finally, between 1950 and 1960 the earth's total shot up to a mark of about 2,995 millions, with the rate of increase in Latin America still in the vanguard. As a result by 1960 the combined population of the twenty countries involved had mounted to 202 millions, or approximately 6.8 per cent of all the people on the earth.

In 1900 only 1 out of every 37 members of the human race was a Latin American, whereas in 1960 this ratio had risen to 1 in 15. In summary form this indicates that a phenomenal change is under way. With the passage of each decade the relative importance in world affairs of the population of Mexico, Central America, the three island republics, and South America is mounting rapidly. Moreover, as will be indicated later, the factors responsible for the rapid increase of population in Latin America will probably retain their force until at least 1980. Then, in all probability, a substantial fall in the birth rate may get underway. In the meanwhile, though, the proportion of Latin Americans among the earth's inhabitants probably will rise to about 1 in every 13 by 1970 and to 1 in 12 by 1980.

RATES OF GROWTH

It is no easy task to determine with a fair degree of reliability the rate of growth of the total population of Latin America or of many of its parts. It is likely, however, that the growth rate for Latin America as a whole from 1950 to 1960 was at least 3 per cent per year, and that the rate for the preceding decade was approximately 2.5 per cent. An annual increase of 3 per cent is of record-breaking proportions. In all probability throughout the entire history of mankind no other large section of the earth, except the United States during the years 1790 to 1860, has ever experienced a rate of growth as high as 3 per cent per year. Such a growth rate indicates, for example, that during the opening years of the 1960–70 decade there were over six million more Latin Americans alive at the end of a year than at its beginning, and that there will be about eight million more Latin Americans on December 31, 1969, than on January 1 of the same year.

The generality of these extremely high rates of increase among the diverse portions of Latin America is another feature deserving of comment. Consider, first, that in the Brazilian half of South America the population growth indicated by the censuses of 1950 and 1960 amounted to 37 per cent. This was closely rivaled, however, by a gain during the same period of more than 35 per cent in Mexico, second most populous of the Latin American countries. Even the phenomenal rapidity of population growth in Brazil during this decade was exceeded, however, by increases of 46 per cent in Costa Rica, 43 per cent in Venezuela, 41 per cent in the Dominican Republic, and 40 per cent in Nicaragua; and the rate in Mexico was less than those of Guatemala, Honduras, and Ecuador, and equaled by that of Panama. Indeed, except for the 13 per cent increase for the small country of Haiti, the lowest relative increases for any of the countries are 19 per cent for Argentina and 24 per cent for Cuba.

The Primary Factors

For most parts of Latin America the data are woefully inadequate concerning the three primary factors that influence the rate of population growth—i.e., fertility, mortality, and migration. In spite of this, however, the role that each of these three primary factors is playing in the phenomenal increase of population is fairly certain. In brief, it is evident that for centuries both the birth rates and the death rates must have been very high in all twenty of the countries, with the former averaging somewhere between 40 and 50 and the latter between 30 and 40 per 1000 population. Except in Argentina and Brazil, and, for a brief period following the close of the Second World War, in Venezuela, immigration from overseas has been so slight as to be negligible in helping to account for population growth. Even in these countries it is unlikely that more than about 10 per cent of the increase during any decade may reasonably be attributed to immigration of Europeans or Asians. The movement from one country to another occasionally has assumed sizable proportions—as, for example, the migrations from El Salvador to Honduras, from Bolivia to Argentina, and from Paraguay to Argentina—but it has had little influence upon rates of population growth.

Since the role of immigration has been relatively unimportant, it is fairly certain that at least until 1900, and probably until 1920, the excess of births over deaths produced the fairly moderate recorded increases of population. Certainly, prior to 1920 there were few dramatic increases of the kind presently going on throughout the twenty Latin American countries.

By 1920 a great demographic revolution had begun throughout Latin America. In large measure this was due to the comprehensive health programs of the Rockefeller Foundation and the world health agencies, working in close cooperation with governments. These programs were highly successful in controlling communicable diseases such as smallpox, malaria, and the dysenteries—all of the causes of death that are susceptible to arrest by such means as vaccinations, injections, and the safeguarding of milk and water supplies. As a result, the death rates in the Latin American countries began to fall sharply and substantially. As yet this dramatic achievement has not been accompanied by a comparable reduction in the birth rates.

As a matter of fact, other than the tendency for the rate of reproduction to fall in some sections of the small, but rapidly increasing, urban population, the fertility rates throughout Latin America have maintained their previous very high levels. This means, of course, that for the areas as a whole the rate of natural increase, or the difference between the birth rate and the death rate, has increased within the last few decades from around 1 or 1.5 per cent to at least 3 per cent per annum. Thus we must attribute the recent large and sustained upsurge of population throughout the Latin American countries to the reduction of the death rate, and almost exclusively to the control of communicable diseases.

There is some evidence to indicate that many residents of the rapidly growing cities are beginning to practice birth control on a fairly large scale. This appears to be the case especially on the part of the numerous descendants of the upper classes who find it extremely difficult to maintain even an appearance of upper-class status; and it also seems evident on the part of those who are genuine members of the middle class. In view of this it is likely that by about 1980 a sharp reduction of the birth rate, comparable to that which took place in the United States between 1900 and 1935, will get underway throughout Latin America. As a matter of fact the fall in the birth rate in Latin America may be even more precipitous and dramatic than that which brought about such tremendous social and economic changes in the United States. Meanwhile, though, the tidal wave of population growth in Latin America is likely to continue rising until it crests, probably about 1970, at a rate of about 3.5 per cent per year. Thereafter the influence of further successes in the control of mortality probably will be more than offset by the quickening pace of a falling birth rate.

REDISTRIBUTION

Rivaling in importance the spectacular rates at which the populations of the Latin American countries are grow-

ing are the drastic changes now underway in their spatial
distribution. The South American continent contains, of
course, a major portion of the unused and underutilized
land on earth. This land is sufficiently favored by climatic,
soil, and other features to permit it, in our present stage of
cultural development, to maintain large numbers of human
beings. There are also extensive areas still awaiting the
fructifying effects of man's efforts in Mexico and the Central American countries. Extensive portions of such countries as Brazil, Venezuela, Colombia, Peru, Bolivia, and
Paraguay are almost devoid of inhabitants, and other
large areas in the same countries are very sparsely populated. In many other parts of Latin America there are also
other immense tracts of land fully capable of supporting
large populations and still awaiting man's efforts to con-
quer the tropics. However, the push of settlement into
virgin territory is involved only to a limited extent in the
drastic changes in the distribution of population now underway in the Latin American countries. Rather, the tendency of overwhelming importance (and that which for
better or worse is affecting economic and social development in all twenty of the countries under consideration) is
the extreme concentration of population growth in the
already densely populated areas of the various countries.
Most of the population increase is accounted for by the
mushrooming of existing cities and by the rapidly mounting numbers of people in extensive suburbs, or "bands of
misery," which surround all of the principal urban centers.
This huge expansion of the urban and suburban populations is most spectacular in the metropolitan districts of
great cities such as Buenos Aires, São Paulo, Rio de Janeiro, Mexico City, Santiago, Lima, and Cali, in which
industrialization is making vast strides. But it is also taking
place in many other localities, such as the cities and towns
of northeastern Brazil, the urban centers of Haiti, and the
population centers of Bolivia, Ecuador, and Paraguay, in
which jobs in industry for the heads of the families involved are conspicuous by their absence. It seems well to
comment briefly in turn about the two important aspects

of the redistribution of population presently taking place throughout Latin America.

The Extension of Settlement. Perhaps the tendency for the population not to push out into the unsettled portions of North and South America is best illustrated by the case of Brazil. For that huge half continent, fully one half of which is almost totally unoccupied, the 1960 census data already are available to use along with those for 1950 in making the necessary comparisons. A study of detailed maps of the changes that took place between 1950 and 1960 indicates that the only portions of the great Brazilian land mass in which in recent years there have been any substantial efforts to bring new areas into agricultural production are the following: the northwestern part of the state of Paraná, the north central portion of the state of Maranhão, the sections of the state of Goiás which are fairly close to the new national capital (Brasília), the northern portions of the state of Minas Gerais, and the extreme northwestern part of the state of São Paulo.

In Argentina the days of the agricultural frontier largely have passed, and it is probable that when the detailed figures from the 1960 census are published, the general pattern will be seen to be one of rural depopulation rather than one of agricultural expansion.

In the Andean countries there is some tendency for settlement to push downward from the densely populated highlands and out onto the plains at the base of the mountains. To some extent this is taking place in Bolivia, Peru, Ecuador, Colombia, and Venezuela. In Ecuador this new settlement is moving into the previously largely vacant sections of the Pacific coastal plain, but in the other countries it is almost entirely down the eastern slopes of the Andes and out onto the plains and into the jungles at their base. Likewise in Central America and in Mexico there are a few areas in which new agricultural settlement is going on, but in Mexico and Central America, as in South America, all of this is dwarfed in importance by the immense flow of population from the rural districts to the cities and into the mushrooming suburban slums that surround almost all the important urban places.

The Phenomenal Growth of Cities and Towns. As mentioned earlier, the rapid growth of cities and towns and the mushrooming of the huge bands of suburban slums surrounding most of them are the most striking features of the great current redistribution of the population of Latin America. The statistical compilations needed in order to determine precisely how the present rate of urbanization in the twenty countries under consideration compares with the rates of urban population growth at various times and places throughout the world have never been made. Nevertheless the developments in this respect probably are among the most unusual in world population history. This is because until recently the level of urbanization in most of the countries was very low; the present rates of population growth in the urban portions of Latin America greatly exceed those in the rural areas; and the entire process is being fed by a rate of increase of the total population of at least 3 per cent per year.

Let us consider a few of the data. In 1950 only about 19 millions, or 36.5 per cent, of the Brazilian population were classified as urban. Nevertheless during the ensuing ten years Brazil's urban population increased by more than 13 millions, or 70 per cent, whereas the rural segment which totaled almost 33.5 millions in 1950 increased merely 5.8 millions, or by only 18 per cent. During this decade 69 per cent of the total increase in Brazil's population took place in her cities and towns. The most publicized aspects of this phenomenal growth of urban population in Brazil are, of course, the immense concentrations of people in the cities of Rio de Janeiro and São Paulo, each of which is now a conurbation containing at least 5 million inhabitants. But the rush of Brazilians to the cities is by no means confined to the migrations to these two huge giants. Between 1950 and 1960, for example, the urban population of the state of Minas Gerais increased by more than 1.6 million and that of Rio Grande do Sul by well over 1,023,000. Indeed, on the relative basis, the burgeoning of such cities as Belo Horizonte (with about 700,000 inhabitants by 1960) and Fortaleza (with well over 500,000 residents in 1960) was even more spectacular than the growth of São Paulo and Rio de Janeiro. Moreover, Recife and Salvador both developed so rapidly that each probably will pass the one million mark before 1970. In Brazil as a whole, places of 2000 or more inhabitants increased from 900 in 1940 to 1,174 in 1950, and to 1,799 in 1960.

Similar developments took place in Mexico, second most populous of the Latin American nations. In 1950 fewer than 43 per cent of its 26 million inhabitants were living in urban centers. Between 1950 and 1960, however, this urban segment increased by 61 per cent, whereas the rural population grew by only 16 per cent. As a result, in 1960 Mexico's urban population actually was slightly more numerous than her rural population, the reported numbers being 17,705,000 and 17,218,000 respectively. In 1960 the Federal District, which now is too small to contain all of the huge community of Mexico City (the nation's capital) alone had 4,871,000 residents. But its rate of growth of 60 per cent between 1950 and 1960 did not quite equal the rate of urban growth in Mexico as a whole. This indicates that the increase of urban population is by no means confined to the capital.

For Argentina, third most populous Latin American country, the recent census data are fragmentary and are still lacking the rural-urban classification that is so essential for present purposes. Nevertheless it is evident that the bulk of the growth of population between 1947 and 1960 took place in the urban districts and especially in the huge half-moon of dense settlement immediately adjacent to the federal capital of Buenos Aires. Thus during the latest intercensal period the seventeen civil divisions, or *partidos,* in this area more than doubled in population, with a numerical increase from 1,741,000 inhabitants in 1947 to a total of 3,647,000 in 1960. Among the most striking increments are those in the following partidos: La Matanza, from 98,000 to 403,000 (309 per cent); Merlo, from 20,000 to 135,000 (241 per cent); Quilmes, from 123,000 to 318,000 (158 per cent); and San Martín, from 270,000 to 541,000 (93 per cent).

In Peru, between 1940 and 1961, the urban population increased by 122 per cent, whereas the rural population grew by only 37 per cent. This difference was produced, for the most part, by the migration of people from the rural districts to Lima. As a result, that capital had almost three times as many inhabitants in 1961 as it had at the time of the 1940 census. At present the city, along with its extensive suburban slums, makes up a metropolitan community of at least 2,500,000 inhabitants. During the same period (1940–61) comparable percentage increases of population were taking place in and about the other important cities in Peru.

Consider also the case of Panama. In 1950 that nation's population was only 805,000, with about 16 per cent of the total in Panama City, capital and largest city in the country. Ten years later, in 1960, the population of the Republic had increased to about 1,076,000; but so rapid had been the growth of the capital that more than 25 per cent of Panama's inhabitants were residents of Panama City. Finally, although recent census data for most of the other countries are lacking, the regular traveler to Central and South America surely must be convinced even by casual observation that the tendency of population to concentrate in the cities and towns of Colombia, Venezuela, Ecuador, Uruguay, and the rest of Latin America is fully as great as it is in Brazil, Mexico, Argentina, Peru, and Panama, the places for which data have been presented.

POPULATION GROWTH AND SOCIAL AND ECONOMIC DEVELOPMENT

In some respects the implications of population growth for social and economic development in Latin America are more puzzling than they are for the development of other parts of the earth. Until very recently the lack of population was generally considered as a factor retarding development in most of the countries. Indeed, the theme song of Brazilian history, *falta de braços,* or lack of hands, had its philosophical counterpart in many of the other countries, as evidenced, for example, by their programs for promoting immigration. Even today in most parts of Latin America a survey probably would show that attitudes in general are favorable to a rapid increase of population.

As larger proportions of the lower classes of Latin American societies assemble in and about the larger cities, however, there is a growing tendency to question the belief that a rapidly increasing population is an evidence of social and economic development. In part this seems to be due to problems inherent in producing and distributing enough food and clothing to meet the most basic needs of the people. But the difficulties encountered in the attempt to build houses, expand public utilities, and establish schools fast enough to keep pace with the increasing population cause many to despair; and others are gravely concerned about the social, political, and ideological complications that arise among the transplanted populations. Today the problem of the suburbs is generally recognized in many of the countries as their most serious social problem, although the nature of the problem is very different in developing and already developed countries.

That population increase can be a problem in countries in which there still are millions of acres of virgin lands strikes many as paradoxical. A few recognize that fundamental reforms are necessary if the problems of rural unemployment and underemployment are to be solved and if any considerable part of the natural increase of population is to be directed to the frontier instead of going to the cities. They know that there must be changes in the systems of surveying and deeding public lands, in the prevailing systems of land tenure, in the existing concentration and control of property in land, in the antiquated systems of agriculture still in use in vast areas, and in the tax system. But there is little agreement about the ways and means of accomplishing such reforms, and there is little reason to suppose that such agreement will be reached in the very near future. Until such reforms are accomplished, however, the rapid growth of population and the maldistribution of the population are likely to serve as severe brakes upon social and economic development throughout much of Latin America.

Summary and Conclusion

1. The Latin American countries make up the great world subdivision in which the rate of population increase is the greatest. This has been true at least since 1920, was especially pronounced between 1950 and 1960, and remains true during the present decade.

2. Between 1900 and 1960 alone, the proportion of Latin Americans among the earth's inhabitants increased from 2.7 per cent to 6.8 per cent.

3. The rapidly falling death rate is chiefly responsible for the currently high rates of population increase in Latin America.

4. Although South America and other sections of Latin America contain a major portion of the earth's usable unsettled lands, very little of the phenomenal increase of population in Latin America is taking place in newly opened agricultural districts.

5. The recent large and significant increases of population are occurring almost exclusively in and about the already densely settled cities and towns of the twenty Latin American countries.

Suggestions for Further Reading

John V. D. Saunders. *The People of Ecuador, a Demographic Analysis.* Latin American Monograph No. 14. Gainesville: University of Florida Press, 1961.

This monograph constitutes the most definitive study yet made of the growth of the population of Ecuador.

T. Lynn Smith. *Latin American Population Studies.* Social

Sciences Monographs No. 8. Gainesville: University of Florida Press, 1961, Chapter 5.

In summary form this chapter sets forth the principal results of a general study of the growth of population in all twenty of the Latin American countries between 1900 and 1950, with emphasis on the changes between 1940 and 1950.

T. Lynn Smith. "The Growth of Population in Central and South America," in *Study of Population and Immigration Problems, Western Hemisphere;* Committee on the Judiciary, Subcommittee No. 1, U. S. House of Representatives. Washington: U. S. Government Printing Office, 1963.

In large measure this document is an endeavor to summarize the materials for the period 1900 to 1950 which are presented in Smith's *Latin American Population Studies* and to supplement them with available information for the years 1950 to 1960.

United Nations. *The Population of South America, 1950 to 1980.* Population Studies No. 21. New York: United Nations, 1955.

This contains population projections by age and sex for each of the South American countries over the period 1950 to 1980.

Nathan L. Whetten. *Guatemala: The Land and the People.* New Haven: Yale University Press, 1961, Chapter 2.

This chapter presents the results of recent study of the growth and redistribution of population in Guatemala.

Chapter 14

THE POPULATION OF INDIA

W. Parker Mauldin

Only a few years ago the word India called to mind
maharajas and jewels, snake charmers, elephants, tigers,
cobras and mongooses. The image of the people was similarly dim and diverse; there was the overwhelming impact
of the sheer numbers of people—teeming masses, crowds
in the cities, crowds at the Ganges; numbers, huge numbers, dense multitudes, a sea of people. There was also the
sad face of poverty, a picture of people poorly housed,
poorly clothed, often living and sleeping on the streets in
misery, squalor, and wretchedness. These vague, inadequate, and misleading images are changing rapidly under
the impact of India's efforts to raise her pitifully low levels
of living, to cast aside the bonds of poverty, of illiteracy,
and of ancient customs.

The numbers of people in India stagger the imagination.
In this single country there are:

—more people than in all of Africa
—more than in North and South America combined
—almost as many people as in Europe
—more than in Russia and the United States combined.

The last census in March 1961 counted 439 million people,
but already that number has grown to 460 million. By
1967 there will be 500 million. During this decade one
hundred million and more will be added, if current growth
rates do not lessen. The rate of increase in population is
high; it may become even higher.

In 1961 less than 30 per cent of the population five
years of age and over was literate: 41 per cent of the

males and 15 per cent of the females. The figures have increased slightly during recent decades, but the problem is enormous and progress is slow. For example, at the beginning of the 1950s, school facilities were so inadequate that more than 47 million children of school age but under fifteen were not in school. There has been an increase in the proportion of children in school, and a further increase is planned during the current or third five-year plan. But by the end of the third plan, during the school year 1965–66, if all school plans are put into effect, there still will be almost 40 million children of school age under fifteen not in school. Enrollment rates during the 1950s increased from about 4 in 10 to 6 in 10 for children six to eleven years of age, and from 1 in 8 to 2 in 8 for children eleven to fifteen. By 1966 it is planned, and hoped, that 3 of every 4 children of primary school age will be in school and that almost 30 per cent of those eleven to fourteen years of age will be in school. The figures for secondary school, ages fourteen to seventeen, are even lower—5 per cent in 1950, 11.5 per cent in 1960, and a planned 16 per cent in 1966.

Average per capita income in 1960 was about 330 rupees or just under $70, using the official exchange rate. In terms of purchasing power for locally produced goods and services, at least in rural areas, the rupee is more nearly equivalent to one dollar than to the twenty-one cents shown by official exchange rates.

The list of indexes of underdevelopment can be extended:

—About 70 per cent of the labor force is employed in agriculture, and this figure has changed hardly at all during this century.

—Per capita consumption is less than 2000 calories per day.

—Production of agricultural products is at a low level and is increasing rather slowly.

—Although India is an agricultural country, it imports

large quantities of food grains, 20 million tons during the second five-year plan.

—Only 196 persons are enrolled in institutions of higher education per 100,000 population.

—Only 11 copies of daily newspapers are read per 1000 population.

—There are fewer than 7 radios per 1000 population.

—Fewer than 4 per cent of towns and villages have electricity.

DISTRIBUTION

Density. The average population density of India in 1961 was very high, 370 persons per square mile. Although less than 1 person in 5 lives in a city, high densities of population are found in many areas of India. The bands of greatest concentration are in Kerala, in Southern India, along the fertile Ganges Plain and in the West Bengal Basin. Density in the entire region is seldom below 500 per square mile and often above 1000 in broad bands astride the river. Indeed, more than half the population of India lives in areas where density is more than 500 persons per square mile, and nearly 1 in 5 lives in areas of more than 1000 persons per square mile. The density of the rural population is twice that of Europe; moreover, at least two thirds of India's population is dependent on agriculture as the principal means of livelihood compared to less than a third in Europe. India has considerably less than one cultivated acre per person.

Rural and Urban Population. India is a rural country; 82 per cent of the population is rural, 18 per cent urban. The growth of the urban sector was relatively slow from 1881 until 1941, increasing from 9 to 13 per cent of the total population. During the 1940s the urban population grew by about 40 per cent, and by 1951 it constituted 17 per cent of the total population. The raw census data show that the total population grew by 21.5 per cent during the 1950s; urban population grew by 26 per cent. Thus the urban population increased only from 17 to 18 per

cent of the total population. Has the tempo of urbanization really slowed down? The definition of urban changed
from 1951 to 1961 so that more than 800 places with a
population of 4.4 million were counted as urban in 1951
but as rural in 1961. If the census definition of urban
had not changed, the urban population would have increased by 48 per cent, an increase more than twice as
rapid as for the rural population.

India has seven areas with populations of a million or
more. In order of size these are Bombay, Calcutta, Delhi,
Madras, Hyderabad, Bangalore, and Ahmedabad. Bombay has a population of more than 4 million, Calcutta's is
about 3 million, and Delhi is approaching 2.5 million.
There are more than 100 places with populations in excess
of 100,000, and 35 million people live in these cities. Yet
India is a rural nation. But it is such a huge nation that
the small urban minority numbers 80 million people—more
than the total population of all but the six other most populous countries of the world.

Growth of Population. The census commissioner for 1951
called the year 1921 the Great Divide because prior to that
time the population of India increased quite slowly and ir-
regularly; after that date the rate of increase was continuous and much larger. Widespread famines and epidemics
visited India with devastating results prior to 1921, but
since then there has been only one famine of statistical significance, and the strength and extent of epidemics have
been greatly reduced. From 1891 to 1901 the population
in India did not grow at all because of severe famines. During the next decade the population increased by a little
more than 5 per cent, a relatively low rate of growth; but
with a base of 236 million people in 1901, 16 million were
added during the decade. Then came another period of no
growth due primarily to the great influenza pandemic of
1918–19, which was especially severe in India.

In the three decades 1921–51, the population grew by
some 44 per cent or 1 per cent per annum. During these
thirty years, there were no extraordinarily severe epidemics
or famines. During the next ten years, 1951–61, the pace

of population growth quickened, averaging about 2 per cent per year; the population increased by 78 million during the decade, more than replacing the population lost to Pakistan at the time of partition.

Birth and Death Rates. Both birth and death rates in India are high, but precise figures are not available. Registration of births and deaths is seriously incomplete, and these statistics must be estimated from census data or from sample surveys. The best evidence available suggests that birth rates ranged from 45 to 50 per 1000 population during the early decades of the century; perhaps the birth rate has declined slightly to the low 40s. The change in the death rate has been much more spectacular. At the beginning of this century it was 40 to 45, and today it is about one half that level, or about 20 per 1000 population.

Thus it is evident that the birth rate is still quite high and that the death rate has been falling. It is this difference in levels of birth and death rates that has led to the increasingly rapid rate of population growth. Detailed data are not available to determine precisely what measures have caused decline in mortality rates, but it is known that there have been some improvements in sanitation, an increase in supplies of potable water, more use of modern sulfa drugs and antibiotics, and widespread application of DDT in malarious regions. Health standards are still woefully inadequate, but it is comforting to note that health conditions have improved appreciably. It is reasonable to suppose that further improvements will lead to lower death rates, for the death rate in modern India is still very high.

Consider now the pattern of fertility rates—that is, the number of children born per 1000 women in the reproductive ages. Fertility rates in India are quite high in comparison with those of the United States or of Western Europe, perhaps twice as high. But they are lower than rates in other developing countries such as neighboring Pakistan or many of the Latin American countries. What are some of the major factors involved, and what evidence is there that these rates are beginning to decline?

Fertility rates in India are high because:

—Almost all Indian women marry at a very early age, and almost all of them have children.

—The Hindu religion places a high value on the eldest son's performing certain rites at the time of death of the father; this religious belief reinforces a desire to have a son, and preferably more than one son.

—Traditional rural societies revere large families.

—For the most part the Indian people have not begun to think in terms of planning family size and determining the number of children they want; accordingly, they have not begun to practice birth control to any large extent.

Fertility rates might well be higher were it not that:

—Mortality has been high, and as a result many marriages are broken by death of one of the partners before the wife is beyond the reproductive age.

—According to Hindu custom widows may not remarry.

—Levels of living are so low that some authorities believe that fecundity—the physiological ability to have children—has been impaired.

—Many Indian women return to their parental home at the time of childbirth and may remain there for many months; prolonged absence of the wife naturally would lead to some increase in the interval between children.

—There are taboos against husband and wife having sexual relations during many days of the year; these taboos are related to special holidays, ceremonies, and religious occasions.

—Age at marriage is increasing gradually and slightly; median age at marriage was thirteen years in 1901–11, 15.4 during the period 1941–51.

A number of scholars have speculated that as levels of living rise, as Indian society modernizes and some of the ancient customs are weakened and abandoned, fertility may actually rise, for a time.

Traditionally, as countries become more urbanized, less dependent on agriculture, as levels of living rise, as education increases—in brief, as modernization increases, fertility declines. India, with 82 per cent of its population living in rural areas, is still a rural country. But 80 million people live in urban areas. Do these urban people have smaller families than do rural dwellers?

Kingsley Davis poses the problem as follows: ". . . the Indian birth rate has remained at a high figure, despite a substantial decline in the death rate. The increasing difference between the two has been responsible for the rapid growth of population. The crucial question is therefore this: Will fertility be brought down in time to avoid either a disastrous growth of population or a calamitous rise in the death rate?" His analysis of differential fertility leads him "reluctantly to a negative conclusion."

In a study in Calcutta, it was found that contraceptive practice has increased in recent years and is greater among upper than among lower social classes. In a separate study of a rural population it was found that those who remained in their fathers' occupational groups generally had higher fertility than those who shifted to another occupation. About a quarter of the working population among this rural sample moved out of their fathers' occupational groups. Rele, in a study of a rural area in Northern India, also found that upper-class Hindus have substantially lower fertility than lower-class Hindus, with the middle class falling in between. Muslims had higher fertility than did Hindus. But these differences in fertility are apparent only after fifteen years of marriage. Further, mortality is higher among children in the lower classes than among those in the upper classes, and this tends to reduce the difference in number of living children among the different social classes.

The data just cited show differences, but relatively small differences, in fertility among various social and economic classes. Another study of fertility in central India found that fertility differentials were trivial among the various occupational, residential, and income groups. Another author concludes that apparent rural-urban differentials in India are based on poor data and that there are no significant differentials. This analysis is based on the ratio of

children under five years of age to women in the reproductive ages. The author concludes that infant mortality
in urban areas has been higher than in rural areas, but that
infant mortality has been declining more rapidly in urban
than in rural areas. The published data appear to show
that urban fertility has been lower than rural fertility, but
this difference has been declining. It appears, however, that
higher infant mortality in earlier decades led to a relatively low child-woman ratio, and that as infant mortality
has improved, particularly in cities, the child-woman ratio
has appeared to rise in cities, and the difference between
rural-urban areas has narrowed.

There is some evidence that many couples in large cities
are using contraceptives and are successfully limiting the
number of children they have. At the same time, some of
the factors just mentioned have tended to increase fertility
rates—better nutrition, weakening of taboos against widow
remarriage, and all the rest. As a consequence of these two
opposing trends, fertility rates appear not to have changed.
Sinha, who found some fertility differentials in large cities
of the State of Uttar Pradesh, summarizes current evidence
as follows: "It appears that, as at present, the differential
fertility trends in India, if any, are without quantitative
significance and there is no imminent problem of a decline
in the biological or social heritage similar to that in the
West. However, big changes are in the offing. That we are
determined to reduce the birth rate is undoubted."

POPULATION GROWTH AND ECONOMIC DEVELOPMENT

The most comprehensive, careful, and impressive analysis of the relationship between population growth and economic development in low-income countries is a book by
Coale and Hoover; and India serves as the case history
that is analyzed in detail. The effect of population changes
on economic development of low-income areas has attracted widespread attention during the past decade because of two trends. The first of these is the rise in expectations, aspirations, plans, and programs for expanding

national output and raising levels of living. The second trend has become popularly known as the population explosion, and reflects the increasingly rapid decline in death rates in areas where until recently mortality risks were high.

India's population is very large absolutely and in relation to its resources. It has a large potential for rapid growth in the near future. Also, because of its size, India must find the solution to its economic and demographic problems mainly within its own borders rather than through international trade and migration. Coale and Hoover state that "Our principal aim in analyzing the possible changes in the Indian economy is to bring out the important qualitative differences in economic development resulting from a choice of a very rapid population growth or a less rapid population growth."

This work, published in 1958, was the first major study to point out that mortality rates were declining rapidly in India, and that future population growth would be enormous indeed. They estimated that the death rate might fall from 31 to 21 per 1000 in the decade 1951–61, and that the rate of population growth—the difference between the birth rate and the death rate—would increase from 1.2 per cent per year at the beginning of the decade to more than 2.0 per cent at the end of the decade. Most other writers on this subject were using smaller estimates of the rate of growth, typically 1.2 to 1.4 per cent per year. The 1961 census shows that population growth was indeed rapid during the 1950s, averaging a bit more than 2 per cent per year.

Three alternative sets of population projections were made. The fertility assumptions were:

1. Current high levels of fertility would continue;

2. A 50 per cent decline in fertility between 1956 and 1981;

3. A 50 per cent decline in fertility between 1966 and 1981.

In each projection it was assumed that there would be no substantial out-migration, and that mortality would continue to decline moderately rapidly. These assumptions were not predictions; rather they were designed to illustrate what effect different rates of growth might have on the economy, on the total output, and on the per capita income. These assumptions lead to very large populations by 1986, a relatively short time ahead.

1. If fertility is unchanged, India would have a population of 775 million by 1986, growing at 2.6 per cent a year. Continuation of this rate of growth would double a population in less than twenty-seven years, or in a single generation.

2. If fertility declines by 50 per cent in fifteen years starting in 1966, the population would be less than the high projection by more than 140 million; but even so, India's population would be 634 million in 1986.

3. If fertility had started to decline in the 1950s, and declined by 50 per cent in twenty-five years, the population would be less than the high projection by 185 million; but India's population would be 590 million by 1986.

The raw figures of population growth and population size are startling enough. But even more startling and important are Coale and Hoover's conclusions about the influence of population growth on economic development. Before giving their conclusions, we should remember that India has a population that:

—is already very large
—is growing rapidly
—is densely settled
—has a large proportion of children, a large dependency load, and, as a consequence, a smaller number of workers relative to the total population
—is both unemployed and underemployed to a considerable extent
—the population is poor, witness the low per capita income and the inadequacy of savings that can be invested in capital goods to improve production.

Population growth, rather than size alone, is the significant demographic factor in economic development in India. This is so because a higher rate of population growth implies a higher level of needed investment to achieve a given per capita output, while there is nothing about faster growth that generates a source of investment. Consider two populations that are equal in size, in accumulated capital, and in output. Assume that population A grows at a rate of 1 per cent a year, and population B at 3 per cent a year. If the ratio of capital stock to current annual output is 3 to 1, population A must invest 3 per cent of current output to maintain its per capita income, while population B must invest 9 per cent of current output. If the supply of capital is limited, as it certainly is in India, a higher rate of population growth forces investment to duplicate existing facilities, preventing an increase in the capital available for each worker.

In addition to population size and rate of population growth, the distribution of the population by age has important economic implications. The principal determinant of age distribution of a population is the course of fertility, if migration is ruled out. A change in the growth rate caused by a change in fertility will generally have associated with it a large change in the age distribution. On the other hand, a change in the growth rate brought about by a change in mortality will generally be accompanied by only a slight change in the age distribution. India has had relatively high fertility, and the fact that in recent years mortality has declined strikingly has not caused much change in the age distribution. As a result India has a relatively large dependency load, or dependent population, and a relatively small proportion of population in the principal working ages. About 58 per cent of the population is in the principal working ages, whereas in low-fertility populations the corresponding figure is much higher, around 65 to 70 per cent.

The calculations of Coale and Hoover indicated that the population will continue to grow quite rapidly for a number of decades, even if fertility should decline rapidly. Thus the population of working ages will continue to grow quite rapidly, and during the period under discussion will not be much affected by a decline in fertility, although of course if such a decline were to start and continue, in time the size of the labor force would also be affected. They also found that *total* economic output would grow faster with reduced fertility than with continued high fertility. Since the number of "equivalent adult consumers" in the high-fertility projection comes to exceed the number in the lower-fertility projections by an ever widening margin, the difference in income on a per consumer basis becomes very marked. With high fertility, a smaller total product must be divided among many more consumers than would be the case with low fertility. Their figures show that income per consumer by 1986 would be about 40 per cent higher with reduced fertility than with continued high fertility. Further, the economic gains from a reduction of fertility beginning ten years later but proceeding faster are only about half as great as the gains to be expected from a decline in fertility beginning immediately.

This bleak picture has been abundantly clear to the Indians. It is this kind of analysis undertaken by the Indians themselves that led them to adopt a national family-planning program.

POPULATION POLICY

There has been concern about rapid population growth in India for a number of years; this concern has been expressed by lay leaders, by scholars, and by government officials. The first five-year plan, which was submitted to the Prime Minister on December 7, 1952, recognized that there was a population problem:

> "The pressure of population in India is already so high that a reduction in the rate of growth must be regarded as a major desideratum. To some extent, improvement in living standards and more wide-spread education, especially among women, will themselves tend to lower the rate. But positive measures are also necessary for inculcation of the need and techniques of family planning."

India was the first country to embark upon a national family-planning program. Its budget has grown from 6½ to 50 to 500 million rupees for family planning during the first, second, and third five-year plans respectively. The program did not get well under way until 1956, during the latter part of the first five-year plan. This program was essentially exploratory in the first and second five-year plans. Little was known at the time the plans were drawn up of the likely public reaction to this program. Further, even if public reaction were favorable, as appears to be the case, an organization had to be developed, procedures instituted, and plans implemented.

There was no relevant experience anywhere else in the world on which India could draw. Declines in the birth rate in the Western world had taken place under very different circumstances. In the West modernization had proceeded much further than it has in India; levels of living were higher; literacy was more widespread; levels of education, particularly among women, were much higher; dependence on agriculture had greatly lessened; and industrialization as well as urbanization had proceeded very far. Also all the institutionalized forces in the West were opposed to family planning: the church, the law, the medical profession, the press, the educational system—in short, almost every governmental and private institution opposed the spread of information about family planning. In spite of this people began to have smaller families; they learned about methods primarily by word of mouth from friends and acquaintances. There was no effective organization, governmental or private, that helped to bring about the major declines in fertility in the Western world.

The decision taken by India to make available information and means so that the poor and uneducated as well as the wealthy and highly educated could voluntarily limit the size of families, if they wished, was a most important decision. It was a decision to rise above the barriers of ignorance and poverty so that peoples of all classes might make a conscious decision regarding the number of children they would have.

How much success has the family-planning program had to date? About 1800 family-planning clinics have been opened, 335,000 sterilization operations have been performed since 1956, demonstration projects have been undertaken in a number of areas, demographic and medical research is in process, institutions for the training of personnel have been established, orientation camps for village leaders have been held, the press has written much about the population problem and about the family-planning programs, and, most important, a basic family-planning organization has been established and staffed, and key personnel have been trained. There are no guidelines by which to measure success, but, in my opinion, moderate success would be some decline in fertility within ten years; a major success would be a decline in fertility rates of ten points in ten years—say from 40 or so per 1000 population to about 30. Effectively, India's family-planning program did not get under way until about 1956. It is still too early to judge whether its program will be successful. Not all of the funds allocated for family planning during the second five-year plan were spent. As is stated in the third five-year plan, "Clearly, the limitations of a programme of the nature of family planning arise not from finance, but essentially from considerations of organization, and personnel, which affect the scale and intensity at which the program can be implemented."

The more than tenfold increase in the budget for family planning for the third five-year plan as compared with the second five-year plan reflects the seriousness with which the Indian Government views the population problem; it also reflects the magnitude of the undertaking. It is easy for one to say that too little in the way of money and of human resources was devoted to the family-planning program in India during the 1950s. It is more realistic, in my view, to say that India was the first to make the momentous decision that the government must undertake to reduce the rate of population growth. Its plans have developed relatively slowly during the early years, but they have continued to advance. Now the Indian authorities believe that they have the knowledge to develop a truly significant national program and the organizational structure with which to implement their expanded program. The resources they have earmarked for this program during the next five years are very large; there is hope, and some expectation, that soon real progress will be achieved.

SUGGESTIONS FOR FURTHER READING

Ansley J. Coale and Edgar M. Hoover. *Population Growth and Economic Development in Low-income Countries.* Princeton: Princeton University Press, 1958.

A systematic and authoritative study of the economic implications of different rates of population growth in a major underdeveloped area, India.

Kingsley Davis. *The Population of India and Pakistan.* Princeton: Princeton University Press, 1951.

A comprehensive historical study of the population of India.

Edwin D. Driver. *Differential Fertility in Central India.* Princeton: Princeton University Press, 1963.

Report of a survey in Central India on the relationship between fertility and age at marriage, occupation, income, caste, religion, education, attitude toward family planning, and a number of other relevant factors.

J. R. Rele. "Fertility Differentials in India, Evidence From a Rural Background," Milbank Memorial Fund, *Quarterly*, April 1963.

Warren C. Robinson. "Urban-Rural Differences in Indian Fertility." *Population Studies*, Vol. 14, No. 3, January 1961.

A review and interpretation of apparent fertility differentials among urban and rural populations in India.

J. N. Sinha. "Differential Fertility and Family Limitation in an Urban Community of Uttar Pradesh," *Population Studies*, Vol. XI, No. 2, November 1957.

Chapter 15

THE POPULATION OF AFRICA

Frank Lorimer

Two hundred and fifty-four million people were living in Africa, midyear, 1960, according to estimates compiled by the United Nations. This figure is only 4 per cent less than the estimated population of America north of Panama, whereas the land area of Africa, including the Sahara, is 25 per cent larger than that of North America, including its artic wasteland. Such global figures, though not wholly useless, tell less than they conceal. This is particularly so with respect to Africa. The popular picture of a typical African landscape is largely a product of distance, ignorance, and romance. Africa is, in fact, a complex of diverse regions offering different conditions for human habitation and influenced by factors that have hampered an efficient adjustment of people to resources in many parts of the continent. This is true within tropical Africa as well as with respect to the major divisions of the continent.

Population statistics for most African countries, though subject to much error in detail, now have a more substantial basis than is generally supposed. Complete censuses or systematic surveys on the basis of scientific sampling have been carried out within recent years in most African countries. Incidentally, the results of sampling inquiries are in some cases superior to those of complete enumerations, because sampling methods permit a more efficient use of scarce resources and closer supervision of field operations. The only large country in which there has never been a census or a systematic survey of the population is Ethiopia, where the mountainous terrain and differences in origin, language and culture among its people

impede administration and communication. The population of Ethiopia is officially estimated at 20 million, but
this figure is viewed with skepticism by many well-informed
persons. It was used by the United Nations in its global
estimates for 1960 (cited above) whereas in prior editions
of the United Nations Demographic Yearbook a much
lower figure (in the vicinity of 12 million) was substituted.
This change in procedure may have caused some inflation
of recent population estimates for northern Africa as a
region, and for all Africa, though this is by no means certain. On the other hand, improvements in the accuracy of
information on the population of most African countries
in recent years have generally led to upward revisions of
the current estimates. It is, therefore, likely that current
estimates for the continent as a whole are too low rather
than too high.

The six predominantly Arab nations of North Africa,
from Morocco to Egypt and Sudan, had a total population
of 66 million persons in 1960. Northern Africa, as here
defined, also includes Ethiopia, Somalia, a small adjacent
area centered on Djibouti and administered by France,
and scattered Spanish possessions in North Africa and the
Sahara. Demographic information on the countries last
mentioned is meager and unreliable—more so than for most
of the countries in tropical Africa. The assumed total for
Northern Africa, 88 million inhabitants, is therefore a
somewhat hypothetical figure.

On the other hand, the estimated rates of birth, death,
and natural increase in this region presented by the United
Nations can be accepted as close approximations to
actual trends; they are probably more accurate than similar
estimates for tropical Africa. The Statistical Office of the
United Nations is able to exercise greater independence in
estimating regional vital trends than in presenting current
population estimates. The fertility of the Arab population
in North Africa is fairly constant from region to region
and is reasonably well known through numerous surveys
and investigations. Similarly, rates of population increase
and, by inference, crude death rates in several of these

countries can be appraised with reasonable accuracy from the results of successive enumerations, in conjunction with various intensive investigations. The estimated increase of the North African population in recent years is 2.2 per cent per annum—sufficient to double the population in thirty-two years. This rate is the difference between a birth rate of 45 per 1000 and a death rate of 23 per 1000. If the assumed rate of increase has not been attained today, it soon will be, through further advances in the control of mortality.

Such increase of population obviously has different implications in different situations. Yet it brings certain serious problems in all underdeveloped countries. It forces the allocation of a large share of current production to meet the immediate needs of the people and thus hampers capital formation. Moreover, the high ratio of children to adults, which is an inevitable aspect of high fertility, impedes the advancement of education and the development of a nation's human resources.

As regards absolute ratios of population to natural resources, Morocco, Sudan, and perhaps Ethiopia appear to be rather favorably situated. We refrain at this juncture from any appraisal of Algeria's economic and demographic prospects. The distribution of population in Sudan poses a special problem. Its functional focus is the tri-city metropolitan district of Khartoum, with some 250,000 inhabitants and, at some distance from Khartoum, the irrigated cotton-growing zone in Gezira. From Khartoum a narrow, broken ribbon of cultivated land along the Nile stretches north through the desert, widening out near the Egyptian frontier into land that will be flooded by the Aswan lake. To the west of the Nile a broad band of dispersed settlements and groups of pastoralists stretches far along the southern fringe of the Sahara. To the south, below and above the great swamps of the Upper Nile, is the homeland of the Nilotes and other indigenous tribes. To the east are settlements along the lower slopes of the Abyssinian mountains and on the shores of the Red Sea. The social and economic development of twelve million people thus dispersed through an area equal to one third the continental United States, excluding Alaska, is a difficult undertaking.

Egypt's population problem is quite different from that of the Sudan. The fertile but narrow valley of the Nile has favored the accumulation through six thousand years of an agrarian population, practicing intensive cultivation of the soil with primitive implements. The population that sustained the Ptolemies was cut back during the Middle Ages by war, starvation, and pestilence, but has increased at a rising tempo in modern times. Though two thirds of the people are dependent on agriculture and there is still much ill health, there are now, on the average, about 2000 persons per square mile of inhabited and cultivated land within a constricted area—an island of fertile land in a sea of burning sand. This population is now increasing at 2.5 per cent per year. Its land base is being expanded at great expense, notably through the construction of the Aswan Dam; but this expansion is hardly equal to the increase of the population. The Egyptian Government recognizes the gravity of this problem and is attempting to popularize family limitation as one aspect of its comprehensive program of economic and social development.

The 1960 census of South Africa showed a population of nearly 16 million persons of whom about 3 million were Europeans and about half a million were South Asians. The proportion of Europeans, 19 per cent, was slightly less than in 1950. Immigration from Asia is rigorously prohibited, but the rate of natural increase of the resident Asian population is higher than that of either Europeans or Negroes. Southwest Africa, administered by the Republic, has about one half million inhabitants, of whom 15 per cent are Europeans.

Tropical Africa, between the Sahara and the Republic of South Africa, held about 150 million persons as of 1960. Its total population is, therefore, only about four fifths as large as the United States in an area that is nearly twice as large. The total is distributed by major divisions somewhat as follows: West Africa over 70 million, East Africa nearly 30 million, Central Africa (including the British High Commission Territories adjacent to South Africa) 44 million, and distant islands in the Indian Ocean, including Madagascar and Mauritius, 6.5 million. Among the mainland countries, Europeans are a significant proportion of the total from a demographic point of view only in Southern Rhodesia (7 per cent), Northern Rhodesia (3 per cent), Angola and the former French Congo (2 per cent). There are also important South Asian minorities in East Africa.

West Africa, which contains nearly half of the inhabitants of mainland tropical Africa, is in general a well-occupied region. The average density of population, if we exclude some uninhabited districts in the Sahara, is quite similar to that of the United States. The distribution of people in East Africa is very spotty, with areas of high density in central Kenya, western Kenya near Lake Victoria, the region around Kilimanjaro, and in Rwanda and Burundi—but also large sparsely occupied districts, mainly in arid areas. On the whole, central Africa as here defined (i.e., the southern part of tropical Africa) is a region of conspicuously low population density. There are, for example, fewer than ten persons per square mile in either of the Congo Republics, Gabon, the Central African Republic, or Northern Rhodesia—though the region also includes some areas of high population density, notably in Nyasaland. The large island of Madagascar has a moderate average density (25 persons per square mile), but the mounting population of Mauritius, mainly dependent on its sugar plantations, is rapidly approaching a density of 1000 persons per square mile.

The distribution of the mainland African population is, of course, largely determined by geographical factors. It may, nevertheless, be significant in this connection that the Niger River Basin was apparently the original center of indigenous African agriculture. This region was also influenced during the previous millennium by trans-Saharan commerce passing in and out of the ancient cities of the Upper Niger Valley. Its people were rather well advanced

in agriculture and political organization at the beginning of
the modern era. There are today three large regions of
conspicuously high density in Nigeria: the ancient Ibo yam
districts in Eastern Nigeria, districts associated with old
Yoruba towns in the west, and the districts around the
Moslem cities of Kano and Katsina in the north. Upper
Volta and the Niger Republic to the north have low average man-land ratios, but cultivation of the land is restricted
to a few months of the year and the region can not properly
support its present population. Its inhabitants, like those
in many other parts of Africa, must periodically leave their
homes as seasonal farm workers or wage earners in other
countries.

Mining and other enterprises promoted with foreign
capital are most important in the south and in parts of
Central Africa. It is in these regions that the bi-polar movement of workers between subsistence farming in their native
villages and wage work in industrial and commercial centers or on plantations takes place on the largest scale.
The same phenomenon is found in varying degrees through
the whole continent. At the same time the development
of commercial agriculture by African farmers is well advanced in Ghana, Uganda, and in varying degrees in several other areas.

Only a small proportion of all Africans are found in urban places at any given time—about 10 per cent in places
of 20,000 or more inhabitants. Moreover in many, though
not in all, African countries a large proportion of those
enumerated in towns are merely temporary residents. However, the cities in most countries are now growing quite
rapidly and are becoming more complex in economic functions and social structure.

Regardless of theories and policies pro and con, movements tending to bring about a very considerable redistribution of the population of Africa during the coming decades would seem to be fairly inevitable.

The population of Africa is probably now increasing at
a rate equal to, or perhaps slightly above, the average for
the world as a whole. It is impossible to appraise rates of

increase and their components in most African countries precisely. Information on this subject from successive surveys that are comparable in coverage, methods, and reliability is very limited. Censuses on substantially constant principles under the same auspices were carried out near the beginning and end of the last decade in two large East African countries, two large Portuguese territories, and the Bantu population of South Africa. The average annual rates of increase per thousand thus indicated are as follows: Tanganyika 18, Uganda (excluding persons of external origin) 22, Angola 15, Mozambique 14, South Africa 25. The apparent average increase in Ghana between the 1948 and 1960 censuses was 40 per 1000, but this is affected both by immigration and by important changes in methods of enumeration. Results somewhat similar to those for Ghana are reported for Southern Rhodesia, but both of the same limitations are applicable with even greater force to these results. Successive estimates on the basis of a population-registration system in the Congo during the 1950s indicate an average increase there of about 20 per 1000 (i.e., 2 per cent) per year.

Birth rates are, as expected, generally high in Africa, but there is substantial evidence of a surprising degree of variability. Official reports on registered births and deaths in selected areas, including in some cases towns that serve the surrounding countryside, may be quite misleading. Better evidence on this subject is obtained from an intensive analysis of the results of nationwide or regional inquiries. For example, the demographic inquiry in the Congo, 1955–57, presents consistent evidence of various kinds on the prevalence of great variation in birth rates, associated with wide differences in the proportions of childless women within this nation. The birth rate for the whole country was in the vicinity of 45 per 1000. Rates over 55 were indicated in some districts, but rates below 30 per 1000 were found in two regions. The people in one of these low-fertility regions live along streams in the Central Congo Basin and have long been active in commerce. The other is an isolated region in the northeastern province. Its principal tribal group, the Azande, spreads into a district in the southern part of Sudan. This tribe was also found in the demographic survey of that country to have conspicuously low fertility. Some other areas of tropical Africa in which evidence of unusually low fertility has been obtained are: part of the Ubangi Valley in the Central African Republic, a Moslem district in northern Cameroun and a Catholic district in the south, a tribal area in Uganda, and the southern and northern, though not the central, parts of Mozambique. Similar conditions exist in some other areas. Even so, such conditions, which are probably pathological in origin, are surely rather exceptional. Birth rates in the vicinity of 45, 50, or more per 1000 prevail in much larger segments of the African population. Moreover, in most African countries fertility seems to be as high in the towns as in the rural districts. Some educated Africans are beginning to practice family limitation, but the effects of such practice in any large segments of the population are as yet negligible.

Variations in mortality among different areas in Africa are probably at least as great as variations in fertility, but evidence on this subject is much more elusive. Rising rates of population growth point conclusively to significant declines in death rates in many African countries in recent years. This conclusion is supported by specific evidence in some regions. This trend may have been interrupted by disturbed conditions in some countries, notably the Congo and Angola. In general, death rates are still very high in Africa, but they will undoubtedly be progressively lowered by the extension of public health services.

The United Nations, in preparing estimates of vital trends in the major regions of the world, offers the following hypothetical figures for tropical and southern Africa: births 48 and deaths 27 per 1000 persons per year, giving slightly over 2 per cent as the average annual rate of natural increase. Though stated explicitly, these figures are intended merely as approximations. They can be accepted as a reasonable, though rough, indication of the actual trend.

The rapid increase of population in Africa undoubtedly hampers to some degree the forces of economic and social development. It raises acute problems in some countries, notably Egypt and Mauritius and, less obviously, in certain areas within the sub-Saharan mainland. But, in general, other aspects of African affairs demand more urgent attention. Even with respect to population trends, major emphasis at present is properly placed by most African leaders on questions relating to the distribution of population and migration and to the formation of a labor force prepared to respond effectively to new opportunities. Leading African statesmen, nevertheless, strongly support a recent resolution in the Economic and Social Council of the United Nations calling for increased attention to population questions.

Suggestions for Further Reading

George H. T. Kimble. "The Pattern of Population," in *Tropical Africa.* Vol. 1, Land and Livelihood. Garden City, N. Y.: Doubleday, 1962.

K. M. Barbour and R. M. Prothero, editors. *Essays on African Population.* New York: Frederick A. Praeger, Inc., 1961.

These references are mainly geographical in approach. There is no comprehensive treatment of the demography of modern Africa, or of particular regions south of the Sahara. Information on Africa is treated, along with that for other continents, in various United Nations publications.

A treatment of problems in African demography by W. Brass, F. Lorimer, and E. van de Walle is included in a symposium on *Social Research in Africa* to be published by Frederick A. Praeger, Inc. for the African Studies Association.

Chapter 16

THE POPULATION OF JAPAN

Irene B. Taeuber

The Japanese are fewer than 100 million people living on mountainous islands off the northeast coast of Asia, but the population of Japan is fact, symbol, and hope to the rest of Asia and the world. Japan's past is the irrigated rice agriculture, the pervasive familism, the unending toil, and the generally quiescent acceptance of the East. Japan's present is the metropolitan vortex, the restless striving, the personal ambition, and the material thrust of the affluent society. People are urban, industrial, and educated. Birth and death rates are very low; vital rates are balanced precariously around long-run replacement. Projections of the future population indicate that whatever problems of numbers there may be are likely to be related to decline rather than to growth. The complaints of the present concern labor scarcity, not labor surplus.

In Japan's long history, population and food have been related problems. In modernization, science and technology, assiduously developed and applied, transformed problems of food along with those of industrial productivity. People are deserting the countryside; most of Japan's forty-six prefectures lost population in the last intercensal period. Increasing unit yields sum to national surpluses of rice that disturb the trade balances of Japan and Southeast Asia alike. The rate of economic growth is 10 per cent or so a year, and current plans involve a doubling of per capita income in a single decade. Population problems are not thereby banished. Perhaps the habit of viewing population as a problem is too deeply ingrained. Definitions and dimensions are altered, however. Declin-

ing numbers of youth are omens of an aging labor force
and increasing proportions of the aged. Rural depopulation
exists alongside rapidly growing urban and industrial concentrations. Metropolitan centers thrust tentacles ever further into areas once rural. Many urban workers live in the
countryside, while many of the men of the farming villages
commute to the cities for work.

This story of Japan is a variant of the familiar one of
economic development, social transformation, and demographic transition among people whose modernization occurred in earlier periods and at slower paces. Thus Japan
is not unique in the fact of demographic transition. But
Japan is the initial demonstration anywhere on earth that
true modernization and comprehensive demographic transition are not restricted as to continent, creed, or culture.
The Japanese are not Western in location, European in
race and culture, or Christian in religion. They are Asian
in origins and associations, Shinto or Buddhist in religion,
basically Confucian in ethic. Modernization has been
achieved in an Asian society. Demographic transition has
been completed by an Asian people.

Japan is significant as a case study in population change,
as symbol of the potentialities of Asian peoples, and as
objective evidence that Malthusian doom is not an inevitable terminus for today's underdeveloping areas. This
case of Japan is a complex one, though. Japan is neither a
model nor a probable future for other Asian nations. Nor
is it a basis for comfortable relaxation in the belief that
declining birth rates and slowing population growth are
natural correlates of industrialization and urbanization.
Perhaps they are. If so, relaxation concerning population
growth in our time would still be hazardous. The major
responsibility for research, planning, and action would be
transferred from demographers whose science and technology are all too limited to economists and sociologists
whose effective operating knowledge is also limited.

Japan was once involved in the intricate and self-per-
petuating web of poverty, illiteracy, low productivity, high
human fertility, and high mortality. The forward move-

ment came in all aspects of life, with varying leads and lags at different periods. The present state of relative advance, relative affluence, and approaching demographic balance at low levels of birth and death rates did not come quickly. It is the result of a century as an independent nation dedicated to the achievement of industrialization and power. Moreover, this Asian nation that was never colonial itself demonstrated full equality with European countries as a colonial and imperial power. Population pressure and population increase were excuses if not reasons for imperial expansionism that began with limited war for major territorial gains and ended in total war and the defeat of 1945. Model for the developing nations? Hopefully not. Omen of the path to modernization in other nations? Again, hopefully not.

A century ago East Asia was responding to internal difficulties and the encroaching West in turmoil and transition. In China, the Ch'ing suppressed the vast Taiping Rebellion, but internal disorder, economic retardation, famine, flight, and pestilence remained the regulators of man's numbers. Korea was still "the land of the morning calm." Imperial Russia had pushed eastward to the Pacific, with Sakhalin Island and Alaska as relics of a dream of the Pacific as a Russian lake. The United States had pushed westward to the Pacific. Japan had withdrawn to seclusion in the early seventeenth century, preserving and unifying her culture but turning aside from the industrial revolution and the advancing science and learning of the outer world. Here, in an insulated island microcosm, there was eventually a population so dense that there was no population growth. There were great cities, though, and there was a commercial development that was reaching major proportions by the middle of the nineteenth century. Change had occurred, but it was pathetically slight if contrasted with that in Europe and the Americas from 1621 to 1852.

Japanese with the mentality, the garb, and the swords of the seventeenth century bowed hopelessly before the guns of American ships, but Japan did not become subservient to the more advanced countries. The complex events of decades may be summarized briefly in the statement that the preservation of independence required power and that power had to be based on industry. There was a sustained drive for that modern industry that meant power, but there were also sustained efforts to preserve the social order intact with its hierarchical discipline that extended upward to the god-emperor. Men were sent abroad to study, and scientists were brought to Japan. Education was made universal and compulsory for boys and girls alike, but the little girls who were educated were also indoctrinated for their roles as wives and the mothers of sons. Agriculture and village life were preserved as the great reservoir of tradition, the stabilizing force in a dynamic society, and the source of taxes that could be diverted to industrial production. Wages were low, and amenities were few.

Japan's economic advance was rapid, but it seemed designed to minimize declines in birth and death rates. However, rapid industrialization and urbanization were conducive to reduced birth rates among increasing proportions of the population. Education proved a force of social change. And the goals of health and reduced mortality gradually permeated people, educated elite, and government.

Japan's population was 35 million in 1872, 55 million in 1920, and 71 million in 1940. Population required two thirds of a century for doubling. The China and the Pacific wars reduced numbers temporarily through the massive exodus of civilians and armed forces, but the price of defeat included the return of all Japanese to the home islands. There were major war losses, and Koreans were repatriated from Japan. In 1950 Japan's population was 83 million. In 1960 it was 93 million. Transition from a premodern balance of births and deaths that yielded negligible or erratic growth to a modern balance that implied no intrinsic natural increase had occurred in less than a century. Population had more than doubled, but it had not trebled.

The relatively slow growth of Japan's population was due to the delayed decline in death rates and the relatively early decline in birth rates. Japan could accept smallpox inoculation and related medical technologies from the West rather than inventing them herself, but she was economically fortunate in that modern biochemical means of reducing death rates swiftly and cheaply had not yet been invented. Japan modernized in a period of time when birth and death rates were alike associated closely with social and economic conditions.

In comments on the levels and changes in vital rates, it is wise to begin with a firm statistical basis in 1920. At that time the expectation of life at birth for men was forty-two years. The gross reproduction rate was 2.7. In more widely understandable terms, the death rate was 25 per 1000 total population, the birth rate 36. Natural increase was a little more than 1 per cent a year. This, it should be noted, is almost seventy years after the opening to the West.

Let us glance at this Japan of 1920 in terms that are comparable with conditions in today's underdeveloped areas. Japan was a relatively developed country. Less than half of the gainfully occupied men labored in agriculture. One third of the total population lived in communes of 10,000 or more. The farming population had long ago ceased to increase, for all the sons beyond the one needed for replacement migrated to cities and non-agricultural employment in Japan or in the empire.

Modernization quickened in the twenties and the thirties of this century, partially in association with militarism and expansionism. The proportion of gainfully occupied men in agriculture had been 44 in 1920; in 1940 it was less than 30. The proportion of the population in incorporated cities of 30,000 population or more increased from 18 per cent in 1920 to 38 per cent in 1940. In this latter year, almost 30 per cent of the total population lived in cities of 100,000 and over.

Death rates declined rapidly as trained public health doctors assumed responsible positions in government; birth rates declined as the industrial society advanced. By 1937 the death rate had been reduced to 16 per 1000 total population, the birth rate to 30. In more refined measurement, the expectation of life at birth was forty-seven years for men. The gross reproduction rate was 2.1. The net reproduction rate was 1.5. Natural increase fluctuated from 1.2 to 1.4 per cent a year.

The declines in birth rates were widespread, and they were associated directly with the various indicators of economic and social advances. In all years, there were high negative associations between the level of the birth rate and the proportion of the gainfully occupied population laboring outside agricultural occupations. Age at marriage was increasing and fertility was declining throughout Japan. Gross reproduction rates declined for each of the prefectures in each intercensal period from 1920 to 1940. Infant and childhood mortality declined throughout Japan, but tuberculosis was an appalling and increasing risk at young-adult ages.

In the late twenties and the early thirties there was mounting concern within Japan on the relations of food production to population growth. The government appointed a commission to study the problem, and the commission made a report that included recommendations for birth control. The government did not note the report officially.

With mobilization for war in China, birth rates dropped, death rates increased, and demographers predicted a future doom of declining numbers. Study of the potential supplies of Japanese manpower in relation to the needs of the Co-Prosperity Sphere led to recommendations for government policy to increase birth rates. This policy was adopted and implemented in ways quite similar to those in Germany and Italy during the same period. But in Japan, as in Germany and Italy, the effects of the population policies were limited except in so far as they influenced economic activities.

The grandiose dreams of continental hegemony ended in disastrous defeat and a return to the limited areas of the Tokugawa Shogunate. All the conquests of the century of imperial advance were lost to Japan. Repatriation of

Japanese brought major increases in the population of the home islands. New marriages and reunited families alike operated to produce the usual postwar baby boom of the type so familiar from European and American experience. In these early postwar years, DDT and the antibiotics and BCG inoculations for tuberculosis were contributing to precipitant declines in death rates. There were 15 deaths per 1000 total population in 1947, 12 in 1949, 10 in 1951, and 7 in 1959. In 1960 the expectation of life at birth for women exceeded seventy years.

As we have already noted, Japan's birth rate had declined to a relatively low level before the Pacific war. Even at the height of the postwar baby boom the birth rate did not reach 35. However, the increase of the birth rate to intermediate ranges combined with the fall of the death rate to low ranges led to rates of natural increase of 2 per cent a year or more. This, incidentally, was the first time in the history of Japan that natural increase had reached 2 per cent a year. Pessimism was widespread and deep, for the demographers and the statisticians projected the vital rates of the period into the indefinite future. The logic of pessimism was enticing, and there was nothing in world demographic experience to gainsay it. Projections of the future population that seemed reasonable yielded numbers so large that Japan appeared destined to remain in poverty, if not indeed on an international dole. Again the government appointed a commission, and again that commission reported. And again the government failed to note the report of the commission it had appointed.

The problem of population and the question of population growth could be ignored by government, but a democratic government could not still the deep public concern over the future of the economy and the relations between numbers of children and the opportunities for those children. The controversy was major. Publicity was compounded when Margaret Sanger was not given a military permit to visit Japan and General MacArthur suppressed a technical report on natural resources that included a factual statement on the necessity for controlled population

growth. The General Headquarters of the Supreme Com-
mander for the Allied Powers remained neutral on the
grounds that population policy was a matter for decision
by the country itself.

The pace of change in Japan has been swift in the years
from 1949 to 1963, and population has been a factor in all
change, whether as cause, as consequence, or as interrelated component. Neither in the specific nor over-all instance is it possible to disentangle economic, social, psychological and political changes, for all were parts of the
same process. In prewar Japan most factors operated to
minimize declines in fertility. In postwar Japan almost all
factors operated to maximize declines in fertility. Means
of family limitation became available to a people determined to limit family size—and this occurred during a
period of rapid economic growth and swift urbanization.
Old verities were vanishing, new values were difficult to
achieve. It is not a "miracle" that Japan's birth rate
dropped so swiftly. It would have been an extraordinary
occurrence indeed if the rapid decline in the birth rate
had not occurred.

In 1948 and 1949, the Diet of Japan passed a eugenic
protection law. The stated purpose of the law was the
biological protection of the race, and indeed it was eugenic if not racial in tenor and in content. Abortion, sterilization, and contraception had been barred under wartime population policies to stimulate births. They were
now legalized under carefully regulated conditions for a
variety of hereditary and presumed hereditary deficiencies
and malfunctionings and to protect the health of mothers
against the hazards of excessive childbearing. The economic factor of poverty was specified in the definition of
excessive childbearing.

The Eugenic Protection Act was received enthusias-
tically because of its provision for the inclusion of contraceptive services in health centers. This provision had little
effect. Sterilizations were permitted, but few people asked
for sterilization. The families of Japan selected induced
abortion as a preferred means of limitation. In the suc-

cessive modifications of the Eugenic Protection Act, re-
strictions were removed until induced abortions became
available on request and without medical consultation.
Financial problems were minor, for private fees were small
and most people were included in health services that provided induced abortion along with other medical services
either free or at nominal cost.

As numbers of induced abortions increased and finally
became almost or even more numerous than live births,
regrets and fears were merged in mounting concern over
the problem as it affected the health of women and the
international stature of Japan. The health services of the
government developed increasingly comprehensive and so-
phisticated activities to spread the practice of contraception. The argument was again health, that most acceptable
of all reasons for government action. Induced abortions
had been made available in the interests of the health of
women. Contraceptive services and supplies were made
available to reduce the presumed harmful effects of induced abortion on the health of mothers, not as an overt
population policy to reduce rates of population growth.

The determination to limit family size was firm and
widespread. The decision to postpone childbearing could
be made firmly in the knowledge that the decision could
be implemented. If there was a failure in contraceptive
practice, induced abortion was available. If induced abortion proved harmful or otherwise undesirable, professional
advice on contraceptive practice was available. The birth
rate dropped from 33 per 1000 population in 1949 to 25
in 1951, 20 in 1954, and 17 in 1957. Decline occurred
throughout Japan, from the Ainu fishing villages on the
Pacific coast of Hokkaido to the slum areas of the great
cities of central Honshu.

In the twelve years from 1925 to 1937, the gross reproduction rate had dropped from 2.5 to 2.1. The rate
was 1.8 in 1950—approximately the continuation of the
prewar downward trend. But then rates of decline became
phenomenal if contrasted with experience elsewhere—from
1.8 in 1950 to 1.4 in 1952, 1.2 in 1954, 1.1 in 1956, and

1.0 in 1957. Decline amounted to almost 40 per cent in the
six years from 1950 to 1956. But decline did not continue
thereafter, for Japan's families were limiting size rather
than repudiating children. Aspiration and the reality alike
are the two-child family. Families have achieved their
goals. The nation has solved its problems of population
growth.

Is the rapid decline in Japan's vital rates in the last decade and a half something that may or can happen in today's underdeveloped countries, or in some of them? It is
tempting to answer in the categorical negative. The Japanese who have modern birth and death rates are themselves modern. The economy is industrial, the labor force
skilled, literate, and disciplined. Residence is metropolitan
or related thereto, and the metropolis is a booming economic unit rather than an agglomeration of the poor and
the dispossessed of the countryside. Education at higher
levels is widespread; science and its technical applications
have world stature. The antennae of television rise in the
farming villages. The liberated women who participate so
abundantly in the labor force have electric irons, cleaners,
and washers.

Before we accept the negative answer, it may be wise
to assume we had looked at Japan against the background
of European and American experience in 1850 and had
asked ourselves the same question. Would or could Japan
repeat the economic, social, and demographic transformations of the European peoples? The answer would have
been negative. Japan could not repeat the transitions of
Europe. She did not do so, but in Japan, as in the other
countries, industrialization, urbanization, and education
were inimical to the roles of women and the rates of reproduction of the traditional societies. All processes of
change were speeded in Japan as contrasted with European countries, for the period of history was later, the
science and technology more advanced, the means of communication more developed.

It may be stated firmly that no modernizing country will
repeat the experience of other countries that modernized

at earlier periods. This is true of Japan with reference to Europe, Oceania, and America. It will be true of countries still underdeveloped with reference to Japan.

We return in conclusion to the incontrovertible fact. Japan has achieved solution to the problems of poverty and population that presumably are inherent in the ancient cultures of the rice lands of monsoon Asia. Japanese experience contradicts the prevalent assumption that the lethargies of the traditional societies of the East prevent rapid social change. Japanese culture has been persistent but ever changing. At different times its values have sanctioned families of quite different sizes, and changes have come swiftly. The Japanese transformation occurred in a period of continuing advances in science and technology, and the changes that they brought were unforeseen. Science and technology continue to advance, not alone in areas relevant to mortality control but increasingly in areas relevant to fertility control. Peoples are alert, awakened, sometimes hopeful, sometimes despairing. The rational anticipation is change whose dimensions and speed cannot be foreseen.

The projection of Japan's past into the future never yielded a description of that future. This may be true for other countries today and in the coming decades. In Japan there were alternatives to demographic doom. It may be presumed that there are such alternatives in other cultures.

Suggestions for Further Reading

Irene B. Taeuber. *Population of Japan.* Princeton: Princeton University Press, 1958.

    Population, economic, and social changes in the century of modernization.

Yoshio Koya. *Pioneering in Family Planning: a collection of papers on the family planning programs and research conducted in Japan.* Tokyo: Japan Medical Publishers, Inc., 1963.

Report by the former director of the Institute of Public Health, Government of Japan.

Ryoichi Ishii. *Population Pressure and Economic Life in Japan.* Chicago: University of Chicago Press, 1937.

A classic study by a Japanese economist, with a balanced evaluation.

Sir George Sansom. *Japan, A Short Cultural History.* New York: D. Appleton-Century Co., 1943.

The indispensable basis for understanding culture, people, and history.

Lawrence Olson. *Dimensions of Japan.* New York: American Universities Field Staff, 1963.

A collection of reports by the representative of the American Universities Field Staff.

Chapter 17

THE POPULATION OF COMMUNIST CHINA

Leo A. Orleans

The subject of population, which only a decade ago was reserved for population specialists—for demographers —is becoming more and more a topic for newspapers and popular magazines. Discussions dealing with the consequences of the rapid growth of the world's population and with the pros and cons of birth control are just as likely to be heard in the family living room as on the college campus. In most countries of the West, however, the problem of excessive population increase continues to be a concern for the future; in many of the so-called developing countries the question is whether economic growth can stay ahead of population growth and whether per capita production can be increased—in other words, it is a question of moving forward or standing still; but the size and rate of growth of the population of communist China are of immediate and crucial concern to that country's leaders. This is because the success of the Chinese communists in being able to cope with their population and manpower problems will, along with food production, determine the success or failure of their ambitious plans and aspirations to make China a modern industrial nation.

Although China has some of the oldest population records in the world, the number of inhabitants living on the Chinese mainland at any one time has always been a matter of speculation. The size of the population, the large land area, the lack of adequate transportation and communication facilities, and the absence of effective administrative controls were some of the most important factors which in the past precluded an accurate count of the country's population. Furthermore, the records that were maintained were generally for purposes of taxation, for conscription of civilian and military manpower, or were designed to serve as police registers rather than to provide accurate population counts. Even more recently, the results of three attempted enumerations between 1909 and 1928 were admittedly incomplete and inconclusive. Thus, prior to the communist take-over in 1949, any figure in the vicinity of 450 million (the 1933 estimate of the League of Nations) was considered to be sufficiently representative of the size of the population of China.

In 1953 the communists carried out what they refer to as the "first modern census" of China, on the basis of which they reported the population of the Chinese mainland at almost 583 million. By Western standards, the 1953 count was not only not "modern" but, strictly speaking, not even a census. The enumeration was associated with elections to the All-China People's Congress and was based for the most part on reports of heads of households, who were required to register at specified locations. On the other hand, fairly efficient centralized controls had been established over the country by 1953. People registered or faced penalties. Also to be considered are the facts that the registration was preceded by an extensive educational campaign and that the questions were limited to habitual residence, age, sex, and ethnic allegiance.

The population density of approximately 150 persons per square mile is deceiving because the population is distributed very unevenly. The extremely densely settled areas of the coastal and central provinces are ringed by regions where the soils are unproductive either because of insufficient rainfall or unsuitable topography and by areas of intense summer heat or long winters where the growing seasons are relatively short. As a result, the overwhelming proportion of the total Chinese population lives on hardly more than 10 per cent of the land area that is presently under cultivation.

Some minor redistribution of the population has been brought about by two major policies pursued by the communists. In an effort to increase agricultural production by expanding the area under cultivation, they embarked on a program of reclaiming new lands, primarily in the northern and western provinces. But, because of climatic conditions, because of lack of water, and because the job had to be accomplished, for the most part, with picks and shovels by hundreds of thousands of laborers, the program has not been a notable success and has been replaced primarily by increased efforts to raise per acre productivity on the lands already under cultivation. Nevertheless, the policy as pursued during most of the 1950s did result in the migration of several million persons into the sparsely settled areas of the country.

The policy of industrialization also resulted in minor interregional movements of people. As a result of efforts to bring industry closer to the source of natural resources, the cities in the western provinces experienced an amazing growth. Of course much of this was the effect of migration from adjacent rural areas, but the expanding industrial and mining activities in the western urban communities also required manpower that was not available locally and had to be brought in from the industrial centers of Manchuria and East China. The volume of migration associated with this industrial development, however, was much smaller than the volume of migration which resulted from the virgin-lands policy. Despite the political and economic upheavals of the past decade, therefore, the spatial redistribution of the Chinese population has been insignificant, especially when viewed in relation to a total population of some 650 million.

The urban population in China in 1953 reportedly constituted just over 13 per cent of the total population. While this proportion is considerably lower than most precommunist estimates of the urban population, it does represent in absolute numbers 77 million people in urban areas.

One of the major reasons for the differences in the various estimates of the number of people living in the cities of China is the fact that no standard definition of the concept of urban population is available. Even the 1953 fig-

ure was never explained in terms of criteria used. Later
reports indicate that some attempts have been made to
draw up such a definition—an urban area has to have administrative significance or a certain minimum population,
out of which a certain number of people are engaged in
non-agricultural endeavors—but it is still questionable
whether the Chinese have the detailed data needed to
determine accurately which of the thousands of populated
points on the Chinese mainland should be classified as
urban or rural.

The two most powerful forces that have promoted urban
growth in communist China over the past dozen years have
been the pull exerted by industrialization and the push
applied by ruthlessly enforced collectivization of agriculture. The resulting serious problems of employing, housing, and feeding the millions of new migrants forced the
regime to return many of the peasants to their native villages and to institute strict controls over any future un-
authorized migration into the cities. These controls were
never entirely successful, and the movement of people in
and out of the cities continued to a lesser or greater extent over the years. For example, during the period of the
"great leap forward" in the late 1950s, millions of peasants
entered the cities, but large numbers were subsequently
again forced to move out of urban centers as a result of
the recent food crisis and the attendant renewed emphasis
on agriculture. Although no exact migration figures are
available, many of these planned and unplanned population movements have been numerically very significant.
Still, any estimate placing the current urban population
in the vicinity of 100–110 million is probably representative
of its actual size.

With regard to ethnic distribution, the 1953 census
registration identified some fifty distinct national minorities
in China, totaling about 35 million persons, or about 6
per cent of the country's population. The Chinese communists, in stressing the equality of status ostensibly offered
under the new regime, have attempted to single out as
many ethnic minorities as possible, even though some of

these cannot be classified in terms of unique characteristics. For example, the Manchus have been completely assimilated—except for a small group in the northeast—and have neither an independent language nor physical characteristics that might distinguish them from the Chinese, yet their number was reported at 2.4 million. The 3.6 million Hui, to take another example, do not represent an ethnic minority at all but are Chinese of Islamic faith. For the most part, the national minorities are located in the thinly populated peripheral areas of the country, with the greatest concentrations found in the southwest and northwest. These regions make up nearly half of China's land area, and the fact that here the minorities outnumber the Han Chinese makes the minority groups much more significant than their small over-all proportion might suggest.

The most important question related to China's population, and one which generates the greatest controversy, pertains to its rate of growth. Over the past half century the increase in the population of China has usually been placed at about one half of one per cent per year. This is an average, however. There have been considerable annual fluctuations, because the rate of growth has depended not only on the consistently high level of fertility common to underdeveloped countries, but on the level of mortality, which varies with natural conditions—such as floods and droughts—with epidemics, and with political circumstances.

As an outcome of their census registration in 1953, the communists announced that the Chinese birth rate was 37 per 1000 total population and the death rate was 17 per 1000, resulting in an annual natural increase of 20 per 1000, or 2 per cent. These rates presumably were derived from a 5 per cent population sample. Since the release of these data in 1954, even higher rates of increase have been reported by the Chinese, implying a considerable reduction in the over-all level of mortality. The question is whether these rates of growth, which would mean an annual increase of from 12 to perhaps 17 million per year, are reasonable and acceptable in the light of our knowledge of demography in general and the conditions in communist China in particular.

Although the reported birth rate is the less controversial of the two rates, it is nevertheless on the low side. A population that does not limit its fertility through widely practiced birth control and whose cultural heritage encourages large families and many sons would be expected to show a somewhat higher birth rate. In addition, more reliable data relating to the observed birth rates of Chinese outside China—for example on Taiwan—and sample studies of small areas within China also suggest higher rates. With these considerations, the plausible range for birth rate in China would be between 40 and 45 per 1000 rather than the announced 37 per 1000.

The possible range of the death rate is considerably wider and deserves discussion in some detail. Although the level of mortality in precommunist China varied from year to year, most estimates placed it anywhere between 25 and 35 per 1000. In fact in the past, during the years in which disaster and adversities were particularly severe and widespread, the population probably suffered actual net deficits. It is difficult to believe that in a period of some three to four years—from 1949 to 1953—the communists would have been able to lower the mortality rate to 17 per 1000—below the 1939 rate reported for the far more advanced Soviet Union.

What are some of the factors that would affect the level of Chinese mortality? Of course it is well known that with present medical knowledge it is relatively easy to reduce the death rate, but to what level, how quickly and with how much effort?

The improvements in the health conditions of the Chinese population are undeniable. Through intensive propaganda, some semblance of sanitation has been introduced even into the rural areas of China. The number of disease-carrying rats and flies, for example, has been substantially reduced and such diseases as cholera, typhus, and smallpox are undoubtedly less prevalent than they used to be. Yet, although diseases and epidemics are fewer, they have certainly not been eliminated. And although the communists have been graduating more and more medical personnel, most of them have only a secondary education. There is still only one doctor trained in Western medicine for every 10,000 inhabitants, medical care is still inadequate, drugs are scarce, and antibiotics are probably known only to a limited segment of the urban population. Of particular significance in terms of health are the conditions at the numerous construction projects, which engage literally millions of people and where many of the most basic sanitary measures are absent. Hard labor, exposure, dirt, disease, and a poor diet are bound to take their toll.

Even prior to the most recent food crisis, there were persistent reports of food shortages from one or another section of China. This does not mean that millions of persons are starving to death. It is a fact, however, that malnutrition accentuates diseases and ailments, weakens resistance, and makes recovery more difficult.

Taking all this into account, it would seem extremely unrealistic to accept as accurate a reported death rate as low as 17 in 1953 and 11 in 1958 or 1959. The latter is a rate that is comparable to those reported in many countries of Europe and only a few points above the death rate in the United States. Obviously the claim of a low death rate—a universal index of a country's achievements —is an important facet of Chinese propaganda.

What are the implications associated with a population that is as large as that of China, a population that is growing at some 10 to 15 million every year? First, of course, there are the obvious factors: the larger the population, the more mouths to feed, the more people to provide with the daily essentials, the more children to educate, and so forth. But there are also economic implications that may not be quite as obvious.

It is true that in absolute numbers China has an immense group of people within the main working ages, but their proportion to the total population is considerably lower than in more advanced countries. During the demographic transition in which China now finds itself, the pro-

portion of children to adults has a tendency to increase
even further. Lower death rates, and particularly lower
infant mortality, in combination with a continuing high
birth rate means increased survival probability for babies
and children; the older cohorts on the other hand are
the product of a period of high mortality rates. In China
children below fifteen years of age constitute at least 40
per cent of the total population, while in more advanced
countries about one quarter of the population is under the
age of fifteen. In other words, China has about 15 per cent
fewer people in the productive age groups to provide for a
much larger non-productive population of children than
does a more advanced nation. This means that China has
about 100 million more children than it would have if its
age distribution were like that of the more developed countries.

Also, the resources that are used in rearing and training
children do not give as large a return in China as they do,
for example, in the United States. An American high school
graduate may have as many as fifty years of productive
work ahead of him; in China a student who has completed
secondary education has, on the average, perhaps thirty
years of gainful employment, by which he repays the state
for the expense of educating him and leaves a certain
"residual" before passing on. And not only that. The
greater productivity and efficiency and the advanced technical base of our economy make it possible for an American worker to compensate the initial outlay that was necessary to raise and educate him in a much shorter time
than can a Chinese worker, whose productivity is much
lower. In the final analysis, all these factors reflect on the
rate of capital accumulation and on the speed with which
the stated goals of economic and social development are
met.

In view of the size and rate of growth of China's population and considering the implications of this growth, what
has been the regime's attitude toward population and what
have been its policies? The initial reaction to the publication of the 1953 census results was one of jubilation. Re-

flecting true Marxist ideology, the stress was placed on people as producers and not as consumers. In other words, the larger the population, the more hands to do the work—but no mention was made of the growing number of mouths to feed, bodies to clothe, and children to educate. It was not long, however, before some concern was expressed in the press and in speeches of various communist officials. The usual line taken in these statements was that the number of children should be limited in order to improve the health of mothers and infants, to advance the education of children, and to allow mothers more time for work and study.

Birth control was never made the law of the land by official proclamation. Nevertheless, by the middle of 1956 it became apparent from the gradual intensification of propaganda that birth control was, in fact, the accepted state policy. Birth-control clinics were established in the cities; teams of medical personnel were sent into the countryside to instruct the peasants in the use of various contraceptive methods; numerous posters proclaimed the need for limiting the size of families. Sterilization and abortion laws were liberalized and the legal age for marriage was raised to twenty for males and eighteen for females. But only seven or eight months after the campaign reached its peak in the spring of 1957 came the first indication of a change in communist China's population policy.

In the fall of that year an article appeared in the *People's Daily*, the official Communist Party newspaper, bitterly attacking "rightists" for taking advantage of the controversy over population and birth control to launch assaults on the party and on socialism. By the summer of 1958 it was apparent that Peking had executed a complete about-face in its population policies. It introduced the now famous "great leap forward," abandoned all propaganda for birth control, "liberated" the women from domestic chores in order to give them the opportunity to work in the fields and factories, and proclaimed a severe manpower shortage throughout China.

Many opinions have been advanced in an attempt to explain why the birth-control policy was abandoned. Some have pointed to the success of the 1957 harvest as the reason for an optimistic approach toward population growth; some have suggested that China could no longer justify birth control as part of Marxist ideology; others have accepted the labor shortage pronouncements as a valid reason for the change. A much more plausible reason, however, is that the reversal in policy followed the realization by the regime that, despite the intensive propaganda, efforts to reduce Chinese fertility proved to be unacceptable because they were a failure. In the first place, the regime could not provide the population with cheap and plentiful contraceptive devices. In the second place, even communist controls could not instill mass motivation strong enough to overcome the ancient cultural and social patterns in an overwhelmingly rural and uneducated population.

It must be remembered, however, that despite the abandonment of propaganda favoring birth control, China did not embark on a pronatalist policy. Birth-control devices continued to be available in limited quantities, particularly in the urban areas; birth-control clinics continued to supply information to interested individuals; and, as far as we know, abortion and sterilization were not made illegal and were available on request.

Following three years of serious agricultural crisis, the communists are once again proclaiming the need to reduce the size of the Chinese family. The current campaign, which started in 1962, is in a lower key, with most of the emphasis placed on the raising of the marriage age. So far, this effort does not represent a radical change in policy, does not involve any significant expenditures on the part of the regime, and is not likely to be much more effective in limiting Chinese fertility than were the earlier measures.

Finally, the basic question: how large is communist China's present population?

The last population series published by Peking brought the data up to the end of 1957. Since then there has not been a single reference in Chinese literature that even pretends to represent a serious estimate of the country's total population. With few exceptions, the only figures quoted during the past few years have been 600 and 650 million, and these have appeared in official publications and speeches in which population data were used only incidentally in discussions of unrelated topics. Current estimates by Western demographers show an even wider range, and some projections to the end of the present century vary by more than 100 million. These variations are particularly surprising since all estimates use the 1953 census registration as the point of departure.

Intercensal population estimates are usually derived from current registration statistics of total population and birth and death rates. The question is: has communist China been able to institute a registration system that would provide the authorities with adequate data for estimating the size and rate of growth of the country's population?

Before 1953 China had no uniform registration system. Efforts on the part of the Ministry of Public Security to maintain a register of the population were limited primarily to the urban areas, and even in these areas coverage was incomplete and figures unavailable. Other records were kept by the Ministry of Interior and by civil administrations at the various local levels. The inadequacy of the existing system was severely criticized in 1955, and in 1956 all the responsibilities related to the registration of population were transferred to the Ministry of Public Security. In 1958 the Minister of Public Security, in announcing still another set of regulations governing population registers, admitted that "the existing system is still far from perfect." The timing of these new regulations was unfortunate, because the dislocations associated with the "great leap forward" and the severity of the national crisis that followed in the 1959–62 period made enforcement even more difficult, and it is to be assumed that the maintenance of population registers became more, rather than less, casual.

As stated before, communist China lacks trained and reliable personnel to maintain population registers; the

primary reason for establishing the registration system was
not to obtain population records but to keep control over
the population; population registration is often integrated
with other types of surveys in which population data
evolves only as a by-product; there are ever present political pressures for population statistics to "serve socialist
construction." The conclusion seems fairly obvious. The
reason that population data have not been reported by the
Chinese communists is that the regime does not have meaningful data.

One may well ask how a planned economy, such as
exists in communist China, can function without accurate
population and manpower statistics. The fact is that the
regime has some of the necessary information. It probably
has a fairly good idea of the country's urban population
and quite adequate data on its urban labor force, particularly on personnel with higher education and special skills.
On the other hand, although a figure in the vicinity of
700 million is probably an adequate reflection of the general magnitude of China's population, it is most unlikely
that the regime's policies and goals would change if the
total population of the country were found to be 25 or
even 50 million above or below whatever figure the Chinese leaders may currently be using.

Finally, no matter what one assumes China's population
to be, it is undeniable that the size and rate of growth of
this population are a deterrent rather than an asset to communist political and economic ambitions. Only a controlled
population and a growing agricultural base will make it
possible for communist China to attain the world status
she seeks.

SUGGESTIONS FOR FURTHER READING

Ta Ch'ên. *Population in Modern China.* Chicago: University of Chicago Press, 1946.

Although the study deals with a sample study conducted in the early 1940s, it also covers some of the
general problems associated with Chinese demography.

John D. Durand. "The Population Statistics of China,
A.D. 2–1953." *Population Studies*, Vol. XIII, No. 3,
March 1960.

Presents a historical perspective for the more recent
Chinese population data.

Warren S. Thompson. *Population and Progress in the Far
East*. Chicago: University of Chicago Press, 1959.

Chapter XI presents an evaluation of communist Chinese population data and discusses potential population
pressures.

*Population Trends in Eastern Europe, the U.S.S.R. and
Mainland China*. New York: Milbank Memorial Fund,
1960.

Includes the following articles on the population of
China: "Present and Prospective Population of Mainland
China," by John S. Aird; "Population Redistribution in
Communist China," by Leo A. Orleans; "Manpower
and Industrialization in Communist China," by Alexan-
der Eckstein; "Questions of Population Growth in
China," by Irene B. Taeuber.

John S. Aird. *The Size, Composition and Growth of the
Population of Mainland China*. U. S. Bureau of the Cen-
sus, International Population Statistics Reports. Series
P–90, No. 15, Washington, 1961.

A comprehensive analysis of population data published by the Chinese communists.

Chapter 18

THE POPULATION OF
THE SOVIET UNION

Warren W. Eason

Thirty-five years ago the Soviet Union embarked on a program of rapid economic development under a system of national economic planning administered by a socialist form of government. In the intervening years, impressive rates of growth have been registered by many economic sectors, and the structure of the economy and society has been radically altered. Some progress has been made toward satisfying the material needs of the population, but primary emphasis has been placed on the development of heavy industry toward the long-run objective of overtaking and surpassing the leading capitalist countries in per capita production and living standards.

Soviet experience has attracted widespread attention from many parts of the world. In countries where the problem of economic development is of immediate concern, there is particular interest in understanding the Soviet case for the relevance it may have to the solution of problems at home.

One of the most important of these problems concerns the interrelationship between economic development and population growth. It is a question, on the one hand, of the implications of economic development for population growth, and, on the other hand, of the implications of population growth for economic development. Experience has shown that the nature of these interrelationships can affect the success of development itself and can help to determine the meaning of development for the people.

Sufficient time has passed with respect to the early stages of Soviet economic development for some of the implications of these relationships to be evident. By the same token, the Soviet Union is far enough along in the unfolding of the developmental process to permit us to make some estimates about the future.

Let us look at the Soviet case by considering, first, the effects of development on population, and second, the effects of the population variables on development, after which we may briefly examine the nature of Soviet "population policy."

From a demographic point of view, the population of a country may be characterized under five headings: the over-all rate of growth; the rate of fertility; the rate of mortality; the distribution of the population by age and sex; and its composition according to various socioeconomic criteria.

What changes have taken place in the Soviet population under each of these headings, and to what dominant influences may we attribute these changes?

The question already indicates that our interest is in the *changes* that typically take place in the course of economic development—declining mortality and fertility, increasing or decreasing rates of growth, and so forth. We shall find that many of these changes have taken place in Soviet economic development, and that their effect is particularly dramatic because they are telescoped in time.

In one important respect, however, the pattern of Soviet population growth may be characterized as inherently *stable*—namely, in the over-all rate of growth. Many underdeveloped countries today are experiencing substantial *increases* in the rate of population growth, to 3 per cent per year or more, as mortality is lowered while fertility remains high. On the other hand, virtually all countries that have succeeded in becoming industrialized have ultimately experienced significant *decreases* in the rate of population growth, to less than 1 per cent per year, as a result of lowered fertility rates.

The Soviet Union has experienced neither of these extreme changes so far. During most *peacetime* years since the Revolution, the rate of increase of the population has remained at the moderately high level of between 1.5 and 2 per cent per year, which is approximately the same as in the decades before the Revolution. Over the Soviet period as a whole—including wartime as well as peacetime—the average rate of increase has been about 1 per cent per year, and this is very close to the long-term average rate over the last century and a half.

What is significant is that the over-all rate of growth has remained stable at the same time that the components of growth have changed markedly. The death rate has declined from near 35 per 1000 in the last half of the nineteenth century to about 7 per 1000 at the present time, while the birth rate has fallen in half, from almost 50 to less than 25 per 1000.

These changes reflect fundamental forces at work in the process of economic development, particularly in the last two decades. What has kept the growth rate stable at a moderately high level is, first, that the changes in mortality and fertility have taken place more or less simultaneously and, second, that a relatively large proportion of the population still lives on the farms, where fertility rates have declined less than in urban areas.

An increase in the rate of growth of the population in the early stages of industrialization takes place typically because mortality rates respond quickly to modern methods of disease prevention, while changes in fertility rates require the transformation of the basic attitudes of the population. The Soviet Union was already experiencing the beginning of such an increase in the rate of growth of the population in the 1920s, arising from the early stages of development set in motion during the Czarist period. Death rates had declined from near 35 to more than 20 per 1000, while the birth rate had declined only slightly, from almost 50 to about 45 per 1000, with the result that the population was increasing for the first time by more than 2 per cent per year. Soviet population projections made at that time assumed a continuing decline in mortality and even an increase in fertility, with the implication of still higher rates of growth than ever before.

In fact, however, these higher rates never materialized. During the period of collectivization and food shortages, in the early 1930s, population growth slowed down precipitously, although in a few years it returned to normal. During World War II, unbelievable population losses resulted in an absolute decline of the population of almost 30 million persons.

But even aside from these exceptional periods, population growth after the start of rapid industrialization, although it remained relatively high, never attained the rates that were projected. The reason is that birth and death rates moved together: they were essentially the same at the end of the 1930s as they had been in the 1920s, but by 1950 each had fallen in half, and they have remained at approximately these levels to the present.

The Soviet Union now has the lowest crude death rate— about 7 per 1000—of almost any country in the world. This reflects in large measure a genuine improvement in conditions affecting mortality. However, the sharpness of the decline in mortality after the war is not unique to the Soviet Union. It took place in many other countries as well and is attributable in part to the availability of antibiotics and other effective drugs and chemicals, such as DDT. Moreover, the rate is as low as it is, compared to some of the other countries, partly because of the young age distribution of the population.

This may be seen by a comparison in terms of life expectancy at birth, an index of survival under given mortality conditions which is not affected by age distribution. Life expectancy in the Soviet Union has risen from 32 years in 1897 to 44 years in 1927, 48 years in 1939 and 69 years in 1959. In spite of this increase, however, to more than double the pre-Soviet level, life expectancy is still less than in quite a number of countries which report a higher death rate than the Soviet Union—for example, the Scandinavian countries, the United States and the Netherlands.

In short, we can attribute the sharp decline in mortality in the Soviet Union, particularly after World War II, to substantial governmental efforts, to the availability of

certain drugs—and also, as far as the crude death rate is
concerned, to the fact that a higher proportion of the population than in many other countries is in the age brackets
least affected by mortality.

It is not as simple to explain the decline in the birth
rate—although once again age structure has an effect, this
time to register *less* of a decline, or a *higher* birth rate,
than otherwise would be the case. On the other hand, the
catastrophic loss of males during the war probably made
the birth rate after the war *lower* than it might otherwise
have been. In any event, with a birth rate near 25 per
1000, the Soviet Union ranks higher than virtually all of
the relatively industrialized countries. But if we measure
fertility in terms of, say, the gross reproduction rate—an
index which is not affected by the age and sex structure of
the population—then the Soviet Union assumes a somewhat
lower position in the ranks of the industrialized countries.

Aside from the effects of age and sex distribution, the
decline in the birth rate after World War II appears to
reflect the same forces that have been at work in other
industrialized countries—namely, urbanization, education,
and various economic and social pressures associated with
economic development. Soviet families in urban areas, and
also to a lesser extent in the countryside, are planning to
have fewer children than formerly. By the nature of
these underlying forces, it typically takes time for their
effect to appear as a significant change in fertility rates.
The fact that the Soviet birth rate dropped sharply in the
decade 1940–50 probably points to the war in hastening
the change of attitudes already underway as a result of
economic development.

This process of change has not yet run its full course,
and it is largely a matter of speculation exactly what this
course will be. The present birth rate of about 25 per
1000 is less than in previous years but higher than in almost all of the developed countries, where rates of 16 to
18 per 1000 are common. Can we expect that the Soviet
birth rate will continue downward, and with it the rate of
population growth, to less than 1 per cent per year? Or

should we assume that the long-run rate will be stabilized near the moderately high levels now prevalent in the United States?

One thing we can say with some certainty is that in the short run—over the next decade or so—the Soviet birth rate will decline, perhaps to below 20 per 1000, as the women and men born during the war, when birth rates were very low and infant mortality high, pass through the reproductive ages.

In the long run, however, there are factors operating in different directions, and it is difficult to see which will become dominant. The possiblity of lower birth rates lies with declining fertility among those segments of the population where fertility is still relatively high. This includes the rural areas in general, which still constitute half of the population, and those parts of the country, such as the Kirgiz and Kazakh republics, where birth rates have remained practically unchanged from prewar levels at about 35 per 1000.

The possibility that the birth rate will not decline in the long run, or will increase after it has declined, lies with the possibility—by analogy with the experience of the United States in the last two decades—that the more established urban areas will experience higher fertility levels than at present. If certain factors which presently inhibit larger families are ultimately removed, centering around the very crowded housing conditions and short supplies of consumer goods, a strong argument can be made that the size of the urban family will increase. Other considerations operating in the same direction include the ultimate prospect of a further decrease in hours of work—to six and even five hours per day, and five days per week—and the expansion of the network of nursery schools and related institutions, enabling women to remain in the labor force and at the same time to care for their children.

What will be the net effect of these forces on fertility and therefore on the rate of growth of the population? One important—perhaps crucial—consideration is timing. Continued rural-urban migration could have its effect in lowering the birth rate within a few decades, while the tendency toward higher fertility rates as a result of improved housing and living conditions in urban areas could take a longer period of time. If such is the sequence, long-run trends would see a decline in the birth rate over the coming decades, followed by an increase. And in the end it is not inconceivable that the birth rate and the rate of growth of the population might return to present or even higher levels.

The immediate effects of economic development on the population, as we have seen, appear in the changing pattern of births and deaths and in the rate of growth of the population. Secondary effects appear in the distribution of the population by age and sex. Under normal conditions, as a country moves from high to low birth and death rates, a gradual "aging" of the population takes place. Soviet progress in this direction has been dominated by two world wars and the rapidity of change in birth and death rates just described. Since the turn of the century, the proportion of the population ages sixteen to fifty-nine and sixty and over has increased, while the proportion under sixteen years of age has decreased. In spite of these changes, compared to most developed countries the Soviet Union still has a smaller proportion age sixty and over but it also has a smaller proportion under age sixteen; in other words, it has a larger proportion in the working ages, sixteen to fifty-nine. This results from the fact, first, that the lower birth rates and higher infant mortality rates of the war "outweighed" the effects of high military losses and excess civilian deaths on the age structure of the population. Secondly, there moved into the working ages right after the war the relatively large numbers of people who were born between the late 1920s and 1940, when the birth rate was relatively high, and who were of an age during the war to escape some of its exceptional hazards.

War losses appear most dramatically in the deficit of males in the adult population. At the turn of the century there were approximately the same number of males as females. By 1926, as a result of World War I and the

Civil War in Russia there were 5 million fewer males than females. By 1939, as a result of some of the difficulties of the early 1930s, there were 7 million fewer males than females. And by 1950, according to estimates from available census materials, there were about 25 million fewer males than females in the adult population. Much of this increase in the male deficit must be accounted for as military deaths, but it is estimated that of a total of 15 million excess civilian deaths during World War II (other than infant deaths) 11 million were males and 4 million were females.

Future trends in the age distribution of the population depend to a certain degree on the projected pattern of births and deaths, although a gradual aging of the population will probably take place in any event. Previous wars will exert their effect in declining degree, as the lowered fertility rates of wartime appear in a smaller number of births in successive generations.

The deficit of males, on the other hand, is already less than 20 million and is confined to the population about thirty-five years of age and older. Barring war or other periods of turmoil, the male deficit as a major social and economic problem should steadily lessen. But the deficit will not be entirely eliminated because, in the Soviet Union as in other countries, even under peacetime conditions life expectancy for females exceeds that for males.

We have now surveyed Soviet population changes of a purely demographic nature. Development also brings with it fundamental changes in the socioeconomic composition of the population. We shall focus on two important and contrasting changes that have characterized the Soviet case.

The first change involves the transformation of economic relationships from those based on the family and "self-employment" to those based on wages and salaries and other wage-equivalent payments. Before the start of rapid industrialization in 1928, approximately 80 per cent of the labor force comprised individuals working within the family as the producing unit—primarily in agriculture. Less than 20 per cent of the labor force earned wages and salaries. Now, through the rapid expansion of state-owned and -operated enterprises and the collectivization of agriculture, all but about 10 per cent of the labor force receives at least part of its livelihood through wages and salaries or other payments in money or in kind. As a step in the direction of the "industrialization" of the population, this is a more rapid and comprehensive transformation than has taken place in any other developing country.

On the other hand, almost half of the labor force is still in agriculture—the same proportion as in the United States in 1880. Such a high proportion in agriculture after more than three decades of rapid industrialization reflects the fact that the Soviet Union began with a higher proportion —more than 80 per cent—than almost any other developing country, and the fact that the rate of growth of the population has been stable at moderately high rates.

These measures of socioeconomic change illustrate the fact that, from certain points of view, the Soviet population has taken major, even decisive, steps in the direction of change implied by a fully industrialized society, while from other points of view the population is still influenced by well-established ties to the preindustrial past.

Let us now examine the question of the effects of population variables on economic development.

If we confine ourselves to purely demographic characteristics of Soviet population growth—that is, to the size and pattern of growth of the population and the distribution by age and sex—then the population variables may be thought of as exerting their influence on economic and social change largely through the medium of *broad quantitative relationships* between human resources and other resources.

By dealing with broad quantitative relationships, we are confining ourselves to only certain aspects of the "human factor" in economic development. Equally important are (1) the "qualitative" aspects, embodied in levels of education and experience and the attitudes of the population toward work; (2) the "locational" aspects, involving the mobility of the population and labor force by industry, occupation, and so forth; and (3) the "institutional" aspects, which determine the effectiveness with which human resources are joined to the production process on the job. Time, unfortunately, limits consideration of these other important aspects.

With a population officially estimated as approximately 225 million persons, the Soviet Union ranks as the third-largest country of the world, exceeded only by China and India, and as the largest of the industrialized countries, followed by the United States and Japan.

With respect to *over-all land area*, the Soviet Union is one of the less densely populated countries of the world, supporting about 10 persons per square kilometer, compared to 20 for the world as a whole, 25 for the United States and 115 for India—although it remains more densely populated than, for example, Canada, with 2 persons per square kilometer. Depending on the future growth of the population, it may be seventy years or more before the population density of the Soviet Union reaches the present level of the United States. With respect to its total land area, therefore, the Soviet Union may be considered as relatively *under*populated.

With respect to *readily available land for agriculture*, however, the country has been characterized—up through early Soviet times—as relatively *over*populated. On the eve of rapid industrialization, there was a "surplus" of labor on the farms, in the sense that migration in substantial numbers would have had a negligible effect on total agricultural production.

The pressure of the "surplus" population moreover, was aggravated by the possibility of an increase in the rate of growth of the population. If population growth had taken place after 1928 as projected, reaching 2.5 or 3 per cent per year—and if there had been no war—the population would now be considerably more than 300 million, rather than 225 million, and the age structure would be inclined more toward the younger and older—that is, unproductive —elements than has actually been the case. The fact that the over-all rate of population growth was lower after 1928 tended to reduce the "surplus" population, or at least prevent it from becoming more serious, and thereby tended to remove one important obstacle to raising over-all labor productivity.

What would have happened if population growth had been significantly higher after 1928? The pressure of human resources on arable land resources would have been greater, but even under present conditions—following the reduction of the "surplus" population in agriculture—labor-intensive methods are still very much in evidence, productivity is lower than in many other countries, and almost half of the labor force is still on the farms. If population growth had not declined, the reduction of the "surplus" of manpower in agriculture might have required more drastic methods.

What is the significance of the condition of underpopulation with respect to over-all land area during these years? Clearly, if Soviet policy had dictated the "balanced" development of the country as a whole from the earliest years of rapid industrialization, the organizational, economic and institutional arrangements necessary to carry out the required population migration and settlement would have raised many difficult problems.

The fact is that population migration to Eastern Siberia, the Soviet Far East and Soviet Central Asia was on a relatively modest scale. Only in recent years has the systematic development of these underpopulated regions become a matter of priority.

The demand for labor in these areas is now greater than at any time in the past, and will probably continue at this high level. Labor supply in the long run must come either from the transfer of manpower already employed in other areas, or from the net increase in the total labor force. Supply, furthermore, is not just a question of "availability"; it is dependent on the whole range of policies and practices that influence labor mobility, and particularly on the effectiveness with which labor can be released from agriculture in the older areas. This, in turn, is a question of raising agricultural labor productivity, a problem that the Soviets continue to find extremely difficult to solve.

In the early years of development, when more than 80 per cent of the labor force was in agriculture, large increases in the non-agricultural labor force, entailing relatively small changes in the agricultural labor force, were possible without radical changes in methods of production in agriculture. Now, with 50 per cent of the labor force in agriculture, given rates of increase of the non-agricultural labor force can be maintained only with a relatively large transfer of manpower from agriculture and therefore a more substantial increase in agricultural labor productivity. The pressure to raise productivity as a source of manpower is rising and will continue to rise as the agricultural labor force becomes a smaller and smaller proportion of the total.

A dynamic but not excessive rate of population growth, under these conditions, tends to lessen the pressure to resort to radical changes in methods affecting labor utilization in order to release labor from existing jobs and areas. A reasonably high rate of natural increase of the population has the same implications for the ultimate development of the Soviet Union as a whole that a high rate of population immigration did for the United States. It provides a growing manpower base necessary for the exploitation and utilization of a broad expanse of territory, and it permits development along these lines without radical changes in the methods of joining labor to the land.

The principal difference is that in the Soviet Union the limits of readily available arable land have already been reached at the same time that the country as a whole is relatively underpopulated. The country must become populated, therefore, by means of an increase in the non-agricultural labor force, whereas the United States was populated by an expansion of both the agricultural and non-agricultural labor force, as more acreage was brought under cultivation.

In the last analysis, perhaps the most significant implication of these relationships between resources lies in the development of policies and practices affecting the training, recruitment and utilization of human resources. Manpower in the early stages of growth is relatively abundant and cheap in relation to capital resources. After sufficient passage of time—through the growth of capital stock and technology and through improvements in the "quality" of labor—rising labor productivity raises the economic value of human resources. In the early stages of development, manpower policies that are "wasteful" of labor are at least consistent with the low economic value of labor. As development progresses, however, the costs of waste become more apparent, and the need to develop enlightened manpower policies more urgent. Other things being equal, the overpopulated country feels this pressure later in the process, because labor is also abundant in relation to land resources.

The Soviet Union has reached the stage where there is a growing awareness that labor is becoming more valuable as an economic resource. As a result, there is underway a comprehensive reconsideration of manpower policies, to utilize the given labor force more effectively.

In our consideration of the interrelation of economic development and population, and the effects of population variables on development, one basic question remains—that of a population "policy." Does there exist in the Soviet Union a set of principles, laws, or regulations that can be said to constitute a "policy" designed to affect the pattern of population growth? And if so, does such a policy have its rationale in the objective of enhancing economic development?

The answer is that in a number of important respects there is a population policy motivated by such an objective. Government efforts to reduce mortality, to educate the population and train the labor force, to provide conditions of full employment—all of these can be considered part of a population policy, broadly defined, which has explicit implications for development.

But is there a corresponding policy designed to affect fertility? The answer to this important question is unclear.

(1) On the one hand, there is a continuing program to give material support and social recognition to mothers with many children, an objective of which is to encourage parents to have more children. On the other hand, contraceptive devices, although of less than superior quality, are readily available.

(2) On the one hand, Soviet leaders call for a rapid increase of the population, and Soviet plans provide for assistance, such as nurseries, to mothers who want to continue to work. On the other hand, free abortions may be obtained in state clinics; and although the objective of reintroducing this program several years ago was to curtail the harmful effects of illegal abortions, nevertheless it is well known that abortions provide a major means of family planning to Soviet families.

(3) On the one hand, Soviet spokesmen criticize so-called neo-Malthusians in the West who propose birth control as a solution to the population dilemma in underdeveloped countries. On the other hand, the Soviet approach to population problems in their own country is to let the *family* decide how many children to have; and under these conditions, as we have seen, families have decided to have fewer children.

How can we explain the apparent contradictions in this summary of principles with respect to fertility? The answer is that the principles may not be as contradictory as they sound. The final principle summarized is really a central idea to which all the others may be logically related.

That is, if the *family* is accepted as the decision-making unit—subject to indirect, but not dominating influences—then encouragement and financial support to mothers with many children, the availability of abortions and contraceptive devices, and the provision of nurseries are all means to carry out the decisions made by the family. Even the argument against "neo-Malthusians" can be construed as an argument to let the family make up its own mind, according to its own traditions and values, without being "educated" one way or another, particularly by outsiders.

The only difficulty with concluding that there is a really

consistent policy toward fertility based on the family is
that Soviet spokesmen do not present it as such with any
degree of elaboration. All of the principles summarized
appear in the relevant literature, but the common, unifying
theme of the family as the decision-making unit is not
stressed or elaborated.

If this is a correct summary of Soviet views at the present time, what of the future? Can we expect a more positive policy—for example, a pronatalist policy—to be introduced? Probably not. One can foresee that Soviet families
will be encouraged to have more children—as housing and
other conditions permit—and that financial and other support may very well be strengthened. But the possibility
that the decision will in some sense be taken out of the
hands of the family seems, at this juncture, to be very
unlikely.

If there is a theme that runs through this whole discussion of the population problem in the Soviet Union, it is
that in a sense there has been no "problem" at all. There
has not been a significant problem of either massive overpopulation or a critical shortage of labor, although elements of both of these conditions underlie the changing
pattern of resource relationships as economic development
progresses from one stage to another. As a result, there has
been no clearly consistent set of population policies designed to correct an extreme situation. The problems arising from the interrelationship between human resources
and other resources have been seen as soluble not through
an attempt to influence the population variables themselves but through the development of policies which utilize human resources effectively in a manner broadly consistent with the given stage of development. The keynote
of the first decades, therefore, has been to transform a
relatively backward and inexperienced labor force into an
"industrialized" labor force, and the keynote of the next
decades will be to reduce the glaring instances of inefficiency and waste that still persist. If this is not really a
population problem, its solution is nevertheless crucial for

the achievement of long-run economic and social objectives.

SUGGESTIONS FOR FURTHER READING

Frank Lorimer. *The Population of the Soviet Union: History and Prospects.* Geneva: League of Nations, 1946.

Although this book is now twenty years old and therefore contains no discussion of the postwar situation (except for some very thoughtful projections), it remains the basic study of the Soviet population.

Population Trends in Eastern Europe, the U.S.S.R. and Mainland China. New York: Milbank Memorial Fund, 1960.

This book contains ten papers and discussions from a conference in November, 1959, addressed to questions of theory as well as those of measurement.

John F. Kantner. "The Population of the Soviet Union," in Joint Economic Committee *Comparisons of the United States and Soviet Economies,* Part I. Washington, D. C.: Government Printing Office, 1959, pp. 31–71.

This is a detailed survey of what we know about the Soviet population as of the end of 1959, by a specialist associated with the U. S. Bureau of the Census.

James W. Brackett. "Demographic Trends and Population Policy in the Soviet Union," in Joint Economic Committee *Dimensions of Soviet Economic Power.* Washington, D. C.: Government Printing Office, 1962, pp. 487–589.

This is an important discussion of Soviet population trends and an evaluation of the primary data, including the results of the 1959 Soviet census, together with a projection of the Soviet population to 1981 by single-year age groups.

Warren W. Eason. "Labor Force," in *Economic Trends in the Soviet Union,* edited by Abram Bergson and Simon Kuznets. Cambridge: Harvard University Press, 1963, pp. 38–95.

This is a survey and analysis of Soviet manpower problems in the light of population trends, also including data from the 1959 Soviet census.

Chapter 19

THE POPULATION OF EUROPE

William Petersen

Europe west of the Soviet Union comprises only about two million square miles, or less than 4 per cent of the world's total area. That it is reckoned a continent rather than the western portion of Eurasia is due less to geography than to history. For this extension of the earth's largest land mass, by global standards no more than a largish peninsula, was the cradle of one of the world's great civilizations, crucial of course to Europeans and their overseas descendants but increasingly so to all other peoples as well. Almost all the forces presently transforming Asia, Africa, and Latin America—whether electricity or nationalism, whether Marxism or public sanitation—are developments of cultural elements that originated on the world's smallest continent.

Europe exclusive of the Soviet Union has a total population of about 440 million, or less than 15 per cent of the world's total. It includes twenty-six nations at least as large as Luxemburg, plus half as many smaller principalities and territories. The four largest countries—the United Kingdom, West Germany, France, and Italy—are very roughly equal in population, each with approximately 50 million inhabitants; and the smaller units range down to Andorra, with about 8000 persons, and Vatican City, with only 1000. Not only in size but also in wealth and power, in level of culture and degree of political freedom, the range is great from one country of Europe to another. Yet underlying this diversity is also a certain uniformity, which defines the continent and sets it off from the rest of the world. Commentators on India have often introduced their subject by pointing out that in many respects this subcontinent of Asia is as heterogeneous as Europe. One might turn the simile about and suggest that in many respects Europe is as much a single unit as India. In reviewing the economic and cultural factors that have shaped Europe's population, thus, we shall have repeated occasion to note both how one European country or region contrasts with another and, on the other hand, how often these differences shrink when they are put against the world-wide range.

Before the development of modern industry, Europe was already distinguished from the other great civilizations by the control that its family system imposed on the rate of population growth. In classical India or China, for example, marriage was all but universal and typically took place at puberty or shortly thereafter. In Europe a quite different pattern evolved, varying from country to country but with certain characteristics common at least to the western region. Guilds generally did not permit apprentices to take a wife until they had finished their training, and this regulation meant that a substantial portion of the urban population had to postpone marriage for a considerable number of years after it was physiologically possible. In agriculture, numerically the most important sector of the late medieval and early modern economies, farmhands were almost members of a farmer's family, and thus were under no social or economic pressure to marry early. Men were induced to put off assuming parental responsibilities until they had acquired the means to care for a wife and children. This meant in many cases that they never married, but lived as fully accepted members of a household headed by an older brother, who, because he had inherited the family plot, was able to be a *husband* (which means, literally, "householder"). As a result of this personally onerous but socially effective system of birth control, population in Europe generally did not press as heavily on the subsistence available to it as in the Asian civilizations; compared with China or India, Europe was relatively free of great famines. And at the beginning of the modern era, the continent was still relatively sparsely populated.

With the rise of European science and industry, one after another the main causes of early death were brought under control. Traditional agricultural practices yielded to greatly improved methods, and such food-deficiency diseases as scurvy became medical rarities. Vaccination against smallpox, discovered at the end of the eighteenth century, made it possible to eliminate this dread disease. When drinking water could be transported through iron pipes, public authorities could finally segregate it absolutely from sewage and thus control cholera and all the other scourges spread by excrement. From Louis Pasteur's hypothesis that each of the infectious diseases is carried by a microscopic organism, to their virtual elimination as causes of death took, in the most advanced countries, only half a century.

Just before the First World War, the high correlation between industrialization and effective control of mortality was evident. In Northwest Europe—that is, the British Isles, the Low Countries, Germany, Switzerland, and Scandinavia—only 15 persons died each year per 1000 of the population; in France, Italy, and the western portion of Austria-Hungary this death rate was about 20; and in Spain and the Balkans it was about 25. Since that time death rates have steadily fallen (apart from the two world wars) throughout Europe, and this regional variation has almost disappeared. Simply the acquisition of an urban-industrial culture, once the major travail of the transition was past, was invariably accompanied by a substantial decline in mortality; but improvements beyond this point depended not on industrialization *per se* but rather on how effectively its benefits were distributed among the whole population. Of the countries of Northwest Europe, thus, those with the fullest and most efficient social services have achieved the most effective death control. In his book on the population of Europe, Dudley Kirk took Holland's record as the optimum and compared it with the rest of the continent, assuming that the age structure was the same in all countries. By this standard, 35 per cent of the mortality even in the rest of Europe was "excess" in 1939—that is, unnecessary if the medical techniques available had been fully used.

A more common measure of a country's all-round ability to combat death is its infant mortality rate. Under the most primitive conditions—typically before accurate statistics are collected—perhaps one out of every three babies dies before its first birthday, or, in terms of the usual convention, well over 300 per 1000 live births. We can illustrate the remarkable decline from this figure by looking at Sweden, whose record is comparable to that of the Netherlands. During the second half of the eighteenth century the rate in Sweden fluctuated around 200 infant deaths per 1000 live births. During the nineteenth century it fell slowly but persistently, reaching 100 by 1900. Since that date the decline has been faster, down to about 15 in 1960. In about six generations, thus, Sweden's infant mortality was cut by 92.5 per cent.

Several generations ago the greatest demographic difference between industrial and non-industrial nations, also on a world scale, was in their mortality. Public sanitation and modern medicine, whose effects were transforming the populations of Europe and its major overseas extensions, were only beginning to spread to most of the countries of Asia, Africa, and Latin America. While this contrast still remains, the world-wide variation in mortality has been reduced greatly since about 1945. With the discovery of antibiotics and powerful insecticides, and with their global distribution through international agencies, every country has been able to bring epidemic diseases under more effective control. Since the less developed nations have proportionately many infants and children, as *their* mortality was reduced the death rates of the whole populations also fell tremendously. In industrial countries, and also in those countries at the periphery of Europe's industrial core, the diseases of advanced ages—cancers and heart ailments, in particular—rank among the most important causes of death, while for the rest of the world these are still relatively insignificant. When in effect old age is the principal cause of death, countries with relatively few elderly persons are especially favored in their average life expectancy.

For the five-year period 1956–60, on the average only 11 persons in Europe died annually for each 1000 in the population. In historical terms this is an astoundingly low figure. Even more remarkably, while Europe's death rate fell to this new low, the difference shrank between it and that of the rest of the world. For the same five-year period Asia's average death rate was only 22 and that of Africa only 25, so that for the world population the rate during this period was 18 per 1000, or a figure that a generation ago was close to the best that had been achieved in the most advanced countries.

Now that the control of early death is becoming characteristic of the whole world, fertility once again marks the greatest difference between Europe and other continents. As we have seen, there were built into the traditional family of preindustrial Europe institutional checks to uninhibited procreation. When large numbers of young people moved to the growing towns and thus escaped from the villages' censorious eyes, it may be that these bonds were broken and that fertility went up from its traditional level. Thomas Robert Malthus, who wrote his famous *Essay on Population* at the very end of the eighteenth century, may have been harking back to this norm of parental responsibility when he propounded late marriage as the prime means of escaping the dire effects of overpopulation. His counsel, obviously enough, was not readily accepted; what is surprising is that the behavioral norm he recommended spread as much as it did.

Especially among the middle classes—that is, those who were most likely to improve their life chances by postponing the formation of their family—the age at marriage rose steadily during the first half of the nineteenth century. In England between 1840 and 1870, for instance, the average age at marriage of clergymen, doctors, lawyers, merchants, manufacturers—in short, aristocrats and "gentlemen" of all types—was almost precisely thirty years. In Ireland, as the extreme case of this European pattern, postponement of marriage was not restricted to the gentry but became the universal standard. In 1946, or just before the new postwar trend, the average age at marriage was thirty-three years for males and twenty-eight for females; and about one person out of four was still single at age forty-five. As compared with many underdeveloped countries, where females, especially, marry shortly after puberty, or even with such overseas countries of European culture as the United States, where the median age at marriage for females is twenty, present-day Europe is anomalous. Throughout the continent marriages below the age of fifteen are almost nonexistent, and even those below the age of twenty are atypical. The European countries where in 1960 the modal age at marriage for females was as high as twenty-five to twenty-nine years included the following: the United Kingdom, France, Belgium, and Switzerland; Ireland and the Netherlands; Norway and Sweden; Portugal, Spain, Italy, and Greece. Over a wide range of European cultures, thus, the norm is still operative that a man should marry and bear children only after he has established the means of caring for his wife and offspring.

That in so many European countries people marry relatively late is all the more remarkable since by and large effective contraceptives are generally available. The opposition to contraception of the Protestant churches and of "respectable" middle-class persons was overcome almost half a century ago, and that of the Nazi and Fascist parties vanished with the end of their regimes. The Catholic ban on contraceptives is truly effective only in Ireland and perhaps in Spain; and the Communist ban applied intermittently in the Soviet Union and mainland China has not been a significant factor in Eastern Europe. Contraceptives are more widely available in the West, but in most of the "People's Democracies" abortions are legal and the number performed is substantial.

If we look at the historical trend in fertility, the first thing we see is that the pattern is essentially similar to the

one in mortality: the lower birth rates started in Northwest
Europe and spread south and east together with the urban-
industrial culture. Within this general pattern, however, a
number of countries stand out as exceptions. In France,
thus, the average family size began to fall very early—
some time in the eighteenth century, while the country was
still a monarchy and before it was in any degree industrialized. By the time of the First World War, the French birth
rate was the lowest in Europe; and as fertility dropped in
other nations, particularly during the depression-ridden
1930s, many European demographers and statesmen
thought that their countries were following the French
path to literal perdition. In the late 1930s the lowest birth
rates (that is, below 17.5 per 1000) were in a strange
assortment of countries in addition to France: England,
Belgium, and Switzerland; Norway, Sweden, and Estonia;
Austria and Czechoslovakia. Many of these countries, as
well as fascist Italy, nazi Germany, and some others, tried
in various ways to induce young people to marry and have
larger families; but the effect of these pronatalist measures
was in most cases close to nil.

The revival of natality came during and immediately
after the Second World War, when there were shortages of
housing and sometimes even of food—when, that is to say,
material conditions hardly favored family life. Fertility rose
enough to make nonsense of the dire forecasts of Europe's
depopulation, but still only to a level that was low by
global standards. For the five years 1956–60—the same
period for which we earlier compared mortality—the average annual rate for the whole world was 36 births per
1000 population, and for Africa it was 47; for Asia, 41;
for North America, 34. Europe had only 19 births per
1000 population, or by far the lowest rate among all the
continents. The 1960 birth rate was higher than 20 in
only a few countries—namely, Ireland and the Netherlands,
which have been demographic anomalies for a century or
more, Poland and Yugoslavia, Portugal and Spain; and
even among these the rate was barely as high as, say, in
the United States.

The balance between births and deaths, or what demographers term the natural increase, has gone through a cycle known as the demographic transition. At the beginning of the modern era many children were born but a large proportion died before reaching maturity, and Europe's population grew slowly. Then, one after another, the causes of early death were brought under control, while for several generations Europe's fertility remained more or less constant or, it may be, even rose slightly. The consequent increase in population was tremendous.

Before that complex transitional period commonly known as the industrial revolution, Europe's cities—those that were then in existence—were no more than small towns. According to a list that the medieval historian J. C. Russell compiled from a wide variety of sources, in the thirteenth to the sixteenth centuries representative town populations ranged from 78,000 (Venice at its height) down to what we would term hamlets. These urban centers were important administratively and culturally, but the proportion of the population living in them was never more than a few per cent of the total. The urban aggregates became large cities only when, with the rise of manufacturing, they acquired an important new economic function. They grew largely by the in-migration of peasants' sons and daughters, whose numbers increased faster than the opportunities that the countryside afforded them.

Almost all of the migration within each European country was ultimately a movement not only to cities but to the largest cities. In England the dominant flow was to the Midlands or to London, in France overwhelmingly to Paris, in Sweden to Stockholm, in Austria-Hungary to Vienna or, if not, to Budapest, and so on. The exceptions to this pattern were countries with important regional differences, such as in language (Switzerland, Belgium, Spain), or in religion (Germany), or in economic development (Italy); and here the same kind of urbanization took place within a smaller unit. And much of the international migration within Europe was another version of this movement of country people to industrial jobs. Irish, Scots, and

Welsh went to England, Poles to Germany and France, Italians to France; the typical movement was from the rural periphery to the industrial center.

During the same period that Europe's cities were filling up, the continent poured forth an emigration of a size and importance unique in world history. Of the estimated 67 million persons who migrated across an ocean between 1800 and 1950, some 60 million were Europeans. They and their descendants founded great new nations in North and South America and in Oceania, and in various spots in the rest of the world they established important outposts of their industrial civilization. The first source of this emigration was Northwest Europe—the British Isles, Germany, and Scandinavia—where industrialization and the concomitant population increase began. Then, as mortality fell in Southern and Eastern Europe and these populations grew at a faster tempo, different countries became the dominant sources of emigration. At the high point of this so-called "new" migration, just before the First World War, some 400,000 left Italy in a single year, and well over half that number departed from each of Austria-Hungary, Russia, and Spain plus Portugal. The tide was stemmed by the war and broken by postwar restrictive legislation in both emigration and immigration countries.

Before 1914 migrants were ordinarily economically motivated; after that great watershed, migrations were largely or wholly political in their origin. The peace treaties following the First World War established a number of new states in Central and Eastern Europe, and in the subsequent period the League of Nations sponsored population exchanges designed to reduce the size of Europe's many ethnic enclaves. Migration from communist Russia and from fascist Italy, or from two of the dominant sources of both intra-European and especially overseas migrants, was prohibited, or, more precisely, was redirected to Soviet Asia and the Italian colonies in Africa. From Hitler's accession to power in 1933 to the beginning of the Second World War six years later, the Jewish population of Germany fell by more than half, presumably mostly because of emigration, partly because of successful evasions of the official count. A considerably larger number of ethnic Germans migrated to Germany, which in the depression of the 1930s now had a labor shortage.

All of these political migrations, however significant compared with past history, were dwarfed by the displacements concomitant with the Second World War. Even if we exclude the Soviet Union, the site of the largest movements, the migrations involved a very considerable percentage of Europe's population; the exact figures are of course not known. The large number of refugees from battle areas was greatly augmented when belligerents on both sides undertook the "strategic" bombing of non-military targets. The nazis rounded up Jews from all their conquered areas and shipped them to death camps. Many thousands of German settlers followed the nazi armies in their victorious march eastward and then rushed headlong back before their retreat. Germany imported about five million forced laborers to supplement the two million prisoners of war working in that country, so that by the end of the war aliens constituted a fifth of the German labor force. In the postwar period those Jews and other displaced persons who survived generally left Germany and were replaced by ethnic Germans expelled from Czechoslovakia, the western regions of postwar Poland, and various other German enclaves. West Germany has absorbed more than seven million of these refugees, and East Germany more than half that number. To every open door, or door that could perhaps be opened, there have come political refugees—from the Soviet Union, fascist Italy, fascist Spain, nazi Germany; the list continues to Hungary of 1956 but does not end there. Especially since 1945, this political push from Europe has been matched by an overseas political pull—the increased efforts of Australia, Canada, and other countries to accelerate the influx of desirable immigrants. The movement typical of Europe in its liberal heyday—when passportless persons left under their own momentum to seek, if not their fortunes, then better working conditions—is gone.

The effect of emigration on Europe's population is difficult to calculate. It is likely that the departure of some 60 million persons, by relieving the economic pressure that largely stimulated the exodus, actually quickened the continent's population growth. This population increase also stimulated Europeans to reduce the size of their families; and by the interwar years, as we have seen, the notion was widespread that this decline in fertility would continue to actual depopulation. In the postwar perspective, we can see rather that Europe's death control and its birth control are both excellent, so that by world standards its growth has been extremely low. During the 1950–60 decade, when the world as a whole increased by an annual average of 18 per 1000, for Europe this was only 8 per 1000. The population explosion, that common metaphor so ominous for Asia and Latin America, applies to very few countries of Europe, and to these in a different sense.

As we have noted at the beginning, Europe's total population of 440 million constitutes less than 15 per cent of the world's total. According to a forecast by the United Nations, in the year 2000 this percentage is likely to be 10 or less. The decline of Europe's population, no longer imminent in absolute terms, is a safe prognosis relative to that of the rest of the world. However, one should not accept too readily the notion that Europe is therefore less well off. The very rapid population growth of India, of China, of Central America, does not constitute an economic, social, or political advantage to those countries, but the contrary. The rational balance of births and deaths that Europe has achieved is a sign of moral health and economic and political strength; it is an example that one day the rest of the world must learn to follow.

SUGGESTIONS FOR FURTHER READING

Dudley Kirk. *Europe's Population in the Interwar Years.* League of Nations. Princeton: Princeton University Press, 1946.

An over-all survey—perhaps the best single work on

the population of Europe. Some historical material, but concentrated on the period 1918–45.

D. V. Glass. *Population Policies and Movements in Europe.* Oxford: Clarendon, 1940.

During the 1930s, when families were typically small and an eventual depopulation of Europe was often forecast, many countries introduced pronatalist measures. These are analyzed comparatively by Glass.

Eugene M. Kulischer. *Europe on the Move: War and Population Changes, 1917–47.* New York: Columbia University Press, 1948.

An analysis of the population of Eastern Europe (including the Soviet Union), concentrating on the effects of war and political disorganization.

Marcus Lee Hansen. *The Atlantic Migration, 1607–1860: A History of the Continuing Settlement of the United States.* Cambridge: Harvard University Press, 1940.

Perhaps the best historical analysis of the Great Migration.

William Petersen. *Planned Migration: The Social Determinants of the Dutch-Canadian Movement.* Berkeley: University of California Press, 1955.

A case study in subsidized migration, emphasizing its inherent limitations.

Josiah C. Russell. *British Medieval Population.* Albuquerque: University of New Mexico Press, 1948.

A study based on the Domesday survey, inquisition records, and poll-tax returns. It is interesting both for its methodology and for its data.

ABOUT THE AUTHORS

ANSLEY JOHNSON COALE is Professor of Economics and Director of the Office of Population Research at Princeton University, from which he received his A.B., M.A., and Ph.D. degrees in economics. He represents the United States at the Population Commission of the United Nations, and is co-author of *The Problem of Reducing Vulnerability to the Atomic Bombs; Population Growth and Economic Development in Low-income Countries;* and *New Estimates of Population and Fertility in the United States.*

WARREN W. EASON is Associate Professor of Economics and Chairman of the Board of Russian Studies, Syracuse University. He holds both M.A. and Ph.D. degrees as well as the certificate of the Russian Institute from Columbia University. He has previously taught at Johns Hopkins University and Princeton University. He has done extensive research and written numerous articles on the subject of human resources in Soviet economic development, dealing primarily with population questions and labor problems. His research has included three trips to the Soviet Union since 1956.

RONALD FREEDMAN is Professor of Sociology and Director of the Population Studies Center of the University of Michigan, where he has served since 1946. He is also Co-Director of the Taiwan Population Studies Center and President-Elect of the Population Association of America. His publications (some jointly with others) include:

Principles of Sociology; Family Planning, Sterility, and Population Growth; and *The Sociology of Human Fertility.* His B.A. and M.A. degrees are from the University of Michigan. His Ph.D. degree is from the University of Chicago.

PHILIP M. HAUSER is Professor and Chairman, Department of Sociology and Director of the Population Research and Training Center of the University of Chicago. He has served previously as Acting Director and Deputy Director of the U. S. Bureau of the Census and as U. S. Representative on the Population Commission of the United Nations. He is Past President and Fellow of the American Statistical Association, and Past President of the Population Association of America. His publications (some jointly with others) include: *A Study of Population: An Inventory and Appraisal; Population Perspectives; The Population Dilemma;* and *Population and World Politics.*

AMOS H. HAWLEY is Professor of Sociology, Associate Director of the Population Studies Center, and Director of the Métropolitan Community Research Project, of the University of Michigan. He has been a member of the University of Michigan faculty since 1941, and was Chairman of the Department of Sociology from 1952 to 1961. His principal publications include: *Human Ecology; Principles of Sociology* (with others); *Papers in Demography and Public Administration;* and *The Changing Shape of Metropolitan America.* His Ph.D. degree was awarded by the University of Michigan.

NATHAN KEYFITZ is Professor of Sociology and Co-Director of the Population Research and Training Center of the University of Chicago. Previously he was Professor of Sociology at the University of Toronto and before that Senior Research Statistician in the Bureau of Statistics in Ottawa, Canada. He has worked in Burma, Indonesia, Ceylon, and India, and most recently in Chile and Argentina, and has published articles on sociological and statistical themes in various journals. A native of Montreal, Canada, he holds a B.Sc. in Mathematics from McGill University and a Ph.D. in Sociology from the University of Chicago.

EVERETT S. LEE is Associate Professor of Sociology and Director of the Population Laboratory of the University of Pennsylvania, where he has served since 1953. His publications include (some jointly with others): *Population Redistribution and Economic Growth, United States, 1870–1950*, Vol. I; and *Migration and Mental Disease*. He received his M.A. and Ph.D. degrees from the University of Pennsylvania.

FRANK LORIMER is Professor of Sociology at American University and Research Associate, Princeton University. He directed the study of the National Resources Committee on *Problems of a Changing Population*. He is a Past President of the International Union for the Scientific Study of Population. His publications include *Dynamics of Population* (with Frederick Osborn); *Population of the Soviet Union;* and *Culture and Human Fertility*. He has traveled in Africa and is now participating in a research program on African population under the Princeton University Office of Population Research.

W. PARKER MAULDIN is Associate Demographic Director of the Population Council, a position he has held since 1957. During this time he was appointed to the United Nations staff at the United Nations Demographic Training and Research Center in Bombay, India. Before that he was Chief of the Foreign Manpower Research Office of the Bureau of the Census. He is currently a member of the board of directors of the Population Association of America. His publications include: *Population of Poland* (with D. S. Akers); "The Population of India: Policy, Action and Research," in *Economic Digest*, Vol. III, No. 2; and "Population Policies in the Sino-Soviet Bloc," in *Population Control*, edited by Shimm and Everett. He was awarded his B.S. degree by Clemson College and his M.S. degree by the University of Virginia.

LEO A. ORLEANS is a Senior Research Analyst at the Library of Congress, where he has been employed since 1951. He spent the first fifteen years of his life in China, emigrating to the United States in 1939. He received his B.A. from the University of Southern California and has done graduate work at American University and George Washington University. In addition to numerous articles, primarily in the field of Chinese population and labor force, he is the author of *Professional Manpower and Education in Communist China.*

WILLIAM PETERSEN is Professor of Sociology at the University of California at Berkeley. He is a member of the board of directors of both the International Population and Urban Research centers on that campus, and the Population Association of America. His publications include: *Planned Migration: The Social Determinants of the Dutch-Canadian Movement; American Social Patterns* (editor); *Population; Social Controversy* (co-editor); *The Realities of World Communism* (editor); *The Politics of Population;* and *The Changing Population of Nevada* (with Lionel Lewis). He received both his A.B. and his Ph.D. degrees from Columbia University.

T. LYNN SMITH is Graduate Research Professor and head of the Department of Sociology at the University of Florida, where he has been on the staff since 1949. Presently he is First Vice-President of the Population Association of America. His publications include: *The Sociology of Rural Life; Population Analysis; Brazil: People and Institutions; Latin American Population Studies;* and *Fundamentals of Population Study.* His B.S. degree is from Brigham Young University and his M.A. and Ph.D. degrees from the University of Minnesota. He also has been awarded the degree of Doctor Honoris Causa by the Universities of Brazil and São Paulo.

JOSEPH J. SPENGLER is James B. Duke Professor of Economics at Duke University, where he has served since 1934. His publications include: *France Faces Depopulation; French Predecessors of Malthus;* and, as co-author and co-editor, *Demographic Analysis,* and *Population Theory and Policy.* His A.B., M.A., and Ph.D. degrees are from Ohio State University.

MORTIMER SPIEGELMAN is Associate Statistician of the Metropolitan Life Insurance Company, with which he has been connected since 1926. He is also Chairman of the Committee on Vital and Health Statistics Monographs of the American Public Health Association. His publications include: *Introduction to Demography; Insuring Medical Care for the Aged;* and (jointly with others) *Length of Life; Money Value of A Man;* and *Facts of Life—From Birth to Death.* His M.B.A. degree is from Harvard University and he is a Fellow of the Society of Actuaries, the American Statistical Association and the American Public Health Association.

GEORGE J. STOLNITZ is a Professor of Economics at Indiana University, where he has served since 1956. He is Past Second Vice-President of the Population Association of America and has been previously connected with the U. S. Bureau of the Census, United Nations, and the Department of Economics and Office of Population Research at Princeton University. His publications include: *Life Tables from Limited Data: A Demographic Approach* and numerous articles in the areas of demography, economic development and statistics. His B.A. degree was awarded by the City University of New York, and his M.A. and Ph.D. degrees are from Princeton University.

J. MAYONE STYCOS is Professor of Sociology, Director of the International Population Program and Director of the Latin American Program at Cornell University. He is a consultant to the Population Council and a member of the Latin American Science Board of the National Academy of Sciences. His publications include: *Family and Fertility in Puerto Rico; The Family and Population Control* (with K. W. Back and R. Hill); and *Survey Under Unusual Conditions* (with K. W. Back). His B.A. degree is from Princeton University and his Ph.D. was awarded by Columbia University.

CONRAD TAEUBER is the Assistant Director for Demographic Fields in the Bureau of the Census, Washington, D. C., where he has served since 1951. His publications, some jointly with others, include: *People of the Drought States; Rural Migration in the United States;* and *The Changing Population of the United States.* His B.A., M.A., and Ph.D. degrees are from the University of Minnesota.

IRENE B. TAEUBER is Senior Research Demographer, Office of Population Research, Princeton University, where she has served since its formation in 1936. She is currently Vice-President of the International Union for the Scientific Study of Population. Her publications, some jointly with others, include: *The Population of Japan; Public Health and Demography in the Far East; The Population of Tanganyika;* and *General Censuses and Current Vital Statistics in the Americas.* Her B.A. degree is from the University of Missouri, M.A. from Northwestern University, and Ph.D. from the University of Minnesota.

RUPERT B. VANCE is Kenan Professor of Sociology at the University of North Carolina, Chapel Hill, where he has taught since 1928. He is past President of the Southern Sociological Society, the Population Association of America, and the American Sociological Association. His books (sometimes with others) include: *Human Factors in Cotton Culture; Human Geography of the South; Population Redistribution in the United States; All These People; New Farm Homes for Old;* and *The Urban South* (joint editor). His M.A. degree is from Vanderbilt University, and his Ph.D. degree is from the University of North Carolina.

CHARLES F. WESTOFF is Professor of Sociology and Assistant Director of the Office of Population Research at Princeton University, where he has served since 1955. Between 1958 and 1961, in addition to a research position at the Office of Population Research, he was Associate Professor of Sociology at New York University. His publications include the co-authorship of *The Third Child* and *Family Growth in Metropolitan America* as well as numerous articles published in professional journals of demography and sociology. He received his A.B. and M.A. degrees from Syracuse University and his Ph.D. from the University of Pennsylvania.

DATE DUE
